AF235528

The Cinema
of Quentin Tarantino

ALSO OF INTEREST
AND FROM McFARLAND

Perspectives on Elmore Leonard: Conversations with Authors, Experts and Collaborators (Andrew J. Rausch, 2022)

Perspectives on Stephen King: Conversations with Authors, Experts and Collaborators (Andrew J. Rausch, 2019)

Fifty Filmmakers: Conversations with Directors from Roger Avary to Steven Zaillian (Andrew J. Rausch, 2008)

The Cinema of Quentin Tarantino

Essays on Race, Violence and History in the Films

Edited by KIERAN FISHER *and* ANDREW J. RAUSCH

McFarland & Company, Inc., Publishers
Jefferson, North Carolina

This book has undergone peer review.

ISBN (print) 978-1-4766-8380-5
ISBN (ebook) 978-1-4766-5601-4

LIBRARY OF CONGRESS CATALOGING DATA ARE AVAILABLE

Library of Congress Control Number 2025018261

© 2025 Kieran Fisher and Andrew J. Rausch. All rights reserved

*No part of this book may be reproduced or transmitted in any form
or by any means, electronic or mechanical, including photocopying
or recording, or by any information storage and retrieval system,
without permission in writing from the publisher.*

Front cover: Samuel L. Jackson in the 2015 film *The Hateful Eight*
(The Weinstein Company/Photofest)

Printed in the United States of America

*McFarland & Company, Inc., Publishers
Box 611, Jefferson, North Carolina 28640
www.mcfarlandpub.com*

Table of Contents

Introduction

Master Filmmaker or Emperor with No Clothes?

Andrew J. Rausch *and* Kieran Fisher

Quentin Tarantino's backstory is as compelling as the stories he writes. It's the story of an unlikely outsider who burst onto the scene and changed the cinematic landscape forever. While he wasn't the first filmmaker to emerge out of (seemingly) nowhere and make a dramatic impact on both cinema and popular culture itself, Tarantino's meteoric rise to superstardom captured the public's imagination in ways that few filmmakers have. An example of this is the fact that the first of his several biographies, Jami Bernard's *Quentin Tarantino: The Man and His Movies* (1995), was published after the filmmaker had crafted only two films. At the height of Tarantino-mania, he was also working as an actor, producing films, and releasing grindhouse flicks through his own A Band Apart Films.

Most filmmakers subscribe to the idea that making movies is the only way to master the artform. Obviously, a good many of the medium's most successful helmers had received formal training before crafting the art that would catapult them into the limelight; much has been written about "The Film School Generation," a group of maverick directors that included the likes of Steven Spielberg, George Lucas, Francis Ford Coppola, Brian De Palma, and Martin Scorsese, who developed their skills attending university filmmaking classes. While their successes undoubtedly inspired many budding creators to attempt to follow in their footsteps, there are just as many stories about directors who opted for more informal routes into the business.

After Tarantino dropped out of high school at age 14 due to an inability to focus on his studies, it was clear that film school wasn't a viable option. Having spent his school years ditching classes in favor of watching television and reading pulp novels and comic books, he received a pop culture education that would serve him well. After he left school, Tarantino's interest in cinema led him to work as an usher in a Hollywood Boulevard porno film theater, take acting classes, and write his own screenplays. At age 22, Tarantino famously went to work at Video Archives, a now-legendary Manhattan Beach, California, video store. While employed there, he made the most of his ability to check out videotapes for free, furthering his pop culture education by consuming (and studying) countless movies. While working at the video store in the early 1980s, he wrote what would become his first produced screenplays, *True Romance* (1993) and *Natural Born Killers* (1994). During this period, he also directed his first film, *My Best Friend's Birthday*, which he funded with paychecks from his minimum wage job and additional funds given to him by his mother. Although Tarantino would ultimately scrap the project, it served as a sort of do-it-yourself film school for future professional filmmakers Tarantino, Roger Avary, and Craig Hamann.

Armed with the knowledge he'd acquired from watching and dissecting a lifetime's worth of movies, along with the lessons he'd learned from his own botched attempt at making his first film, Tarantino was ready for Hollywood. His official directorial debut, *Reservoir Dogs*, first screened at the 1991 Sundance Film Festival, was met with equal parts acclaim and controversy, and it gained an immediate cult following. And the rest, as they say, was history. Tarantino's journey to creating *Reservoir Dogs* has been forever immortalized as a Rocky Balboa story of unlikely triumph, which in turn elevated him to superstar status in the eyes of critics and film fandom. While Tarantino wasn't the first filmmaker to bypass film school, even in his generation, he became the *de facto* face of an entire movement of mavericks who skipped film school and instead made films by any means necessary. It is for this reason that this movement has, in some quarters, been called "Generation Tarantino."

His unconventional path to success lent him an almost mythical quality from the start, leading to the cult-like status his followers give him today. This is partly because of his well-earned reputation as an outspoken cineaste who fills his films with overt nods to films, television shows, and works of literature. As a filmmaker, Tarantino has never been interested in simply making movies. According to the director, he's fascinated with "participating in, and reflecting on, film history." This dedication to cinephilia has even extended to the way his films are released, as evidenced by the decision to originally release *Death Proof* (2007) as a drive-in–inspired double feature with Robert Rodriguez's *Planet Terror* (2007) and the 70mm roadshow that accompanied *The Hateful Eight* (2015).

Of course, referencing pop culture and being an outspoken cineaste doesn't equate to importance, per se. What separates Tarantino's work from all the Easter egg–loaded films that have followed is the sheer quality and influence his films have had on the cinematic landscape in the decades that have followed.

Tarantino's films are postmodern in their approach due to their refusal to conform with the ideas, theories, and trends that are popular in contemporary filmmaking and storytelling. These postmodern qualities include non-traditional narrative structures, the rejection of "grand narratives," and a propensity for mixing high- and low-brow art. One of the most fascinating elements of Tarantino's approach to storytelling is his use of literary devices such as fragmented structures accompanied by chapters.

Virtually everyone in the United States (over the age of 12) knows the name Quentin Tarantino. Even if they have zero knowledge of his body of work or maybe even who he is or what he does, they know the name. "Tarantino" has become a part of the cultural lexicon, a familiar brand alongside Coca-Cola, Ford, McDonald's, and Stephen King. Similar to fellow creative King, Tarantino's name has become a shorthand label for a specific genre. In King's case, that genre is horror (which is patently unfair since King has worked in almost every existing genre). But in the instance of Tarantino, the specific genre the name signifies is difficult to articulate, although instantly recognizable. Is it crime thriller? Western? War drama? This is where the difficulty in definition comes into play. While a Tarantino film isn't specifically any one of the types of films listed above, it's *all* of them. And yet none of his films are truly like any crime, Western, or war picture that preceded it (beyond surface similarity). For a long while, as Tarantino himself acknowledged, he was known as "the gun guy"; even though he worked in different genres, they were always genres in which his characters could realistically brandish firearms. But then, in 2019, Tarantino wrecked even this most basic of labels by making *Once Upon a Time in Hollywood*—the gun-less story of a washed-up actor and his semi-blacklisted stunt double/buddy. And while the filmmaker has even come to be recognized for his history-bending films (*Inglourious Basterds, Django Unchained*, and *Once Upon a Time in Hollywood*), that element only represents a portion of his work. So what is Tarantino's genre? It's simple— his is *the Tarantino genre*; he's a genre unto himself, and entries in this genre can be identified by the writer/filmmaker's unique voice and aesthetic. No song sounds like a Beatles song, just as no novel or story reads like a Kurt Vonnegut tale. Similarly, no film looks and feels like a Tarantino film. Sure, the Beatles, Vonnegut, and Tarantino have all had their share of imitators, but those pastiches come short of capturing the *je na sais quoi* of the originals.

Tarantino's films have inspired countless filmmakers to adopt a like-minded approach to their own films, resulting in a phenomenon that has been called the "Tarantino Effect." These films have been labeled as being "Tarantinoesque," a term that was officially recognized by the Oxford Dictionary in 2018 to describe films that are "typically characterized by graphic and stylized violence, non-linear storylines, cineliterate references, satirical themes, and sharp dialogue."

By no means did Tarantino invent these postmodern sensibilities, but he's applied them to his art in a way that's unmistakably unique, recognizable, and impacting. It's a style that has brought him commercial success (at the time of this writing, his films have grossed more than $2 billion at the international box office) and spurred endless debate among his fans, peers, and film critics. There are no rules or traditional logic when it comes to a Tarantino story, which has earned him the reputation of being a rule-breaker, much like Jean-Luc Godard and the other auteurs after whom he's modeled elements of his style.

Tarantino's detractors claim that his films are derivative. Again, looking beyond *surface similarities*, such claims are undeniably false. Like Mary Shelley's Dr. Frankenstein, Tarantino takes pieces of preexisting things and reassembles them, crafting something new from the parts. This is akin to sampling in hip-hop music. While there are certainly examples of songs that completely rip-off preexisting recordings, there are other producers who snatch small pieces from old songs and then assemble them in such a way as to create art that is fresh and different.

Since the beginning of his career, Tarantino's detractors have sought to convince the world that he's some sort of flavor-of-the-month pop culture fad—a hack devoid of true talent. But consider this: Tarantino's career continues to be successful (both critically and commercially), and he has remained relevant for more than three decades. Additionally, his older works continue to be praised and reappraised with some (*Jackie Brown* in particular) growing in stature and popularity with the passing of time. Flavor-of-the-month pop fads don't do that. If you want proof, consider the likes of Paula Abdul, MC Hammer, and *My Big Fat Greek Wedding* (2002), all of which were cultural darlings at one time or another.

None of this is to say that Tarantino's work or aesthetic is above reproach. There are critics who label his work as being sexist. Others point to his films as examples of "toxic masculinity." And, as anyone who has followed Tarantino's career even the slightest bit knows, assertions that his films are "racist" and appropriate black culture have long plagued him. Depending on whom you ask, Tarantino is either a master filmmaker or a cinematic plagiarist and a hack. Because of the divisive way in which his work is viewed and interpreted, volumes such as this are important and necessary.

Whether or not critics' and academics' assessments and theories are correct—some are and some aren't, simply by the nature of such things—it is only through studying and considering a variety of opinions and assertions that we can properly "see" these works. This book contains 10 essays, all written expressly for this volume. We, the editors, do not claim that this book is the final word on the study of these films; it is not. For some readers, it will be just the tip of the iceberg—an introduction into Tarantino academia. For other readers, this volume will illuminate new facets of the filmmaker's work, provide further insights into specific areas that have previously been studied, or reaffirm beliefs the reader already possessed. Unlike most other collections of this nature, there is no singular theme; no connecting through-line, if you will, other than they are essays about the works of Tarantino.

Is Tarantino a master filmmaker or an emperor with no clothes? Are his films racist? Sexist? Is he merely a hack retreading already well-traveled ground? Most importantly, *are there definitive answers to these questions?* These questions are ones cineastes and academics must answer for themselves, and to reach a satisfactory conclusion, it is important that we examine the filmmaker's cinematic output. This volume is intended to provide additional insights that will further the discussion.

Vitae Necisque Potestas

Quentin Tarantino's Pulp Fiction (1994) and the Sacred Machinations of Exception

Dara Waldron

> In an amazing acceleration, the generations precipitate themselves. A work can become modern only if it is first postmodern. Postmodernism thus understood is not modernism at its end but in the nascent state, and this state is constant.
>
> —Jean François Lyotard,
> *What Is Postmodernism?* (1982)

First Date

It was a cold winter evening in 1994 when I first encountered Quentin Tarantino's *Pulp Fiction*. Along with my fellow undergraduate humanities students, I had digested some hash yogurts before heading out to the cinema. Three hours later, I knew we had experienced a special film, yet I couldn't remember any of the details. My only memory pertained to the interchanging of beginning and ending, the first time I had encountered a narrative so circular in its form. I vaguely recalled Vincent (John Travolta) getting shot while reading a magazine on the toilet. The finale's return to the diner from the perspective of Vincent and Jules (Samuel L. Jackson), altering the basic Chronos of time, brought its genius to bear down upon us. When I returned the next day in a sober state to see *Pulp Fiction*, I was no less intrigued by the inventive dialogue, all of which begged the question, "Where is the place on screen?" In addition, a strong burgeoning desire grew in me to know what was in the suitcase Jules held so tight.

A year later, I went to England to study for an MA in criticism and theory at Exeter University and brought a VHS copy of two films with me: *Pulp Fiction* and *Withnail & I* (1987). Whenever I was feeling low, missing friends and family, and in need of a pick me up, I watched one of the two films. One of the modules for the first semester was modernism/postmodernism and *Pulp Fiction*, in my eyes, typified the latter. The corridors of low culture, the cross-references to cinematic culture, most notably *Bande à part* (1964) as a high point in French new wave cinema, drugs, the gangsters, intrigued, coupled with a noir undercurrent most visible in the mercurial figure of Winston Wolfe (Harvey Keitel). Fredric Jameson alludes to a celebration of mass culture in the postmodern, artifacts previously settled beneath the lens of academic scrutiny, to explain a fascination with the oxymoronic concept of postmodernism.[1] *Pulp Fiction*, with its Big Kahuna burgers and its Royale with Cheeses, ticked many of the boxes outlined in Jameson's now classic text. The penchant for low-brow culture, the black and white suits gleaned from late noir classics like *Kiss Me Deadly* (1959), boxing, and S & M is not "the stuff that had enraptured the great modernists in their pomp." Yet, as suggested in the essay that follows, it is not the Jamesonian penchant for low culture that is most intriguing for an exegesis of *Pulp Fiction* as canonical postmodern text, but the reification of the ambivalent indistinction between the sacred and profane that operates at an unconscious level in the film revealed only, in its vital import, with Jules's departing monologue in the final scene.

Jules's monologue closes the circle in full: returning in time to the original scene that had opened *Pulp Fiction*, Honey Bunny (Amanda Plummer) and Pumpkin's (Tim Roth) hit on the café. Jules leaves the game, in perhaps the most remarkable scene, claiming that he has chosen to walk the earth: a sacred man who must help resist the monopoly in the world by the profane forces of evil (no doubt exemplified by the figure who is facing him in the café). Not only is the scene perplexing from the perspective of time, subverting the teleological dance that still pertains to the classical modernist form, but also spectacular in the way it brings the sacred and profane together. The world of *Pulp Fiction* is made up of petty criminals, profane criminals trying to make a buck. However, there is also the sacred. To this end, I will argue that the finale's turn to the sacred man in Jules, with specific reference to Italian philosopher Giorgio Agamben's reading of *homo sacer*, can be gleaned as an expression of the modern in its nascent form, formulated by Jean François Lyotard in his canonical essay "What Is Postmodernism?" (1982).[2] To understand the postmodern in this way is to find the thing suppressed in the early days of modernism at the core of what comes after. In the case of *Pulp Fiction*, I contend it is the sacred life of the *homo sacer*, understood as a person who can be killed without sanction from the law (as the figure of the sacred exception) that illustrates the repressed "nascent" concern of *Pulp Fiction* (as sacred exception). The coming to consciousness of this concern as a realization in the film is a coming to consciousness of that Lyotardian "nascent" form in the film text. It is the bare life of the *homo sacer* that ends *Pulp Fiction*. Jules is the figure of bare life that manifests as the sacred machination of the exception. There is still a space, at once obliterated in the modern, for the bare life of the sacred.

Homo Sacer

Giorgio Agamben's philosophical project is inseparable from his consistent turn to the concept of *homo sacer*. Tracing the concept's evolution (and its materialization) from ancient Roman law through Christianity to a concentrated focus in academic theology in the 19th century, Agamben finds in the attributed meaning of sacred and profane a soon-to-be elicited ambivalence of form. For Agamben, this same ambivalence is concentrated in a duality that cuts into the age of reason, taking specific form in the modern era. Intense theological debate about the sacred arrives when Nietzsche is famously declaring that "God is dead," the exclamation ringing out around Europe.

The concern, for Agamben, is political in that the *homo sacer* is the required exception particular to the coordination of a modern subject. A "subject," not a subject, is cast out by the political sphere for that sphere to exist. This contradiction haunts modernity most evidently in the Holocaust. Agamben ends *Homo Sacer: Sovereign Power and Bare Life* (1998) with an extended analysis of the death camps. The Jew, reduced to bare life, is the exception, characterized as the cancerous tumor that must be expelled from the political system for the body politic constitutive of that system to maintain its longevity and health. Bare life is the term Agamben expunges to describe the Jew as *homo sacer* par excellence. He returns to the concept of *homo sacer* throughout his philosophical career, setting bare life up against the political forms that a life takes, the management of which increases in modernity. Agamben traces the scholarly focus on the *homo sacer* as a limit point from antiquity through to the Victorian period, focusing on the theological debates surrounding the "ambivalence of the sacred" that shaped the thinking of Marcel Mauss and later Freud. He says of this,

> In the body of the surviving devotee and, even more unconditionally, in the body homo sacer, the ancient world finds itself confronted for the first time with a life that, excepting itself in a double exclusion from the real context of both the profane and the religious forms of life, is defined solely by virtue of

having entered into an intimate symbiosis with death without, nevertheless, belonging to the world of the deceased.[3]

Bare life is the life of a person that can be killed but not sacrificed; it is both profane, in that it cannot be included in the legal remit of the state that constitutes the political subject, but also sacred, in that no human-made law protects its place in the social order. Bare life exists in that zone of indistinction required by the social order. The figure of bare life is in "an intimate symbiosis with death, without," and herein is the contradiction, "belonging to the world of the deceased." The contradiction in question governs the social order in the form of an exception, collapsing the profane into a once-opposing category of sacred. This collapse is just one of the many reasons Agamben, who ends his masterpiece *Homo Sacer: Sovereign Power and Bare Life* with sustained analyses of the death camps (as indicative of modernity), prefers the word Shoah as a de facto denominator for the extermination of the Jewish race during World War II. The mass killing of the Jews in the concentration camps, Agamben attests, is the killing of bare life: there is no attributable "meaning" for the genocide. This is not to undermine the criminality in question but, conversely, to indicate precisely what is meant when Theodor Adorno says there is no poetry after Auschwitz. The crime is so big that it eludes any categorical meaning. "After the First World War, what appeared was Nazism and fascism," Agamben writes, "that is, two properly biopolitical movements that made of natural life the exemplary place of the sovereign decision."[4] "Natural life," now the product of state power, issues from a legal domain rendered now as a specific political category. The sovereign exception produces the state of exception afforded to the *homo sacer*. One state of being produces the other in the exertion of life over death. It is from this position that Agamben moves to uncover the foundational contradiction structuring human life in the modern biopolitical era that he traces from antiquity to the 19th century in his text. Bare life, once the preserve of the banished exception, is indistinguishable from the modern subject. In the modern era, the subject citizen is *homo sacer*. There is no space outside.

With this thesis in mind, I want to propose *Pulp Fiction* to be a postmodern text for two reasons of note. It is postmodern in its Lyotardian fascination with what is nascent in the modern: the sacred exception still removed from politics. There is still a space to cultivate pure Being. The second reason it is postmodern is that it centers on the exception as the consistent problem of modernity. The modern is invested in forms of life, with all the overriding issues for Agamben coming from modernity's politicization of life. This is also the resounding concern of *Pulp Fiction*. From the very outset, the narrative bumps up against rules and exceptions in daily life. The film opens with Honey Bunny and Pumpkin discussing the unspoken rules of robbing the diner they are sitting in. The diner has a near-sacred status, not just in Hollywood cinema (think of Hopper's *Nighthawks* [1942] or the pivotal scene from *The Godfather II* [1974] when Michael plants a gun in the toilets of the diner) but in French cinema also. As mentioned above, the diner in *Bande à part* is a little disguised influence on *Pulp Fiction*. As a result, from the outset, the question "what is a law and what is the exception?" dominates. The opening scene centers on codes and binds defined by the exception. In the remainder of this essay, I want to explore some reasons why the *sacred* exception (regarding the sovereign and *homo sacer*) is an explicit concern of Tarantino in *Pulp Fiction* (and one that resurfaces across his *oeuvre*), exploring the way the film envisages sacred spaces free from an overreaching sovereign power. I will do this with a particular focus on the "rape scene"—when Marsellus (Ving Rhames) and Butch (Bruce Willis) united against Zed (Peter Greene) and the Gimp (Stephen Hibbert)—before turning, finally, to the end when Jules is fashioning his own self as the real sacred exception, experiencing what is arguably the most famous "moment of clarity" in the history of cinema.

The Sovereign Marsellus

Who is the crime boss Marsellus Wallace? Why do we not see him up close? Why do we not get to know him firsthand? Almost everything about Marsellus is revealed through conversations those who work for him have directly: most notably Vincent and Jules. The main narrative of *Pulp Fiction* revolves around these characters, both tasked with giving meaning to the "gangster morality" they are subject to, or what Martin Rossouw calls "hypervalues" that are set up against the legal binds of the state.[5] In one of the earliest scenes of *Pulp Fiction*, Vincent and Jules are deliberating on whether a foot massage can be decoded as a sexual act or whether it is simply a friendly exchange between friends. They start to question the rumor concerning their boss Marsellus' response to a similar act performed on his wife Mia (Uma Thurman). The spectator is also encouraged to assess the role rules play regarding a sovereign who controls the desires of those under his watch. They assume Marsellus is powerful enough to have someone thrown over a balcony for giving a foot massage to his wife: he controls desire in *this* world. The task Vincent and Jules face as hit men working for him lies in decoding his rules—those that manifest as internal rules for them—in the everyday. Vincent is tasked with bringing Mia Wallace out for dinner when Marsellus is away. His foremost concern is etiquette: if he crosses the line, he too can be thrown off a balcony. Marsellus can punish him because he is exempt from the coded laws in their world: he is the sovereign and ultimate lawgiver.

Another compelling scene revealing the crime boss figure as an all-powerful sovereign, whom many commentators point to as pivotal to the narration, is the rape. Marsellus had bribed Butch to cheat in a boxing match, but Butch bets his payment on him winning the fight. Having won, he returns to the city to collect a watch bequeathed to him by his dead father from an internment camp, as an enraged sovereign confronts him there: the figure who yields the power of life and death. Marsellus chases Butch into a shop, where he is captured and turned into a sexual object for the pleasure of Zed and his Gimp accomplice. Butch has the option to leave Marsellus: allow the sovereign who rules to be raped and potentially killed. However, in a change of heart, he rescues Marsellus. As a recompense for this, Marsellus, lawgiver and ruler, makes Butch an honoree exception. He is spared if he agrees to leave the city walls for good.

Many strands of narration begin to coalesce in this scene to humanize Marsellus. The sovereign believed to give meaning to the sexual advance is himself the victim of sexual violation: turning the tables and making of the sovereign the object of bare life. Nonetheless, just as Marsellus is being raped, Butch intervenes. Marsellus is reduced to "bare life" when one of his subjects rescues him. Butch wants to know if they are good, given that he has risked his life to save him, to which Marsellus replies affirmatively. The sovereign speaks of "getting medieval" on the ass of Zed and the Gimp in perhaps the film's definitive quip. Medieval torture, overseen by a sovereign, is a preferred form of justice. The sacred, defined by the sovereign who oversees the state of exception, is also the figure of "bare life": she who can be killed but not sacrificed. The film pivots on the relationship between the sovereign and *homo sacer*.

For Agamben, the Holocaust as genocidal crisis has been studied—in the main—from the perspective of racial politics, a perspective that often underplays the alignment of life with politics that shapes modernity. The collapse of nature into "life" shapes the biopolitical moment when life, in every instance, becomes inseparable from politics. "Insofar as its inhabitants (of the concentration camps) were stripped of every political status and wholly reduced to bare life," Agamben notes, "the camp was the most absolute biopolitical space realized, in which power confronts nothing but pure life without any mediation."[6] If there still exists a sacred machination of the exception, the *homo sacer* driven from the city by the sovereign, it exists in a zone of indistinction. "The *biopolitical body* that constitutes the new fundamental political subject" is, Agamben believes, "the site of a sovereign political decision that operates in the absolute indistinction of fact and law."[7] The exception that was always on the outside now seems to play a key role in defining political life, as the "body" is subjected to the Law.

This pivotal insight here, at first glance, seems alien to the experience of a film set in the late 20th-century United States, celebrated for its nihilist vision of a world void of sacred value, where characters are made to make constant efforts to find sense in a consumer everyday world (most evident in the discussion between Vincent and Jules regarding Vincent's trip to Europe). But it is the less obvious concern with the relationship between power and life, and its jurisdiction in law, that cultivates the sacred exception particular to the film's final narrative turn, so important as an end, when Jules decides to "walk the earth." This is important because, like Butch, Jules can flee the sovereign.

Perhaps the key moment of *Pulp Fiction* then is Butch's decision not to leave the sovereign he has defeated to die at the hands of his sexual abusers and run off into the sunset with a bulging bank balance. He decides to do otherwise. We watch as he moves through Zed's shop surveying the objects of potential harm he can use to enact revenge and set Marsellus free. He decides on a chainsaw before pivoting and changing his mind when a large sword presents itself. This is an exhilarating scene that brings redemption to Butch. Once Butch bursts through the curtains that designate inside and out—a visual metaphor for the designation of inside and out of the state and the state of exception—he confronts a gagged Marsellus reduced to an object of sexual violation. He saves him from further abuse and offers him the opportunity for revenge. At this point, the film pivots back, away from the bare life of pure bodily objectification (he is being used as a piece of flesh in a game of sexual depravation) designated by the mouth gag, to the sovereign who still bears the power of life over death. Another crucial pivot follows this, one captured in Marsellus' assertion to Zed in response to Butch's intervention. Butch then asks Marsellus, "What now?" and Marsellus replies that he intends to take revenge by "getting medieval." Butch is unclear where this leaves him regarding the sovereign's power over his life.

Thus, he asks, "Are we cool?" He is seeking confirmation that he can leave safely. Marsellus replies that they are cool on the condition that he tells nobody of the events in the dungeon and leaves Los Angeles for good. Butch cannot know the law that subjects him; there is no correlation between fact and law. As is the case throughout *Pulp Fiction*, the sovereign Marsellus yields power over life, but nobody can know for sure what the law binds and what its exception is. Butch is exempt not because the sovereign Marsellus is applying the strict rules that govern gangsta morality, the law, but because Marsellus simply says so. In the medieval-cum-modern Los Angeles of *Pulp Fiction*, life is subject to the all-powerful word of the sovereign. There is no distinction between the sovereign and the judicial. Butch leaves with only the word of the sovereign: there is no contract or bind. There is simply the honor of Marsellus. At this point, the earlier conversations between Vincent and Jules considering the meaning of a foot massage controlled not by the dictates of a law but by the whims of the sovereign power echoes in the voice of a sovereign Butch makes his plea to. It is perhaps the most pivotal scene of the film, revealing the sovereign power hinted at in earlier scenes: it distills the sovereign against the traces of bare life.

The next phase is so incredibly smart in flipping over the generalized flow of time again, bringing Vincent back to life after his shooting by Butch (after taking a shit). We arrive at the final scene, also the beginning (disquieting to those viewers succumbing to a hash-induced stupor), when Jules announces his decision to "walk the earth." For certain speculative critics of the film, the suitcase Jules guards with his life contains the soul of sovereign Marsellus. A bright light radiates from the case when open, but what is inside is never clear: we can only imagine what is there. The noir influence is prevalent. Not only are Vincent and Jules, in their classic black and white suits, noir-like protagonists in a fallen world, but the glowing suitcase is an inside reference to the McGuffin in Robert Aldrich's noir-class *Kiss Me Deadly* (1995). Paying homage to Aldrich's infamous suitcase, Tarantino suddenly changes focus. A *Dazed & Confused* article from 2014 to mark the 20th anniversary of *Pulp Fiction* pushes the theory of the case containing Marsellus' soul, having sold it to Satan in return for financial gain. The author Carmen Gray makes the exact point,

> The most persistent and ingenious theory is that what is inside the case is nothing short of the soul of gang kingpin Marsellus Wallace, who sold it to Satan and is trying to get it back. The imposing mob boss wears a Band-Aid on the back of his neck, reportedly because actor Ving Rhames has a scar there he wanted to hide for the iconic over-the-shoulder shot, but it has also been argued that when the devil takes your soul he takes it from the back of your neck.[8]

This theory fits with the general reading of the film proposed in this essay, in that the sovereign Marsellus has become sovereign by collapsing his role as ruler into that of the judicial decree. Such a collapse has made him all-powerful in designating the meaning of the law and its exception: from the meaning of a foot massage to the "we cool" that ends his beef with Butch. In *Pulp Fiction*, the modern state that Agamben believes brings life and politics into unison, spreading sovereign power across the state bureaucracies, reverts to the pre-modern. Here sovereign power is still the sole preserve of a decree. Unlike the modern-day refugee, who is subject to the biopower of state politics—and who cannot move freely without jumping through bureaucratic hoops that define citizenship within a given territory—Jules will "walk the earth" according to the terms he discovers laid out in his own version of Ezekiel 25:17. Until his "miracle," when he survives multiple shootings, he executes God's vengeance upon the tyranny of the world. But he changes. He becomes the merciful one, walking the earth to find those in need of help (there is even a theory that he turns up in Vince Gilligan's TV masterpiece *Breaking Bad*). In the final part of this essay, I want to propose that Jules affirms his status as *homo sacer*. This time, far from the redeemer, he confirms—tout court—the sacred machination of the exception.

Jules as Homo Sacer

> "From here on, you can consider my ass retired."
> —Jules, *Pulp Fiction*

Jules *becomes* the sacred machination of an exception. When he takes on this role in the film, *Pulp Fiction* begins to operate as a postmodern text in a Lyotardian sense, a film that orients us back toward what lies nascent in the modern. Jules is banished from the polis. "It may be that only if we are able to decipher the political meaning of pure Being," Agamben says, "will we be able to master the bare life that expresses our subjection to political power."[9] Furthermore, as Agamben notes, "his entire existence is reduced to a bare life stripped of every right by virtue of the fact that anyone can kill him without committing homicide; *he can save himself only in perpetual flight or a foreign land*."[10] It is not merely that Jules identifies with a *homo sacer* beyond the gates of the polis, a boundary that predates his own world, but that he confronts the modern condition for what it is, the political subjection of all beings. He designates a space where the exception is still sacred and merely beholden to God.

Sovereign power is predicated on the state of exception. Marsellus Wallace, as the sovereign figure of *Pulp Fiction*, rules precisely because he defines the exception. This power to designate is made abundantly clear, as I outlined above, in the constant attempts by the many protagonists throughout the film to delineate the distinctions in their criminal world. What constitutes a nonsexual foot massage? Is such an act even possible? Is it acceptable to dance with Mia when she asks Vincent? Is it an exception?

Pulp Fiction makes for kind of triumph of revelation over these concerns. Jules tells Vincent, in the diner where the film begins, that he has decided to "walk the earth." He is intent on giving up a life of crime that he has been integrated into overtime. It is not that Jules wants to turn away from his profane existence to embrace the role of sacred man but that his very decision pays homage to the collapse of one into the other in the exception. This is the realization that ends *Pulp Fiction*. Maybe it is an urban myth that Jules turns up in *Breaking Bad*, a TV show also about the biopolitical order; that is, Walter White's (Bryan Cranston) evolution from cancer patient to drug kingpin. Jules's decision to "walk the earth" casts him—speculatively—as an escapee, not belonging within a specific nation-state. Jules will become a man who simply walks the earth, driven from the polis as the sovereign's sacred exception.

   Pulp Fiction, therefore, ends with aplomb: it is possible to escape the biopolitical order. There is a space for pure Being beyond the space where the state decides who is subject to the law and who is the exception. As in many of his later films, Tarantino presents us with a character that can choose a route out of the biopolitical. The sacred machinations of the exception, in the form of a subject's monologue at the end of *Pulp Fiction*, involves walking the earth as *homo sacer* answerable only to God. It is an ending particular to the Tarantino oeuvre. The sovereign and exception run through his films, buoyed by a gangster morality in his first three (think of Ordell [Samuel L. Jackson] in *Jackie Brown*), filtering down in the casting of David Carradine as the sovereign Bill in *Kill Bill 1 & 2* (2003, 2004). Carradine also had a significant presence in my youth: *Kung Fu* aired after *Match of the Day* every week on Irish TV. I begged my father to stay up to watch it with him, my fascination with Carradine, the actor, slowly developing. It was only when pausing to consider the sacred machinations of the exception around Jules's decision to walk the earth, just like Caine in *Kung Fu*, I thought of Kwai Chang Caine, wandering the earth in search of a brother. The sacred man of *Kung Fu* is a monk, an expert in martial arts who is a protective shield against the worst excesses of the American West. Carradine, who plays Chang Caine with real panache, is later cast by Tarantino as Bill in his *Kill Bill* series. Moreover, the American West Kane wanders through comes to life in later Tarantino films, in particular, *Django Unchained* (2012) and *The Hateful Eight* (2015).

   Jules's decision to walk the earth along lines of flight that know no boundaries or territory is a fantasy panacea for all his ills and for two reasons of note. On the one hand, it is presented as an escape from the "tyranny of evil" that Jules considers to inhabit the world he lives in, a world where facts are separate from law and nobody seems to know who yields power (is it the sovereign Marsellus, or some powerful edifice invisible to man?). On the other hand, it is desire—or what I have argued is a prevalent "theme" in the Tarantino oeuvre—to separate bare life from politics, to wander the earth as a pure Being, no longer hindered by the politicization of life, no longer subject to the whims of the sovereign figure, whatever form their power takes.

Tarantino films the conversation between Vincent and Jules from a side angle so that each perspective on the opposing take on the desire "to walk the earth ... like Caine in *Kung Fu*" is given equal weight. The conversation hinges on the distinction between fact and law. Was it a miracle that Jules was spared from the bullets shot at him? Or was it simply a "freak occurrence" still in the domain of the rational? The either/or of this conundrum is brilliantly espoused by the subtlety of Tarantino's camera work, from a side profile of Vincent increasingly frustrated with his partner, back to Jules, who is set firmly in his decision. Vincent is adamant that Jules will become a bum. Jules, however, digesting his food, is adamant that he is submitting to God's sacred decree.

"When life and politics—originally divided and linked together by means of the no man's land of the state of exception that is inhabited by bare life—begin to become one," Agamben informs us, "all life becomes sacred and all politics becomes the exception."[11] *Pulp Fiction* ends in a full-scale rebuttal of this truism, turning to the cinematic medium by retreating into a world where open spaces still exist for the *homo sacer* to walk outside the injunctions of state law: a space for pure Being. "If my answers frighten you, Vincent, you should cease asking scary questions," Jules says to Vincent just as Pumpkin calls out "*garcon*" and the film pivots back to its beginning. We are seemingly caught within the circular loop of time, but will Jules escape from it? We already know that Vincent will be killed a few days after the diner scene (he is already dead in the film) and that Jules's declaration might well be the thing that saves his life. Not only does Butch later kill Vincent, but he is also killed after taking a shit. His quick demise is so utterly profane an event that it sits in clear opposition to the sacred aspirations of his partner. That Vincent's fate is sealed when he confronts Jules makes his decision to do so more fascinating: Jules will "walk the earth" as a sacred man.

The Law Is Known by Its Exception

"The exception is more interesting than the rule. The rule proves nothing; the exception proves everything. In the exception, the power of life breaks through the crust of a mechanism that has become torpid by repetition."
—Carl Schmitt, *Political Theology: Four Chapters on the Concept of Sovereignty*

What, then, is God's law? And is the *homo sacer* subject to this law? These questions linger long after Jules's declaration that he will stop walking the earth when God tells him to, a riposte to those—such as

Vincent—who cry *qua* Nietzsche that "God is dead." Here an affinity can be drawn between K in Franz Kafka's masterpiece *The Trial* and Jules, who will wait to hear God's call.[12] How will he know it when it comes? Both are convinced that they know the law, yet each is beholden to an exception. Over the course of K's journey, he is thwarted in his attempt to determine the nature of his crime, a journey that is distilled in the parable "Before the Law," the parable of a man who seeks to gain entry to the law. The same man is kept in suspension, endlessly bribing the doorkeeper. He eventually confronts the doorkeeper with the question of why nobody else has sought him out, why nobody else has tried to access the law directly while he is there. He tells him that the door is meant only for him. Many have interpreted Kafka's parable in starkly different ways, with some seeing a reference to tyrannical authoritarianism used to keep people in check. Others see it as a parable concerning Judaism: the Law a metaphor for an all-powerful and invisible God. *Pulp Fiction* presents K's problems in something of a different light. As argued in this essay, it is the question of the law and its exception—mediated through the sovereign Marsellus—that dominates from the film's outset. When is a foot massage a massage? What does Marsellus want when Vincent is asked to take Mia out for an evening? Do the terms of the contract change when Butch comes to the sovereign's rescue? The film's characters are caught in a noir-like universe of shades without clear light. Because facts do not translate into a singular legal "truth," the characters seek something that is without reserve. According to Agamben, there is no natural link between the registered facts and law.

Kafka's protagonist cannot know the law that governs. Everyone is guilty under the law; nobody can determine the precise cause of this guilt. The state of exception is the truth of *the* modern world: once life is politicized, everyone is an exception. *Pulp Fiction* reorients things, as I argued in this essay, by harking back to a space before life takes on this form: when the *homo sacer* is still a truly sacred exception, exceeding the state while free to walk the earth. This focus, I suggested, makes *Pulp Fiction* fittingly postmodern as a text in the Lyotardian sense of the term over any proper Jamesonian direction. This is not to deny that the film has many features employing the standard postmodern tropes outlined by Jameson in his scholarly work. Nonetheless, we need to acknowledge that there is something unique to the Tarantino worldview that manifests in *Pulp Fiction* alone: that we come to know the law through the sacred exception. Underlining the often-witty dialogue of Tarantino films then is a preoccupation with spaces such as these that manifest in time: life before it is subject to the political. There is still a way out, still lines of flight compatible with pure Being. Perhaps the main reason Jackie Brown (Pam Grier) is so memorable as a heroine in the later *Jackie Brown* is that she, too, escapes the clutches of the sovereign Ordell. "She knows she needs to pull off a flawless crime," Roger Ebert notes, "or she'll be dead." *Jackie Brown*'s end complements the end of *Pulp Fiction*. Jackie visits her "partner" Max (Robert Forster) to tell him she never used him.

The film's heroine sits on an office couch, asking if Max is afraid of her. Max uses his small fingers to indicate that a portion of him is and then says a little bit. She looks up from the couch to invite Max to accompany her to Spain before suddenly standing up as both characters edge close together. They kiss. Like the end of *Pulp Fiction*, when the camera cuts from a side profile of one character to another to indicate the strength of Vincent's and Jules's bond, the camera moves from Jackie to Max. Then Jackie drives away in her car as Max looks on, intimating he could drop everything to be with her. He appears "torpid by repetition," a subject of the profane Law and Jackie a sacred exception. Again, as in *Pulp Fiction*, the film ends with an escape from the polis: Jackie is not so much intent on walking the earth Jules walks, yet not indifferent in her desire to do so. "*Jackie Brown*," for David Roche, along with "*Kill Bill, Death Proof*, and even *Inglourious Basterds* to an extent," relates the downfall of a perverse patriarch at the hands of one or several female protagonists.[13] The perverse patriarch is the sovereign who yields power over life, like the sovereign Marsellus. *Jackie Brown* ends with a powerful heroine escaping the city, her gaze staring outward. Bobby Womack's "Across 110th Street" comes on the soundtrack, a song about escaping the ghetto. The world is one big ghetto, but Jackie, like Jules, is checking out. These are the sacred exceptions in a world of sovereigns and overriding state power. They walk the earth, leaving the big smoke in that ineluctable state of pure Being.

NOTES

1. Fredric Jameson, *Postmodernism or, the Logic of Late Capitalism* (Durham: Duke University Press, 1991).

2. Jean Francois Lyotard, "Answering the Question: What Is Postmodernism?" in *Modernism/Postmodernism*, ed. Peter Brooker, 139–51 (London: Routledge, 1992).

3. Giorgio Agamben, *Homo Sacer: Sovereign Power and Bare Life*, trans. Roazen, Daniel Heller, 99–100 (Stanford: Stanford University Press, 1998).

4. *Ibid.*, 129.

5. Martin P. Rossouw, "Loyalty, Women and 'Business': Ideological Hyper-Values in Quentin Tarantino's *Pulp Fiction*," *Arts Academia* 45 (2013): 84–118.

6. Agamben, *Homo Sacer*, 145.

7. *Ibid.*, 171.

8. Carmen Gray, "*Pulp Fiction*: What was really in the briefcase?" *Dazed*, 2014, https://www.dazeddigital.com/artsandculture/article/19937/1/pulp-fiction-whats-in-the-briefcase?

9. Agamben, *Homo Sacer*, 182.

10. *Ibid.*, 183.

11. *Ibid.*, 146.
12. Franz Kafka, *The Trial*, trans. Will Muir (London: Vintage, 2001).
13. David Roche, *Quentin Tarantino: Poetics and Politics of Cinematic Metafiction* (Jackson: University of Mississippi Press, 2018), 87.

WORKS CITED

Agamben, Giorgio. *Homo Sacer: Sovereign Power and Bare Life*. Trans. Daniel Heller Roazen. Stanford: Stanford University Press, 1998.
Bande à part. Dir. Jean-Luc Godard. Orsay Films, 1964.
Breaking Bad. Written and produced by Vince Gilligan. AMC, 2008–2013.
Django Unchained. Dir. Quentin Tarantino. Columbia Pictures, 2012.
Ebert, Roger. Review of *Jackie Brown* in *Chicago Sun-Times*, 1997.
The Godfather II. Dir. Francis Ford Coppola. Paramount Pictures, 1974.
Gray, Carmen. "Pulp Fiction: What Was Really in the Briefcase?" *Dazed*, 2014. https://www.dazeddigital.com/artsandculture/article/19937/1/pulp-fiction-whats-in-the-briefcase.
The Hateful Eight. Dir. Quentin Tarantino. The Weinstein Company, 2015.
Jameson, Fredric. *Postmodernism or, the Logic of Late Capitalism*. Durham: Duke University Press, 1991.
Kafka, Franz. *The Trial*. Trans. Will Muir. London: Vintage, 2001.
Kill Bill Vol. 1. Dir. Quentin Tarantino. Miramax Films, 2003.
Kill Bill Vol. 2. Dir. Quentin Tarantino. Miramax Films, 2004.
Kiss Me Deadly. Dir. Robert Aldrich. Parklane Pictures, Inc., 1955.
Kung Fu. Written by Ed Spielman. Warner Bros. Television, 1972–1975.
Lyotard, Jean François. "Answering the Question: What Is Postmodernism?" in *Modernism/Postmodern*, ed. Peter Brooker, 139–151. London: Routledge, 1992.
Pulp Fiction. Dir. Quentin Tarantino. Miramax Films, 1994.
Roche, David. *Quentin Tarantino: Poetics and Politics of Cinematic Metafiction*. Jackson: University of Mississippi Press, 2018.
Rossouw, Martin P. "Loyalty, Women and 'Business': Ideological Hyper-Values in Quentin Tarantino's *Pulp Fiction*." *Arts Aacdemia* 45, no. 4 (2013): 84–118.
Schmitt, Carl. *Political Theology: Four Chapters on the Concept of Sovereignty*. Trans. George Schwab. Chicago: University of Chicago Press, 2015.
Withnail & I. Dir. Bruce Robinson. Handmade Films, 1987.

Putting the Punch in Elmore Leonard's *Rum Punch*

Jackie Brown *as Homage*

CHARLES J. RZEPKA

In style, themes, and characterization, the works of Quentin Tarantino and Elmore Leonard share a family resemblance so striking that only
the disparity in their ages might challenge the assumption that they're
twins separated at birth. Perhaps adoption offers a better analogy. As
director Steven Soderbergh told Sheila Johnson in 1999, referring to the
first of three successive box-office hits in the late '90s inspired by Leonard's
crime novels, "Quentin Tarantino's rise has so much to do with Elmore
Leonard's world ... that by the time a 'real' Leonard adaptation showed up
in the form of *Get Shorty*, everyone had been prepared by *Reservoir Dogs*
and *Pulp Fiction* for that tone" (Kaufman).

Soderbergh's "everyone" could not have included anyone familiar
with Leonard's history of writing for the movies, or the older writer's fictional world in general, which had originated in the Old West and was
chugging merrily along under its own steam by 1963, the year Tarantino
was born. Far from preparing them for the "tone" of *Get Shorty* (1995) on
screen, *Reservoir Dogs* (1992) and *Pulp Fiction* (1994) would have struck a
familiar chord to any reader of *Get Shorty* in print (1990). That was no accident. "Elmore Leonard ... was the first novelist I read as a kid that really
spoke to me," Tarantino told Adrian Wooton less than two weeks after
Jackie Brown, his film adaptation of Leonard's *Rum Punch* (1992), pre-
miered on Christmas Day, 1997. Tarantino's enthusiasm began at age 12
and got him in trouble three years later when he tried to shoplift a copy of
Leonard's *The Switch* (1978) from a local Kmart.[1] Which reminds us that in
cases of artistic influence, the adoptive metaphor must always be reversed:
it's the younger *epigone* who chooses a *mentor* to emulate, not the other

way around, and his gratitude is expressed by imitation. Leonard's books helped a young Tarantino to perfect the "tone" that, as Soderbergh suggests, prepared the way for Leonard's successful return to film prominence after decades of sporadic Hollywood misfires.

From the beginning of his career, writing Westerns in the 1950s, Elmore Leonard had his eye on the movies, conceiving his stories and books cinematically well before he began to write screenplays. Successful movie versions of Leonard's fiction like *3:10 to Yuma* and *The Tall "T"* (both released in 1957), *Hombre*, starring Paul Newman (1967), and *Valdez Is Coming*, featuring Burt Lancaster (1971), held out the promise of more to come as Leonard, beginning in 1965, began the tough transition from horse operas to crime capers, the genre for which he was to become famous.[2] That promise dimmed at the outset with *The Big Bounce* (1969), starring Ryan O'Neal. "The second-worst movie ever made," he later told Neely Tucker of *The Washington Post*. "God, it was awful," he said, adding, "The worst movie ever made was the second version of *The Big Bounce*," directed by George Armitage and released 25 years later (Tucker).

Until his *fin de siècle* celluloid renaissance, the only film based on a Leonard book or screenplay comparable in popularity to his movie Westerns was, arguably, *Mr. Majestyk* (1974), a Charles Bronson vehicle that began life as a screenplay commissioned by Clint Eastwood. Leonard re-wrote it as a book to be published simultaneously with the movie's release.[3]

Leonard's crime novels were generally mishandled by the studios until *Get Shorty* made its debut in 1995, "one of the first films to surf the post–Tarantino wave," in Oliver Lyttleton's opinion (Lyttleton). The most important reason for its success? "This is Leonard's voice on screen pure and simple," writes Lyttleton, crediting Scott Frank's screenplay as well as Barry Sonnenfeld's direction. While there are certain features of Leonard's "voice" in prose that can't be replicated on film, even in dialogues,[4] Frank and Sonnenfeld, like Tarantino in *Jackie Brown* (1997) and Soderbergh himself working with Frank in *Out of Sight* (1998), did manage to capture, even when they didn't copy to the letter, the diction, rhythm, and tone of Leonard's dialogues and internal monologues.

They also grasped the most fundamental element necessary to any successful adaptation of a Leonard book: adhering to the author's deadpan sense of humor.

As Leonard himself told Sonnenfeld before the filming of *Get Shorty* began, "When someone delivers a funny line, I hope you don't cut to another actor to get a reaction, like a grin or a laugh or something, because these people are serious" (Orr para. 11). Sonnenfeld listened, but Leonard had little reason to expect he would, or Tarantino or Soderbergh either, for that matter. His advice to Sonnenfeld echoes his criticism of Burt Reynolds, director of the 1985 movie version of Leonard's *Stick* (1983), which the author found appalling. As he wrote Reynolds afterward, "When I'm writing I see real people and hear people ... but when I view [your] picture I see, too often, actors acting.... I hear what seems to me too many beats between exchanges, pauses for reactions, smiles for the benefit of the audience—like saying, get it?" (quoted in Vasquez).

Of the three directors responsible for resurrecting Leonard's Hollywood career as he entered the seventh decade of his life, Quentin Tarantino probably came closest, by familiarity and temperament, to both hearing Leonard's voice and understanding his sense of humor, as the author himself acknowledged. "That was not an adaptation," he said after seeing *Jackie Brown*, "that was my novel" (Wooton)—a remarkable compliment, considering that one of the most often cited departures from Leonard's original was Tarantino's decision to cast a Black actress, Pam Grier, in the title role. In *Rum Punch*, Jackie Burke (as she's known) is white. As we'll see, however, Leonard's handling of color suggests there was a Jackie *Brown* hiding inside Jackie *Burke* all along.

One advantage Tarantino had over Sonnenfeld and Soderbergh, besides his life-long admiration for Leonard's work, was that he wrote the screenplay for the film he directed, so he had two tries to get it right. During the filming, he could change what he'd written to better fit the performances, or encourage improvisations in the same key.

Here's a minor example. Preparing for the "trial run" of a gun money sting at LAX, Detective Mark Dargus (Michael Bowen), Federal Agent Ray Nicolet (Michael Keaton), and money "mule" Jackie Brown (Pam Grier) argue briefly over Nicolet's description of the Del Amo mall shopping bag to be used for carrying the cash, a description Nicolet is recording. It's purple, he announces. No, white, says Mark. White, with pink lettering, says Jackie. Mark corrects her: the *image* is purple, with pink lettering. Ray, exasperated, announces that the bag is "white, it's got purple on it, and the lettering's pink" (1:26:00–1:26:16). Neither book nor screenplay includes this 16-second spat, but it's in keeping with Leonard's and Tarantino's shared taste for random, comic digression. Whether improvised by the actors or by the director on the spot, it was Tarantino's decision to let this exchange play out and to keep it.

I've chosen four broad categories for sorting out the affinities and differences between Leonard's book and Tarantino's adaptation: structure, style, themes, and characterization. "Tone," which includes "sense of humor," will be considered further under "Style." Tarantino's boldest move, casting a Black woman in the role of Leonard's white Jackie Burke, will come last under "Characterization."

Structure

Given how much of *Rum Punch* had to be left out of the movie, even at a playing length of two and half hours, it's a wonder that what did make the cut should adhere so closely to Leonard's main plotline, despite Tarantino's relocating the action from Miami to Los Angeles' South Bay, the director's home turf. This may not have been the case had Tarantino followed his original intention to produce the film without directing it when Miramax first obtained the rights in 1994, along with two other Leonard novels, *Freaky Deaky* (1988) and *Killshot* (1989). He'd originally read the book in galleys just before it was published, but on rereading it, decided to adapt and direct the movie himself. "Lo and behold," he later told Wooton, "I saw the same movie I saw the first time, when I read [the galleys]. It just came back again. I thought I wanted to do this" (Wooton). Turning a book into a film seemed to Tarantino the right next step in his evolution as a screenwriter and director following the rapid-fire successes of *Reservoir Dogs* and *Pulp Fiction*: "Original writers need to do an adaptation … every once in awhile so a certain sameness doesn't creep into the work," Tarantino said at a press conference to promote the film (Sherman 156). He had long admired Leonard's handling of character and motivation, and wanted to see if he could do justice to the original using the same characters in a movie version. That's one reason, observes Dale Sherman, that he spent "the first hour introducing the characters to the audience before the real action begins," a departure from his standard practice (156).

Tarantino introduced his main character last, along with the two cops that were about to put the screws to her. This delay, too, indicates the director's respect for his source, for Leonard waits until chapter four to introduce his female protagonist. The delay, along with Leonard's shift to the cops' surveillance point of view (255), adds some mystery to Jackie Burke's personality. We don't know at first who these two men are or why they're watching her, and once we do, we still don't know if she's done what Mark and Ray accuse her of. Similarly, aside from the opening credits, we don't lay eyes on Jackie Brown until almost half an hour into Tarantino's film (00:27:32), right at the moment she's arrested at LAX smuggling $50,000 into the country in her flight bag.

That's well beyond the legal currency limit, and all of it is headed for Ordell Robbie (Samuel L. Jackson), an illicit gun dealer who launders his money through a Mexican bank. Working for tiny Cabo Air, which shuttles between Cabo San Lucas and LA, Jackie is the ideal courier for Ordell's loot. Once Mark and Ray catch her with the goods, however, she has no choice but to cooperate in a sting operation aimed at Ordell if she wants to avoid being charged as his accessory. Half the fun of *Jackie Brown* is watching Jackie play Ordell and his two hangers-on, former prison buddy Louis Gara (Robert De Niro) and surfer-girl Melanie Ralston (Bridget Fonda), against her police handlers long enough to avoid getting killed or imprisoned. Along the way she latches onto $500,000 in cash and Ordell's black Mercedes.

The other half of the fun is watching the romantic relationship between Jackie and Max Cherry (Robert Forster) bud and bloom, only to fade suddenly at the very end.

Cherry is the bail bondsman Ordell hires to post bail for Jackie so he can kill her before she starts giving the police information in exchange for a reduced sentence. Max falls in love with Jackie at first sight, when he comes to pick her up from her holding cell, and is soon inveigled into helping her execute the elaborate shell game she's contrived in order to make off with the bulk of Ordell's money, leaving Ordell and the cops with the petty cash.

Because *Rum Punch* was an unplanned sequel to *The Switch* (the coveted prize of Tarantino's adolescent larceny), serious Leonard fans, including the director himself, would have already known something about the shared history of Ordell, Louis, and Melanie. All three were featured in the earlier book, which pivoted on a botched kidnapping scheme. For those not in the know, Leonard had enough room to allude to their backstory, enriching and complicating the characters' decision-making in the present. Tarantino hasn't the luxury to include any of this. His Ordell and Louis have done time together, but the rap isn't specified, and Melanie is a recently acquired beach bunny with just enough intelligence to think she can scam some cash off Ordell during the final money-switch at the Del Amo mall. As in the book, however, she ends up dead, as do Louis and Ordell, in that order.

Occasionally, Tarantino has to stitch together pieces of scenes and snatches of dialogue, re-locate some scenes, and add to others to make connections and provide character insights Leonard achieves through his allusions to *The Switch*. Chapter 14 of *Rum Punch*, for instance, was mined for three separate scenes in the movie. The first is the opening scene with Ordell and Louis watching a video promotion for automatic weapons ("Chicks Who Love Guns"). In the second, an hour into the film, Louis and Melanie get to know each other better following their introduction. After a brief cut-away and return, Melanie urges Louis to help her rip off Ordell. Most of this scene was written by Tarantino. The exception is a handful of lines that include an exchange taken from page 338 of Leonard's novel:

MELANIE: Wanna fuck?
LOUIS: Yeah.

"Three minutes later" (according to a subtitle over black), Louis says, "That hit the spot," and Melanie agrees: "Now, we can catch up" (1:07:54–1:08:25).

Here, Tarantino's stitching (or that of his editor, Sally Menke) seems to have left a thread hanging from *The Switch*, since Melanie's reply suggests that she and Louis first met a long time ago. A more appropriate response would be something like "Now we can get to know each other." Because Melanie's line doesn't appear in the published screenplay, it gives the impression of something overlooked when Tarantino edited an earlier draft, as though he'd originally meant to include some references to *The Switch* but changed his mind. This impression is reinforced by an exchange occurring a few moments previously, where Melanie asks, "When was the last time I saw you?" and Louis replies, "Oh, six, seven years ago" (1:05:35). These lines in the film, referring directly to a shared history, are also missing from the published version of the screenplay.

The third scene from Chapter 14 occurs in the film not long after the three-minute fuck: Jackie's first meeting with Ordell in the Cockatoo Bar. There she lays out her plan to get him his money by playing along with Ray and Mark's sting operation, which goes very wrong for Ordell and the cops but oh-so-right for the woman they all believe they have under their thumb.

Tarantino wisely dropped two of Leonard's major subplots: Max Cherry's decision to divorce his separated wife, Reneé, a narcissistic art gallery owner, and anything having to do with how Ordell acquires his weapons for resale, including his raid on the rural compound of a wealthy fascist sympathizer (Gerald, aka "Big Guy") in order to steal his cache of rocket launchers and AK-47s. Unfortunately, the latter cut also meant leaving out the meth-crazed "jackboys" that Ordell uses for his home invasions—a dependable go-to whenever Leonard wants to serve up his trademark cocktail of violence, stupidity, and humor. Even a scene between Ordell and Louis that the screenplay originally set at the rented storage locker where Ordell keeps his guns was relocated to the bar at the Cockatoo Inn.

Style

Nearly any feature of a movie or book can come under this heading. Aside from themes and characterization, which will be treated separately, tone and point of view are the most important. We'll start with tone, which includes voice, pace, and affect.

Considering that movie makers as a rule eschew voiceovers, it's remarkable that so many directors faltered when translating Leonard's fiction into film, for cinema's narrative silence matches Leonard's narrative *desideratum*. Leonard told anyone who would listen that he tried to remain "invisible" in his books by letting his characters' voices—their characteristic diction, syntax, turns of phrase, and rhythms—seep into his prose, to the point where any sense of an authorial persona simply disappeared. It was as though he took "I am a camera," Christopher Isherwood's famous statement from the first page of *Goodbye to Berlin* (1939), literally. "For the most part I'm copying a sound of speech," Leonard has said, "so that my 'sound' or style or attitude is the sound of the characters. You never hear me. You're never aware of words used by an author because I never use a word that my characters wouldn't or couldn't" (Skinner 41).

In short, all any screenwriter or director has to do to capture Leonard's vocal tone is remain true to what his characters say and, more importantly, how they deliver their lines. Despite numerous minor changes in phrasing and word order, Tarantino's characters sound like their prose counterparts, whether the latter are speaking aloud or talking in their heads. Jackie Brown and her cohorts use more obscenities and speak in shorter bursts under the temporal constraints that film inevitably imposes on a novel's verbal expansiveness. Still, the prevailing tone of voice in Tarantino's movie is a close match to its fictional original, despite its deviations from Leonard's prose. As Tim Lucas puts it in "Breaking Down *Jackie Brown*," a panel discussion led by Elvis Mitchell that accompanies Lionsgate's Blu-ray DVD release, Tarantino is not so much echoing Leonard but "constructing his voice" as if from scratch ("Breaking Down").

Contrary to what we might expect, Tarantino's more staccato rhythms in dialogue don't carry over to his pacing of events, which matches that of the book. Sherman's comment about letting Leonard's sense of character emerge is relevant here. Indeed, compared to Tarantino's standard product, and especially *Jackie Brown*'s immediate predecessors *Reservoir Dogs* and *Pulp Fiction*, the held close-ups—as when Max first sees Jackie (00:40:21–00:41:20)—and the getting-to-know-you conversations—between Max and Jackie, for instance (00:53:28–1:00:17), or even Louis and Melanie (1:03:00–1:08:45)—are more frequent. The slower pace contributes to what Scott Foundas, in Mitchell's roundtable discussion, calls the "autumnal quality" of the film, reflecting the midlife crisis that prompts both its romantic leads to take desperate measures that might otherwise seem out of character. It also makes *Jackie Brown* a disappointment at first to Tarantino fans like Andy Klein, a fellow panelist, who expected another *Pulp Fiction* but found the film "terrific" the second time around ("Breaking Down").

Tarantino's and Leonard's shared sense of humor is relevant to any discussion of affect, a prominent feature of style, in *Jackie Brown*. Mark,

Ray, and Jackie's disagreement regarding the color of the shopping bag Jackie will be carrying is a case in point: it works because this isn't the time to be arguing over something as trivial as the bag's exact color. *Rum Punch* contains many such moments of situational humor. In one scene left out of the movie, the jackboys try to figure out the directions for firing a shoulder-mounted rocket launcher at the cops who have trapped them in Ordell's storage locker. Being almost entirely illiterate, however, they succumb to a stun grenade before they can figure out how to release the safety (405–7). "Couldn't read it, could you?" Nicolet asks the jackboy named Zulu. "See? You should never've dropped out of school" (407).

This scene is funny, in part, because its violent payoff is never realized: no one ends up hurt or dead.[5] However, both Leonard and Tarantino are known for mixing more overt violence with humor, if in different proportions, and the aesthetics of violence, like an author's or director's sense of humor, is also a matter of tone. Tarantino is more graphic in his violence than Leonard (the torture scene in *Reservoir Dogs* marks a limit case for many viewers and reviewers) and he more often uses revenge as motivation, which tends to mitigate our revulsion: we feel these victims deserve what they get. At times, however, Tarantino invites us to laugh at horrifying punishment for its own sake, as if we were watching a cartoon. *Jackie Brown* is an outlier for the director in this respect as well. Its four *coups de grâce* are, for a Tarantino film, brief and tidy (in Melanie's case the victim even gets it off-camera) and thus more aligned with Leonard's relatively discreet handling of violent crime. Also, none of these four are revenge killings.

This is not the place to discuss the merits and demerits of Tarantino's use of violence, which has sharply divided viewers and critics alike.[6] But his and Leonard's mix of humor with violence does raise a stylistic question: is there a difference in how each of them tries to make laughter compatible with fear, pain, and suffering? Though often couched in moral terms, this is really a question about the aesthetics of violence, not its morality, and typically depends on a corresponding vocabulary of evaluation, e.g., "gratuitous" or "meretricious" on the negative side, "serious" or "meaningful" on the positive. Because aesthetics focuses on the formal integration of all elements in the work of art into its structure, themes, and characterizations as a whole, any violence that can't be integrated in this way raises a moral suspicion, like gratuitous sex, that it's there just to pander to our baser instincts and, by extension, turn us into bad people.[7] Thus, the aesthetics of violence may provoke moral questions, but these are secondary to what aesthetics is all about. They are also unrelated to the *moral attitude* the work of art conveys toward human action within the world it represents, which is something that belongs under the heading "Themes" and intersects with the idea of poetic justice.

Several critics who have focused on the aesthetics of violence in Tarantino's films have mounted a stylistic defense, turning on its head the accusation that the director celebrates violence "for its own sake" by, in effect, invoking the "art for art's sake" motto of early modernism. Jeva Lange, for instance, considers the gore in Tarantino's movies as "yet another tool to emphasize the artifice—and, contained within that, the *possibility*—of filmmaking as a medium," which would turn it into a commentary on film itself (Lange). Because the violence is "unnatural, unrealistically bloody, and heavily stylized," she considers it integral to at least the visual meaning of the director's work. Elmore Leonard's use of violence elicits no such defense because it never rises to the level of needing one. Cormac McCarthy's handling of violence in a book like *Blood Meridian* is probably a closer match to Tarantino's than you'll find in anything Leonard ever wrote, with the possible exception of a few pages in *Split Images* (300–5), where the morally numbing effect of stylized violence is the aesthetic point.

Tarantino is accused of pandering not only because we often feel he's inviting us to take pleasure in the infliction of pain, but also because he makes no bones about admitting that he likes cinematic violence. "If you ask me how I feel about violence in real life, well, I have a lot of feelings about it. It's one of the worst aspects of America. In movies, violence is cool. I like it" (quoted in Kornhaber). While Leonard is famous for saying he "accepts" all of his characters and even has "an affection for them," including the violent ones, he's quick to add, "Doesn't mean that I like them," or, presumably, what they do (Grobel 282). Accordingly, as in the case of Ordell's illiterate jackboys, Leonard invites us to laugh *at* rather than *with* even his scariest psychopathic killers. In *Jackie Brown*, Tarantino follows his mentor's lead, which is one reason why you won't find this movie cited by those who deplore violence in his films. Not only is the carnage here less graphic and drawn out, but when Tarantino mixes humor with violence, he either invites us to laugh at, not with, those inflicting it or he uses a comic element to intensify by contrast the horror of the act rather than to mitigate it. Louis Gara's shooting of Melanie illustrates the first option.

Louis and Melanie become involved in the money switch at the Del Amo mall when another female participant, Simone, backs out after the trial run-through, disappearing with $10,000 of Ordell's illegal profits. Melanie is there to fill in for Simone, and Louis is there to make sure Melanie doesn't follow Simone's lead. Louis's irritation with Melanie's lackadaisical attitude grows throughout this scene. She makes them late for the drop-off and seems constantly distracted; he's a professional bank robber who understands the importance of promptness and timing. Plus, he suspects she's trying to pull a fast one. After Melanie receives the shopping bag full of cash from Jackie, Louis tears it away from her and heads for the parking lot. But he doesn't remember where they came in, or where they parked. Melanie begins needling him in a sarcastic voice, asking how "Lou-isss" ever robbed banks if he couldn't remember where he parked his car. She continues as they wander up and down the lot until Louis orders her to shut up: "I mean it. Don't say one fuckin' word, ok?" (1:53:07). Unable to resist, Melanie can't help replying, "Okay, Lou-isss." Whereupon Louis pulls out his gun and shoots her, twice. Spotting the van, he hurries toward it, shouting, "See, just where I said it was!" (1:53:21). In the screenplay he adds, yelling out the window as he drives away, "Hey, look, I found it!"

Louis's sarcasm is not entirely lost on us, the viewers: these one-liners (both taken from Leonard's text) do make us laugh, in part because we, too, found Melanie annoying. But her fecklessness and needling has turned Louis into the stumblebum bank robber she took him for. Not only did he forget where he entered the store and where he parked the van, but he also shot a gun, twice, in a public parking lot and now he's trying to one-up a corpse. He even stalls the van as he backs it out. In short, we laugh at Louis even as we laugh with him, just as we laugh at his embarrassment and confusion in a subsequent scene, where he tries to explain to Ordell what happened to Melanie and finally blurts out, "I shot her" (2:00:22). This is the same Louis we meet in *Rum Punch*, the one who tries to hold up a liquor store by putting his hand in his pocket and pointing his finger at the owner, who replies, "Why don't you take your finger out of there and stick it in your ass while I go get my shotgun" (294). Louis later returns with a real gun, but it's obvious he's gotten rusty in the joint and isn't thinking too clearly out of it.

When Tarantino can't, like Leonard, direct our ridicule at characters that inflict pain, he uses humor to heighten our revulsion rather than lessen it. Ordell's murder of Beaumont Livingston, another member of his crew, shows us how.

Beaumont, a parolee arrested for possessing illegal drugs and carrying an unregistered weapon, is facing a sentence of 10 years, and Ordell fears he might make a plea deal. Beaumont's already told the cops about Jackie's role as Ordell's money mule, which is why she's about to be stopped and searched on her next arrival at LAX. Ordell bails Beaumont out of jail, as he will Jackie, in order to kill him before he can cough up any more vital information. "Beaumont don't got a doin' time disposition," he tells Max Cherry when making the arrangements (00:15:03). The evening of Beaumont's release, Ordell asks him to help out as security for an arms delivery by hiding in the trunk of Ordell's car with a shotgun. It makes no sense, of course, but Beaumont eventually agrees despite his misgivings because he feels obliged to Ordell for springing him.

Stand-up comedian Chris Tucker earned Tarantino's praise for his performance as Beaumont, which he plays in broad comic strokes ("Interview"). Tucker's high, loud, whiny voice sings a comical *recitative* of complaints and refusals right up to and just past the moment the trunk slams down, stopping only when Ordell starts the car. In a cinematographic *tour de force*, Tarantino then uses a continuous, slowly elevating crane shot to track the car as it circles the block to enter a fenced-in empty lot across the street from Beaumont's motel. During these two long minutes (00:21:04–00:23:01), we hear nothing but the laid-back soul music on Ordell's cassette player, fading with distance, until the moment the car stops and Ordell gets out and opens the trunk. Beaumont's cartoonish voice, now diminished with distance, comes bursting out as though it had never stopped. With two quick shots, Ordell puts a stop to it (00:23:02). He slams the trunk down and restarts the car, and as the cassette resumes playing, he drives slowly out of the lot.

Whatever laughs Tucker's performance may have earned up to the point where he's locked inside the trunk of Ordell's car, those laughs are silenced the instant Beaumont is silenced forever. That's when the calculated cruelty of Ordell's ruse, growing on us from the moment we first realize he's only driving around the block, registers in direct but inverse proportion to the hilarity of Tucker's previous routine, which now serves, in stark contrast, to heighten rather than diminish its emotional impact.

Visual and aural distancing is crucial to achieving this somber effect, and that depends on Tarantino's mastery of point of view.

A director's options in controlling point of view are generally limited to what can be seen or spoken diegetically, within the world depicted on screen.[8] The movie audience necessarily adopts the impersonal, exteriorized perspective of the camera, which can occasionally, through a facial close-up, establish a specific character's point of view for the shots that immediately follow. However, no camera can allow us to overhear that character's silent thoughts or experience what they smell, taste, or touch. Writers of fiction can lead us into the deepest recesses of a character's thoughts, impressions, and sensations through direct description ("he considered...," "it seemed to her that...," "they smelled smoke...," "it tasted salty...") or through what's known as free indirect discourse (FID), where thoughts and sensations described in the third person and in past tense make us feel as though we're overhearing an interior monologue silently running through the character's mind ("She entered the room. What was that smell? Smoke!"). FID, a prominent feature of Leonard's style, particularly resists translation onto the screen, dependent as it is on grammatical markers like verb tense, person, and mood.[9]

However, the limitations on point of view imposed by film also offer opportunities unavailable to a writer. The pathos registered by distance in the tracking crane shot of Beaumont Livingston's murder would be impossible in a book unless the author gave us visual instructions: "Imagine Ordell's car driving away as you rise into the air...." That kind of direct address would be fatal to the narrative invisibility that Elmore Leonard prized more than anything else. Elsewhere, Tarantino circles the camera around Jackie Brown's head to convey her (feigned) panic as she looks for her handlers, Ray and Mark, after the money handoff goes (apparently) wrong (01:45:05–01:45:20). That, too, is beyond the capabilities of fiction. Meanwhile, Tarantino can exploit to the full Leonard's chameleon tendency to tell the story from his characters' perspectives by using establishment or point-of-view tracking shots whenever necessary. FID may be off the table, but Tarantino shows tremendous agility in trying to recreate Leonard's shifts in narrative perspective without leaving the viewer dazed and confused.

For instance, Chapter 22 of *Rum Punch* follows the complicated events of the real money transfer at the Del Amo mall (the first was a rehearsal) through 12 changes in point of view using four different characters in a span of only 15 pages. Tarantino re-shuffles these 12 fragments into three scenes, each dominated by a particular character's point of view (Louis's dominates the scene that includes Melanie) and integrates each of these three scenes into a continuous, self-contained narrative sequence, in the following order: Jackie, Louis, and Max. Establishment shots, frame composition, entrances and exits, and tracking shots anchor each scene in its dominant character's point of view, while superimposed time markings in the lower left of the screen at the start of each scene indicate that all three overlap roughly within the same chronological span.

Thus, Tarantino manages to capture Leonard's perspectival relativity without leaving the viewer feeling vertiginous.

As in the movie's handling of structure and pacing, characterization—so important to Leonard—here provides Tarantino with the rationale for organizing this 16-minute span of shifting perspectives at the Del Amo mall into a unified narrative arc embracing three distinct but internally coherent points of view, all focused on the same sequence of events. Except in this one case, Tarantino generally resists the temptation—clearly irresistible in his other films—to overlap or scramble chronologies. In *Jackie Brown* the complete sequence of events is, with a few minor exceptions, straightforward and easy to follow.

Themes

The way Tarantino and Leonard see the world is rooted in their similar childhoods. Both were raised by firm but loving mothers, with the father largely absent during their formative years, and both fell in love with movies while quite young.[10] With the exception of the all-male *Reservoir Dogs*, Tarantino has included strong, assertive, independent women in nearly every film he's ever made or written. With some exceptions, like Jackie Brown, they are extremely violent, but like Jackie Brown, they are all tough as well as smart. Leonard included tough-minded female characters in many of his early sagebrush sagas, but the Code of the West dictated that, except for rare exceptions, they played a secondary role to the male protagonist and his opponent.[11]

This pattern continued after Leonard turned to crime writing until, in the late '70s, his second wife, Joan Shepard, urged him to catch up with Second Wave feminism. In *The Switch*, Leonard paid his dues. Mickey Dawson's kidnapping for ransom elicits little more than a shrug from her wealthy, alcoholic, and emotionally abusive husband, Frank, because he's keeping a mistress he intends to marry and is about to file for divorce.

Frank's mistress is Melanie, who actively discourages Frank from paying Mickey's ransom since his money is about to become her money. Mickey's kidnappers are Ordell Robbie, Louis Gara, and a loser named Richard Monk. Aided by Louis, who has developed a crush on her, Mickey escapes, "gets in touch" with her anger at Frank and Melanie, empowers the "new Mickey" inside her, and takes her revenge by making the male kidnappers a proposal they can't refuse: she and Melanie will "switch" places!

No wonder Tarantino wanted to shoplift the book.

Rum Punch resurrects the criminal cast of *The Switch*, minus Richard, to reprise the prequel's basic theme of female empowerment using a similar plot device. Like Mickey, Jackie Burke is tired of being victimized by the men in her life—husbands, criminals, cops—and gets the upper hand by "switching" two shopping bags—one containing $50,000, the other $500,000—and beguiling Max Cherry into retrieving the bag containing the half million. Max thus has a major thematic function in both *Rum Punch* and *Jackie Brown*. He introduces a romantic interest into what would otherwise amount to a fairly straightforward crime caper of the shell-game variety.

Fascinated by news accounts of Bonnie Parker and Clyde Barrow as a kid and drawn to *film noir* and the *femme fatale* as a young adult, Leonard began introducing romance elements into his crime fiction formula with his very first crime novel, *The Big Bounce*. It wasn't until later in his career, however, that these elements began to assume the recognizable features of romantic comedy.[12] The formula is hard at work not only in *Rum Punch*, but also in the other two Leonard novels that became big-screen successes in the '90s, *Get Shorty* and *Out of Sight*. What makes *Rum Punch* unusual, as we've noted, is the more advanced ages of its lovers. Part of what motivates Jackie Burke and emboldens her in the risky attempt to outsmart both the criminals and the cops is her 40-something realization that this may be her last chance, ever, to escape a life lived on the brink of poverty. "I feel like I'm always starting over ... and before I know it, I won't have any options left" (325), she tells Max, who is facing a similarly bleak end-game. Having "written something like fifteen thousand bonds" (289), he's tired of the business and decides to quit the night he bails Jackie out of prison and falls in love with her (353). Accepting her invitation to become her accomplice seems, in retrospect, inevitable.

Tarantino's screenplays and movies often include "romantic" pairings. Alabama and Clarence in *True Romance* and, more perversely, Mickey and Mallory in *Natural Born Killers* are perhaps the most conspicuous, but even in *Pulp Fiction* they number no less than three: Vincent and Mia, Butch and Fabienne, and "Pumpkin" and "Honey Bunny." The epic revenge saga *Kill Bill*, in two volumes, pivots on the failure of Bill and the Bride's previous relationship. Thus, it's no surprise that Tarantino should give the romance between Max and Jackie the same prominence it has in *Rum Punch*. In both the book and the movie, moreover, the reciprocity of the couple's romantic interest is put in question. Max is clearly smitten with Jackie, and would have helped her even without any prospect of sharing the loot. But is Jackie smitten with Max? Or, like the typical *femme fatale* of *noir* fiction and film, is she just using him, exploiting his infatuation to further her scheme? Here Leonard takes a page from the work of James M. Cain, where the amorous motivations of deadly females like Cora Papadakis in *The Postman Always Rings Twice* and Phyllis Nirdlinger in *Double Indemnity*, both of whom seduce their male partners into helping them murder their husbands, are repeatedly placed in doubt.[13] Tarantino follows Leonard's lead, but only up to a point, a topic to be examined more closely under the heading "Characterization."

The moral attitude that informs *Jackie Brown* closely resembles that of its source material and finds expression in choices that determine the value and consequences of human action and the justice of outcomes. This is a matter of theme and not tone, which seeks to elicit a specific affective response in the reader or viewer—laughter, fear, anxiety, love, sadness, joy—rather than share with them a vision of the world. Some viewers detect a bold streak of nihilism running through films like *Pulp Fiction*, which according to Mark Conrad offers a grim critique of America's pop-cultural mirage of values. But Tarantino doesn't see himself that way. "Some people have told me I'm a nihilist," he said to Geoffrey Campbell in 1994. "But I'm not a nihilist at all. I'm an optimist" (Campbell 95). So is Leonard. Tarantino's optimism finds expression in the poetic justice that, sooner or later, imposes itself on the anarchy, chaos, and random violence of his films and that, minus his standard depiction of revenge as a cathartic moral good, dictates the outcome of events in the make-believe world of *Jackie Brown* just as it does in that of *Rum Punch*. The bad guys lose and the good guys win (the cops, sort of), and the heroine and her accomplice get away with the money despite their duplicity and technical criminality: aiding and abetting a gun smuggler, absconding with evidence in a Federal crime, and, for Max, serving as an accomplice in the latter. This is standard practice in Leonard's fiction, where protagonists may engage in morally dubious, even criminal, behavior, but are just good enough, at least compared to their antagonists, to earn our desire to see them rewarded for it.

Characterization

If a director's options in manipulating point of view are more limited than an author's, the tables are turned when it comes to characterization. In addition to the vast array of past heroes and current types available to an author, a director can include in each frame many more visual and aural details of an actor's performance, as well as exploit memories of their previous film roles, to provide nuance to the character they are playing. Casting in particular is a means of characterization for which Tarantino is famous (Bailey). Many a forgotten regular of the "grindhouse," B-movie, exploitation, and horror genres that Tarantino loved as a kid have the director to thank for reviving their careers by choosing them for roles in his films, including Robert Forster, who plays Max Cherry, and Pam Grier, who plays Jackie Brown. As we'll see, even a minor role in *Jackie Brown* can benefit from the aura of past roles hovering around the actor playing that character, or from the actor's off-screen biography.

The Melanie that Tarantino created on screen differs in several obvious respects from her counterpart in *Rum Punch*. Both survive by gold digging, neither can be trusted, and each has a well-developed sexual appetite. However, Leonard's Melanie (no known last name) is a thirty-something blonde coyote with big breasts and lots of experience.

Tarantino's is a surfer-girl. Resetting the action from Miami to LA, the director wanted a younger, slimmer, SoCal atavism of the beach party movies of the '60s. Bridget Fonda's performance as Melanie Ralston fits the bill perfectly, and benefits from the mystique attached to the Fonda name. Her father, Peter Fonda, launched his career playing countercultural misfits and rebels in '60s films like *Easy Rider* (1969). Tarantino alludes to Papa Fonda's reputation at one point by showing Melanie and

Louis smoking pot and watching a scene from *Dirty Mary, Crazy Larry* (1974), a car-chase caper starring Peter playing opposite Susan George, a Bridget Fonda look-alike.

Casting Robert De Niro as Louis Gara, a role requiring little display of emotion until the final money switch at the Del Amo mall, was a counter-intuitive stroke of genius on Tarantino's part. Some viewers may have trouble connecting the affectless couch potato of the film's early scenes with the impatient, furious Louis who shoots Melanie twice in the Del Amo parking lot.[14] Why waste De Niro's talents on a loser like this? But the role as Tarantino wrote it is true to the character Leonard created: an easy-going, habitual offender and ex-con recently released from prison and unable to adjust to life outside it, where things have changed so radically in just four years that he has trouble understanding the keyless entry on Ordell's Mercedes. Louis Gara is out of his element, amiably disoriented and passively following along wherever he is led, not only by Melanie ("Wanna fuck?") and Ordell, who wants to recruit him into his posse, but even by Simone, who insists on entertaining him with her patented Diana Ross routine while he sits rocking, mildly curious but vacant-eyed, in her upholstered glider (00:23:36–00:24:16). Once Melanie reveals her treacherous plot to cheat Ordell, however, Louis's prison habits and loyalty to Ordell, both acquired the hard way when the two were inmates together, kick in and Melanie becomes their target.

Leonard, through free indirect discourse, uses Max's point of view to convey the problem with Louis:

> It was his eyes that gave him away.
> Max saw it. Those dull eyes that didn't seem to have life in them but didn't miss anything. Three falls, you don't come out, put on a new suit of clothes, and become a normal person again. That life changed you [266].

De Niro has those eyes. His amiable cluelessness accords perfectly with Tarantino's succinct restatement of Max's view in his screenplay: "While acutely aware of the rhythm of life inside a correction facility, in the real world his timing is thrown. It's like a song he doesn't know the lyrics to but attempts to sing anyway." As in Fonda's case, film history helps to enhance the credibility of De Niro's sudden transformation into a furious, cold-blooded killer. Watching him onscreen, it's difficult not to recall his breakthrough role as Travis Bickle in *Taxi Driver* (1976), a quiet, almost catatonic guy who goes off the rails not long after returning to civilian life from a tour in Vietnam. The trauma of prolonged incarceration takes the place of Bickle's Vietnam in shaping the PTSD personality of Louis Gara.

Samuel L. Jackson came to the part of Ordell Robbie trailing clouds of glory from his Oscar-nominated performance as Bible-spouting hitman

Jules Winnfield in *Pulp Fiction*, a role that catapulted him to stardom at the age of 42 after two decades of relative screen obscurity. Winnfield was a character Tarantino wrote specifically for Jackson, but in creating his version of Ordell the director also drew on three of Jackson's recent named roles in movies directed by Spike Lee: a super-cool DJ named Mister Señor Love Daddy in *Do the Right Thing* (1989), Madlock, a brutally sadistic loan shark enforcer, in *Mo' Better Blues* (1990), and "Gator" Purify, a jivin' and lyin' crack addict in *Jungle Fever* (1991). These three roles, along with Jackson's very brief but memorable appearance in the Tarantino-scripted *True Romance* as hitman "Big Don," were smelted in the furnace of Winnfield's ruthless fury to give the actor's cool, savvy, jive performance as Ordell Robbie an underlayer of bad-ass treachery and menace that breaks the surface whenever he feels threatened.

But there's another side to Jackson's Ordell Robbie that isn't apparent in these previous roles, and it conforms to the profile of villainy that dominates Elmore Leonard's fiction. Leonard described it in an interview he gave to Tim Adams, of *The Guardian*, in 2003. When asked if "living with gangsters in his head" is difficult, the writer replied, "It's really never hard.... I think of them either as stupid or just playing a role. I like to think of what they were like as children—that helps."

Whatever else he may be or thinks he is, the Ordell Robbie that Tarantino creates on screen and that Jackson plays with such élan shows himself to be, at the most crucial moments of the film, as stupid as his fictional counterpart. He lets a flight attendant get the drop on him when he goes to kill her because, instead of grabbing and strangling her when she opens her door, he decides to toy with her. Then, just as he places his fingers around her neck, he hears a "click":

ORDELL: Is that what I think it is?
JACKIE: What do you think it is?
ORDELL: I think it's a gun pressed up against my dick.
JACKIE: You thought right. Now take your hands from around my throat, nigga [00:50:43].

Once Jackie has the drop on him, Ordell has to listen as she explains her plan to get him his money back. Worse, he agrees to it. Thinking he can renege on his end of the deal once he's got his $500,000, he lets Jackie string him along to the bitter end, leaving him not only penniless, but dead. His desire to get his money out of Mexico blinds him to every glaring sign that Jackie is using the cops against him. When Ordell learns that she's told them everything she knows about his operation in order to earn their trust, he's visibly upset, but doesn't opt out. Even after the switch has gone down and Ordell realizes he's been swindled, he agrees to meet Jackie at Max's office so she can return his money. She's afraid she'll be named as an accessory, says Max over the phone, or that Ordell will shoot her before she can explain what happened. Every lame excuse Max and Jackie can come up with for meeting at Max's office, at night, where the cops are waiting for him just as he suspects, Ordell swallows—with hesitation, yes, but completely. Once he's there, it's Jackie who makes sure he's shot dead and not thrown in jail, where he might sooner or later reveal how she cheated him and snookered the cops into helping her do it. The astonished look on his dead face at the end of this scene, held for six full seconds, tells us all we need to know about Ordell's criminal IQ (2:24:19–25).

This is Ordell Robbie as Leonard originally conceived him, the Ordell who botched Mickey Dawson's kidnapping in *The Switch* and, along with Louis, ended up serving time for it. In Tarantino's film, as in *Rum Punch*, Louis admires Ordell's operation, but Melanie sees through the gun-dealer's street smart façade, telling Louis, in words taken almost verbatim from Leonard's book (342), "He's acting like he's this big international arms dealer, when, come on, face it, the only people he ever sold to were dopers.... You got to admit, he's not too bright." Louis disagrees, to which Melanie replies, "He moves his lips when he reads.... Let's say he's streetwise, you know? I'll give him that. He's still a fuck-up" (1:13:14–1:13:54). Melanie may be a bimbo, but she nails Ordell.

Ordell is not only stupid, but he's also, in Leonard's words, "playing a role." His cool demeanor is fake, as demonstrated by how quickly he loses it when Jackie tells him what she's told the cops, and as anyone with an ounce of real street savvy can detect.

Max Cherry, for instance. Robert Forster's Max is singularly unimpressed by the gym bag full of cash that Ordell has brought with him as collateral for bailing out Beaumont.

Forster's laconic, all-business voice and poker face tell us that, after writing 15,000 bonds, he's seen more than his fair share of flashy street trash like Ordell. In this respect, too, Tarantino's conception of the man remains true to the original. "Ordell got a kick out of people wondering about him," writes Leonard in *Rum Punch*, indicating the character's interest in how well he performs (240). That sliver of self-consciousness tells us Ordell is not only playing a role, but it's a role he feels insecure playing. In short, he lacks authenticity. As Max puts it a moment later, in free indirect discourse, "The kind of guy who worked at being cool, but was dying to tell you things about himself" (242). Jackson's loquacity, not just in this scene but throughout the movie, fits Max's description perfectly. When Max asks what Jackie "does" for Ordell and Ordell replies, "Why should I tell you anything?" Max says: "Because you want me to know what a slick guy you are. You got stewardesses bringing you fifty grand" (37:54–58).

Unlike Melanie, Louis, and Ordell, Max Cherry and Jackie Burke undergo significant changes in making the transition from text to screen. Taken together, these alterations underline a point more subtly registered in Tarantino's source material: the enigmatic but tantalizing threat posed by the *femme fatale* to her partner in crime.

At first glance, Pam Grier's replacing Leonard's white female protagonist seems the more radical of the two transformations. It brings the enormous cultural and political significance of skin color to bear on the heroine's personality, all of it magnified by Grier's secure position in America's pop-cultural imaginary as the doyenne of '70s blaxploitation flicks. But the omission of Max's fictional backstory from Tarantino's adaptation has, arguably, a more marked impact on our impression of Leonard's male protagonist than Grier's Blackness does on our impression of Jackie Burke. Being African American lends a certain degree of street-cred to Jackie Brown's angrier personality and more obscenity-laden speech patterns when pushed to her limits. As we'll see, however, it doesn't alter our general impression of the character she's based on or the type that both of them represent: the alluring but dangerous *femme fatale*. Jackie Burke is just as cool, determined, and wily as her screen counterpart. Just more demure.

Tarantino couldn't help but omit Max Cherry's backstory because so much of it involves his separated wife of 27 years, Reneé, and Max's gradual realization that he needs to divorce Reneé occupies a good deal of page-space. Max married Reneé back in the '60s, when he was a young cop facing anti-war demonstrators in the streets. But as he gradually rose in the ranks to Homicide Detective, Reneé expressed dissatisfaction. "She said she was worried sick all the time something would happen to me," Max tells Jackie. "Also, she said, I put the job first" (299). "Did you?" asks Jackie.

"You have to," Max replies. "So I quit. She didn't like being married to a cop—she *hates* being married to a bail bondsman" (300).

The Reneé subplot lays bare two contradictory sides to Max's personality. On the job, he's not just your ordinary bail bondsman. He's a seasoned veteran of policing and detective work who knows how criminals, male and female, operate. He's comfortable in dangerous situations, can calculate the risks, and knows how to deal with fear. In short, he's just what Jackie needs to pull off her switch. In contrast to Ordell, he's authentically cool in the only sense Leonard recognizes, or rather, he was: he knew how to do his job and did it well.[15] Off the job, however, Leonard's Max was and continues to be hen-pecked, submissive, and indecisive. The fact that he sacrificed the career he loved for the tedious paper shuffling of a bail bondsman just underlines Max's amative susceptibility, which is further emphasized by his refusal to follow through on the couple's separation two years ago and get a divorce, all the while supporting Reneé's financially disastrous pretentions as owner of an art gallery. His factotum, Winston, finds such behavior in his otherwise hard-boiled boss a constant cause for amazement. Max expresses his softer side in his love of poetry, and the Beats in particular, "Ginsberg and Corso," whom he once read to an uncomprehending Reneé while trying to woo her (298). He also tends to develop crushes on actresses, Terry Moore back in the '50s and, most recently, Annette Benning (299).[16]

Leaving this material out of his movie makes Tarantino's Max tougher and less sentimental. But without his professional backstory he also seems, oddly, more naïve. Forster, who languished in B-movie action and horror flicks after a promising start as a supporting actor in films like *Reflections in a Golden Eye* (1967) and a starring role in the critically acclaimed *Medium Cool* (1969), brings to the part of Max something of the hard-boiled world-weariness of his role as Officer David Madison, who is assigned to investigate the mysterious deaths and disappearances occurring in the 1980 cult monster flick, *Alligator*. As played by Forster, Taratino's Max Cherry would have worn Leonard's sentimental backstory like an ill-fitting suit. His sudden infatuation with Jackie is already sanctioned by the laws of romantic comedy. This is simply how "the meet-cute" always happens: in the unlikeliest of circumstances to the unlikeliest two people. Nor does this Max need a previous history in law enforcement to make his familiarity with the mean streets of life plausible. He's walked down enough of them in his present job to persuade us that, despite his skepticism, he's up to the task of helping Jackie outsmart Ordell and the cops.

What the policing backstory added to the character of Leonard's Max—and to good effect—was experience with women like Jackie, and an awareness of the possibility that she could be using him for her own ends. In the book, driving home after bailing her out of jail, Max starts "putting up pictures of Jackie Burke in his mind."

> The ones where she had that gleam in her eyes, the look saying, *We could have fun.*
> Unless she was appraising him with the look, making a judgment, and what it said was, *I could use you.*
> Maybe.
> Either way it was a turn-on [300].

In *Jackie Brown*, it never seems to occur to Max that Jackie might be using him until the point at which she gets Ordell killed. The Max in Taratino's movie is never seduced into sleeping with Jackie, so he has no reason to think she's using sex to manipulate him; Leonard's Max is, so he does.[17]

Nevertheless, the possibility doesn't deter him because, having been a professional cop, he can handle it.

In short, Tarantino's Max is more trusting than Leonard's original, even if he is less sentimental. That trust comes across most forcefully at the moment it's broken, in the scene where Ordell is shot and killed by Ray Nicolet (Michael Keaton) in Max's darkened office right after Jackie yells, "Ray, he's got a gun" (2:23:01; page 447).

Both Leonard and Tarantino make it clear that Ordell has yet to draw his weapon at this point, and although what Jackie says is technically true, its motivation is cynically performative. She says it to get Ordell killed, but only partly because she fears he's going to kill her. Knowing the cops are listening, she needs to silence Ordell before he can say anything to incriminate her and Max. This is clearly conveyed in the book when Max and Jackie go over their plans to lure Ordell to Max's office, where Ray and Mark will be waiting to arrest him. "Nicolet—is he already there, or does he come busting in while we're chatting?" asks Max.

> "He's already there."
> "What if he hears something he's not supposed to?"
> "We won't let that happen."
> "You still have a gun?"
> Jackie looked up now. "Yeah, why?"
> "Don't bring it" [441].

At first glance it looks as though Jackie is assuring Max that, with the cops overhearing all, the two of them will have to take care not to refer to her elaborate scam. But Max's question, and especially his instruction, "Don't bring it," should make a careful reader suspect what Leonard's Max already suspects: that Jackie is capable of shooting Ordell to shut him up before *he* says anything to incriminate them. That would only get Jackie back in hot water with the law, since self-defense would be off the table unless Ordell pulled his weapon first and, with a gun at hand after inviting Ordell to meet her, Jackie could also be charged with premeditation. That's a risk the experienced homicide detective inside this Max isn't willing to take.

Tarantino doesn't have time for all this. His Jackie brings her gun (the one she took from Ordell in her apartment) and spends several minutes before Ordell and Max arrive practicing a quick-draw from Max's desk, each time failing to pull out the gun fast enough. This scene, which is not in the book, has the same effect on a viewer's understanding of her intentions in exclaiming, "Ray, he's got a gun!" as Max's telling her, at the end of the previous chapter, not to bring her gun with her. Jackie means to get Ordell killed before he can say more than "Hi!" Our last clear view of Ordell before Ray reveals himself and Jackie tells him Ordell is armed shows both of Ordell's hands empty and at his sides. But an instant after Ray steps over to check his victim's vital signs, we see him kick a gun away from Ordell's right hand. This ostensible inconsistency actually corresponds to Leonard's description of what happened: "Max saw Ordell's face change. Saw his eyes come open wide with a look of surprise and then panic. Saw him pulling at his shirt to get to the pistol and did have it in his hand, cleared. But Nicolet beat him" (447).

Ordell doesn't draw his weapon until Jackie tells Ray he's got one and he knows he's about to be blown away. By then, of course, it's too late.

It can be argued that Tarantino's editing has left Jackie's culpability in doubt—did Jackie see Ordell draw his weapon before she warned Nicolet? But we should remember that it was Jackie, not Ordell, who turned off the lights before he and Max arrived. For what purpose if not to make it difficult, if not impossible, for Nicolet to tell if Ordell had drawn his weapon? In the dark, all cats are black, and all black cats (to white cops) are armed. Even if Jackie turned out to be "mistaken," well, it *was* dark, after all.

In short, Jackie Brown, like Jackie Burke, is quite literally a *femme fatale*, and Tarantino spends almost a minute and a half after Ordell is shot cutting back and forth between Max's and Jackie's faces (three times, in fact) as they stare at each other while the conversation between Max, Winston, and the two detectives continues around them. Max's face conveys stunned bewilderment, Jackie's guilt. Max's face says, "I never suspected." Jackie's says, "Now you know."

Thus, we aren't too surprised when, at the end of the film, Max turns down Jackie's offer to run off with her to Spain in Ordell's Mercedes with a suitcase of money in the trunk (2:26:06–2:26:22). "Thanks," he replies, "but you have a good time." After a second refusal, Jackie asks, "Are you scared of me?" Holding up his thumb and index finger close together, Max smiles and says, "Mmmm … a little bit." He settles instead for two, long, tender kisses before his phone rings with a frantic mother on the line trying to arrange bail for her son—exactly where we, and Ordell, came in more than two hours earlier in the film.

Rum Punch ends more ambiguously, but leaning distinctly in the opposite direction. Max keeps hesitating until, just as it looks as though he's going to say no, he asks instead, "Where would we go?" "'I don't know,' Jackie said, and he saw her eyes begin to smile. 'Does it matter?'" (451).

Leonard's novel ends here, leaving us hanging. But although we never learn for sure if Max agrees to join Jackie, the "smile" in her eyes, recalling the "gleam" that told Max "*we could have fun*," indicates the likeliest outcome, and its likelihood is made more plausible by our awareness of Max's history as a cop and a detective. If Jackie is as dangerous as she's shown herself to be, we feel Leonard's Max can handle it, or rather, that he has reason to believe he can. And he doesn't mind in the least being used.

I've saved Pam Grier's performance as Jackie Brown for last not because it has the least impact on Tarantino's adaptation of Leonard's book but because it has the most, which also means, the most obvious. For that reason, it needs the least commentary. Grier dominates the film throughout, from its opening credits—printed in the same font as the posters for her 1974 Blaxploitation hit, *Foxy Brown* (1974) (Gunst 45)—to the very end, when she walks out Max Cherry's door, drives away in Ordell's car, and starts lip-synching the tune that accompanied those opening credits: Bobby Womack's "Across 110th Street," one of Blaxploitation film's best known theme songs, from the film of the same name (1972). Jackie Brown is the riveting center of attention every time she appears, an atavism of her cinematic sisters in *Coffy* (1973), Grier's first hit, and *Foxy Brown*, her star vehicle—violent, action-packed revenge flicks of the kind that Tarantino grew up loving. But it's not just her race that carries Grier's performance, even though, as noted, it adds to Jackie Brown a layer of hard-knocks experience and street toughness missing from Leonard's Jackie Burke. Grier's Jackie is more obscene, less patient, and more prone to outbursts of rage and sass than Leonard's, and physically bigger, a veritable Amazon whose stature is magnified in the opening credits by Tarantino's waist high camera angle.

But there's an argument to be made that Jackie Burke herself was, all along, Jackie Brown in whiteface. When Leonard told Tarantino *Jackie Brown* "was my novel," he tacitly admitted as much. As Zach Vasquez observes, Tarantino's change in race saved Leonard from the dubious honor of having "noble white antiheroes" killing "vicious, half-smart Black male villains" in all three of his late-'90s screen hits (Vasquez). But Leonard has always been canny about race. From early in his career, when books like *Hombre* were anticipating the pro–Indian anti–Westerns of a decade later,[18] to the height of his crime-writing fame, when Black readers would sometimes mistake him for an African American author, Leonard never stopped ridiculing white assumptions of superiority.

While Black characters take center stage only twice in Leonard's fiction,[19] Hispanic and *mestizo* characters often do, and some of his most memorable protagonists come from mixed racial heritages. The two central male characters in *Rum Punch* are a case in point.

Ordell, for instance, is so light-skinned that his "people" call him "Whitebread." "Or they say just 'Bread' for short," he tells Max, who is dark-skinned: "Eyetalian," thinks Ordell, "except [he] had never met a bail bondsman wasn't Jewish" (239). Max thinks Ordell is Jamaican, until Ordell sets him straight, to which Max replies, "You're African-American,

I guess I'm French-American, with maybe some New Orleans Creole in there, going way back" (241).[20] From the outset, Leonard goes out of his way to establish Ordell and Max as reciprocal and reversed mirror-images of racial mixing—a "white" Black man trying to con a "Black" white man—and the book's thematic color-coding extends to Jackie Burke as well. Despite her Caucasian features, including blonde hair and a face so white that Ordell thinks it "whiter … than any white face he had been this close to" (he's just about to strangle her) (305), Burke is consistently associated with the color tan, the shade of *brown* that matches her Cabo Airline uniform and accessories. The coding begins in the first sentence introducing her to the reader (255) and extends to "the tan Bic" lighter "that matched her uniform" (260; also 323) and in particular, the "tan bag" in which she smuggles Ordell's money into the country (327).

For a writer as parsimonious with visual details as Leonard, this amount of color repetition would appear superfluous unless it were there for a reason. There's a "brownness" about "white" Jackie Burke that's more than skin deep and not a matter, as it is with Melanie, of tan lines (336). Nor is it just accessorized, because these particular accessories have to do with the particular features of her flight attendant's job that enable her to function as Ordell's money mule. Thus, by association, tan comes to represent Jackie's ability take risks and (what is flicking her Bic if not playing with fire?) stay cool[21]—an authentic cool: brisk, confident, and self-assured, as opposed to that of Ordell, Leonard's "white" Black man.[22] Like Max's self-possession, Jackie's has also been honed by her professional training: flight attendants must keep their composure in the most trying circumstances, even when facing the threat of impending disaster. Finally, as in "When the Women Come Out to Dance," a Leonard short story where color coding is also important, Jackie Burke's eyes are green—the color of money.[23]

It's unlikely that Tarantino noticed Leonard's racial color code when reading *Rum Punch*, and even unlikelier that it could have inspired his decision to cast a Black woman as Jackie. But it's not as though Leonard hadn't anticipated such a move, and his crediting Tarantino for having fully realized, on screen, the novel as he conceived it implies as much.

Conclusion

Movie adaptations are like foreign language translations, argues Lawrence Venuti, insofar as the director's aim, like the translator's, is never simply communicative, an attempt to maintain fidelity to the original, but necessarily hermeneutic, an attempt to interpret the original by producing an independent creation whose meanings are determined by its "intertextual" relations with "the receiving situation" it is forced to navigate (31). In both media, interpretation proceeds by means of an "interpretant," a set of assumptions—formal or thematic, conscious or unconscious—regarding the meaning of the original text that shapes the process of its transformation into an intertext (31).

Thus any film adaptation, like any foreign language translation, demands analysis and interpretation as a creation independent of its relationship to an original.

Every choice that Quentin Tarantino made in adapting Leonard's original text to the requirements of the big screen—what Venuti calls a director's "shifts" of material—demonstrates the validity of evaluating *Jackie Brown* as an independent cinematic intertext rather than a communicative artifact. These shifts include not only the "additions, deletions, and substitutions" (Venuti 33) demanded by the different formal resources and limitations of film itself, but also those freely chosen by the director as points of thematic emphasis or narrative reorientation. And yet, in his extravagant compliment, "that *was* my book," Leonard recognized his acolyte's ironic commitment to a communicative rather than hermeneutic model of adaptation within the interpretive constraints necessarily imposed by the director's medium of choice. That is to say, the primary interpretant guiding Tarantino's interpretation of *Rum Punch*, despite any liberties he may have taken with structure, style, theme, and above all characterization, seems to have been, from the start, fidelity—a concept anathema to Venuti's hermeneutic ideal.

Does *Jackie Brown*, then, represent an anomaly in Venuti's application of translation theory to our understanding of film adaptations? For whatever other interpretants we may bring to our analysis of its hermeneutic impact, the one that stands out as dominant in the eyes of author and director alike is also the one that seems the least hermeneutic and strives hardest to adhere to a transparently communicative model. A "Brown" Jackie Burke seems, by this standard, blatantly unfaithful, but perhaps it only makes evident a salient reality that was latent in Leonard's *femme fatale* all along, as his color-coding suggests. Is it possible to maintain fidelity to a feature unapparent to begin with? Or is that, after all, what faith is, taking "the evidence of things not seen," as Paul said (Hebrews 11:1), and bearing witness to it in one's actions?

However we choose to answer such questions, the fact remains that *Jackie Brown* is as close to a faithful adaptation of its source text as any we are likely to find in the annals of film history, and it is so precisely because of, rather than despite, Tarantino's numerous "shifts" from Leonard's original, including and especially his decision to make white Jackie Burke "Brown."

NOTES

1. Wensley Clarkson, *Quentin Tarantino: Shooting from the Hip* (Woodstock, NY: The Overlook Press, 1995), 42.

2. Charles J. Rzepka, *Being Cool: The Work of Elmore Leonard* (Baltimore: John Hopkins University Press, 2013), 75.

3. Oliver Lyttleton, "From Best to Worst: Elmore Leonard Adaptations," IndieWire, May 14, 2013, https://www.indiewire.com/2013/05/from-best-to-worst-elmore-leonard-movie-adaptations-98187/#!.

4. Rzepka, 16–24.

5. Rossita Terzieva-Artemis, "Moral Luck and Determinism in *Rum Punch*," *Critical Essays on Elmore Leonard: "If it sounds like writing,"* ed. Charles J. Rzepka (Hoboken: Wiley Blackwell, 2020), 6–7.

6. The pros and cons are neatly summarized by Jeva Lange, who defends the director, and Roy Chacko, who considers Tarantino's most brutal scenes misogynistic. Jack Wareham, also taking the negative side, adds a cultural dimension to the discussion, and the unnamed writers at *Exploring Your Mind*, adopting a largely neutral position, include a consideration of the psychology of violence going all the way back to Aristotle.

7. Thus, the formal justification set forth by District Judge John M. Woolsey in the landmark case regarding sex in James Joyce's *Ulysses* similarly applies here: "Whether or not one enjoys such a technique as Joyce uses is a matter of taste on which disagreement or argument is futile, but to subject that technique to the standards of some other technique [designed to excite sexual desire] seems to me to be little short of absurd" (Woolsey, John, 5 F. Supp. 282: *UNITED STATES v. ONE BOOK CALLED ULYSSES.* December 6, 1933). Ultimately, the aesthetics of violence depends on a Kantian concept of "disinterestedness" or impersonal objectivity: if the work of art leads us to put our personal "interest" in *what* is expressed above our appreciation of *how* it is expressed, then it is not really "art" but entertainment or propaganda or pornography.

8. The rare exception is an extra-diagetic first-person voice-over, like Fred MacMurray's in Billy Wilder's *Double Indemnity* (1944).

9. For details distinguishing point of view from grammatical person, as well as the relation of both free indirect discourse, see Rzepka, 16–17.

10. For a concise summary of Tarantino's early life, see Sherman, 1–16; for Leonard's, see Rzepka, 24–46.

11. The exceptions include Amelia Darck in "The Colonel's Lady" (1952) and, in a supporting role, Martha Cable, the wife of beleaguered homesteader and Civil War veteran Paul Cable, in *Last Stand at Saber River* (1959).

12. On Leonard's debts to romantic comedy, see Sinowitz.

13. Leonard's early admiration of Cain is reflected in the first short story he ever wrote, "One Horizontal" (1950). His love of *noir* in general get a thorough airing out in *La Brava* (1983).

14. My colleague, Boston University professor emerita Julia Brown, is one of them. In an email of 6/11/20, she writes, "I'm not convinced that De Niro's character really works. It didn't make sense to us that a man who would be unable to interrupt Melanie (Bridget Fonda) in the bathroom would kill her so easily later in the day. Tarantino let De Niro improvise and the result, to me, was an unconvincing statement about how he shot her because she was nagging him,"

15. See Rzepka, 40–41, on *techne* ("skill"), or acting according to rules, as opposed to *praxis*, acting according to custom or principles, in achieving authentic "cool."

16. Tarantino includes this feature of Max's personality, including the Benning reference, in the screenplay, but not the movie.

17. To keep their relationship chaste, Tarantino rewrote a chat between the two that, in the book, leads them to Jackie's bed (388–89). In the film, it takes place entirely over the phone (1:28:33–1:28:58).

18. On this topic, see Powers. Leonard's very first publication, in 1951, a short story titled "Trail of the Apache," features a long speech by Indian agent Eric Travesin on how

whites have abused the Apache nation, and the deplorable (and predictable) result of their policies (8–9).

19. The first is Army veteran Harold Jackson, who shares the spotlight with the Hispanic/Apache convict Raymond San Carlos, in *Forty Lashes Less One*. The second is another vet, former rough rider Bo Catlett, in "Hurrah for Captain Early!"

20. New Orleans was Leonard's birthplace.

21. In Tarantino's film, Detective Mark Dargus remarks on Jackie's "cool" demeanor when he and Nicolet first spot her at LAX.

22. On authentic vs. inauthentic "cool," see Rzepka, 1–46.

23. Leonard uses color coding in a similarly programmed (and more easily recognized) way in his short story "When the Women Come Out to Dance." Here yellow indicates subservience, blue refers to lost virginity, and their combination, green (the color of envy), signifies the money that compensates for both.

WORKS CITED

Bailey, Frankie Y. "Visual Clues: Dress, Appearance, and Perception in Elmore Leonard's Crime Fiction," in *Critical Essays on Elmore Leonard: "If it sounds like writing,"* ed. Charles J. Rzepka. Hoboken: Wiley Blackwell, 2020, pp. 57–72.

Clarkson, Wensley. *Quentin Tarantino: Shooting from the Hip.* Woodstock, NY: The Overlook Press, 1995.

Grobel, Lawrence. *Endangered Species: Writers Talk About Their Craft, Their Visions, Their Lives.* Cambridge, MA: Da Capo, 2001.

Gunst, Stephanie. *Pam Grier and the Articulation of Female Subjectivity in Blaxpoitation Theme Songs.* MA Thesis. Tufts University, 2011.

Kaufman, Anthony, ed. *Steven Soderberg Interviews.* Jackson: University Press of Mississippi, 2015.

Kornhaber, Spencer. "Tarantino's Ultimate Statement on Movie Violence." *The Atlantic,* August 2, 2019. https://www.theatlantic.com/entertainment/archive/2019/08/once-upon-a-time-end-tarantinos-message-on-violence/595168/.

Leonard, Elmore. *Rum Punch, Four Later Novels,* ed. Gregg Sutter. New York: Library of America, 2016, pp. 229–451.

Leonard, Elmore. *Split Images.* New York: HarperCollins, 1981.

Leonard, Elmore. "Trail of the Apache," in *The Complete Stories of Elmore Leonard,* ed. Gregg Sutter. New York: Morrow, 2004, pp. 1–36.

Leonard, Elmore. "When the Women Come Out to Dance." *When the Women Come Out to Dance: Stories.* New York: HarperCollins, 2002, pp. 40–56.

Lyttleton, Oliver. "From Best to Worst: Elmore Leonard Movie Adaptations." *IndieWire,* May 14, 2013. https://www.indiewire.com/2013/05/from-best-to-worst-elmore-leonard-movie-adaptations-98187/.

Mitchell, Elvis. "Breaking Down *Jackie Brown.*" In Quentin Tarantino, *Jackie Brown.* Burbank: Miramax Home Entertainment, 2002. DVD.

Orr, C. "The Elmore Leonard Paradox." *The Atlantic,* January/February, 2014. https://www.theatlantic.com/magazine/archive/2014/01/the-elmore-leonard-paradox/355734 (accessed 31 May 2019).

Powers, Korine. "The Man with Five Names: *Hombre* on Race and the Cinematic Western," in *Critical Essays on Elmore Leonard: "If it sounds like writing,"* ed. Charles J. Rzepka. Hoboken: Wiley Blackwell, 2020, pp. 95–111.

Rzepka, Charles J. *Being Cool: The Work of Elmore Leonard.* Baltimore: Johns Hopkins University Press, 2013.

Sherman, Dale. *Quentin Tarantino FAQ.* Milwaukee: Applause, 2015.

Sinowitz, Michael. "Elmore Leonard and the Romantic Comedy, or 'Get Some Love Into It,'" *Critical Essays on Elmore Leonard: "If it sounds like writing."* Rzepka, Charles, ed. Hoboken, NJ: Wiley Blackwell, 2020, pp.27–39.

Stamm, Robert. "Beyond Fidelity: The Dialogics of Adaptation," in *Film Adaptation*, ed. James Naremore. New Brunswick: Rutgers University Press, 2000, pp. 54–76.

Tarantino, Quentin. *Jackie Brown*. Film. Burbank: Miramax Home Entertainment. Distributed by Lionsgate. 2011. Blu-ray DVD.

Tarantino, Quentin. *Jackie Brown*. Screenplay. The Internet Movie Script Database (IMSDb). https://www.imsdb.com/scripts/Jackie-Brown.html.

Terzieva-Artemis, Rossitsa. "Moral Luck and Determinism in *Rum Punch*," in *Critical Essays on Elmore Leonard: "If it sounds like writing,"* ed. Charles J. Rzepka. Hoboken: Wiley Blackwell, 2020, pp. 147–164.

Tucker, Neely. "A Blast of Bullets." *The Washington Post*. May 27, 2008. https://www.washingtonpost.com/archive/style/2008/05/27/a-blast-of-bullets/33b2e0de-d136-44ad-b2c4-b2e3c0c21f20/.

Vasquez, Zach. "The Great Elmore Leonard Renaissance of the Late '90s." *CrimeReads*, May 22, 2020. https://crimereads.com/the-great-elmore-leonard-renaissance-of-the-late-90s/.

Venuti, Lawrence. "Adaptation, Translation, Critique." *Journal of Visual Culture* 6, no. 1 (2007): 25–43.

Wooton, Adrian. "Quentin Tarantino Interview (I)." *The Guardian*, January 5, 1998. https://www.theguardian.com/film/1998/jan/05/quentintarantino.guardianinterviewsatbfisouthbank1.

Quentin Tarantino's Sole Aspect

Foot Fetishism in His Films

KEVIN QUIGLEY

"I have a foot fetish," Quentin Tarantino's character Clarence Poole admits in the director's first, incomplete film, *My Best Friend's Birthday*. This revealing line comes during a story in which the character is reminiscing about working in the ladies' footwear section of a department store, kicking off a theme that would recur over and over in the director's career. Tarantino's focus on feet—particularly women's feet, specifically *bare* women's feet—would later become so prevalent that Brad Pitt would remark, "Seriously, Quentin has separated more women from their shoes than the TSA."[1] TV talk show host Tyra Banks would drop her feet into guest Tarantino's lap, showing off her recent pedicure. A mid-career *Vulture* article, commenting on a photo shoot in which Tarantino is photographed fondling Diane Kruger's feet, shouted, "Okay, Okay, Quentin Tarantino Has a Foot Fetish, We Get it!"[2]

But is that all it is? A prurient preoccupation with feet, a kink Tarantino is helpless to resist throwing onscreen in a combination of titillation, explanation, and popularization?

Perhaps not. *The Village Voice*, eschewing the shock and exasperation that generally comes bundled with a discussion of Tarantino's quirk, explored it a little more deeply: "It's not just that he's a foot fetishist, but that he takes what he cares about—personal, quirky stuff—and transforms it into art."[3]

Directors are famous for their motifs, and Tarantino is no exception. His fascinations—genre films, off-kilter sequencing, and '60s and '70s American culture among them—define and occasionally pigeonhole him. Just as each of these directorial choices come to shape the movies he makes, so too does his fondness for feet. No mere fetish writ large, Tarantino's examination of the toes and soles of his actresses is far more interesting.

Yet curiously, this facet appears nowhere in the director's first full-length feature, *Reservoir Dogs* (1992), in which virtually no women—apart from victims "Shot Woman" and "Shocked Woman"—are even present. Only in its absence is this trope important; in retrospect, *Reservoir Dogs* becomes, no pun intended, something of an odd man out. Its depiction of a robbery gone wrong and its aftermath is a paroxysm of male camaraderie and chaos, the only real female presence being the Madonna song the gang dissects at the start.

Crucially, though, *Reservoir Dogs*' most famous scene—in which Mr. Blonde severs Marvin Nash's ear—offers foreshadowing. Tarantino is forcing us to focus on a single body part, separate from the whole of the person but representing a fundamental shift in how that person is perceived. Mr. Blonde discards the ear carelessly after playing with it like a toy. Nash's entire life is reduced because of a few seconds of sadism. While Tarantino will not utilize feet as horror objects until the much later *Death Proof* (2007), this pivotal scene points the way toward his use of individual body parts as synecdoches, standing in for the whole of a person even as they command more specific attention.

Pulp Fiction launches right into things, as gangsters Vincent and Jules' discursive discussion angles swiftly into a philosophical debate: whether giving a man's wife a foot rub is cause for defenestration. It's an interesting question, one that really sparked the misconception that Tarantino's interest in feet is entirely sexual. Was throwing Tony Rocky Horror out of a window for touching Marsellus Wallace's wife Mia's feet justified? Maybe, but that's not really the issue. That's the text. The subtext is far more interesting: does a foot rub imply sex? Is a foot rub even more intimate than sex? Would Wallace have been less inclined to throw a man from a window if he'd caught his wife during intercourse with him?

The scene pivots to the hit before we get answers, but it's not too long before we are shown Mia's feet—answers unto themselves. When Mia Wallace first appears, we don't see her in full, only close-ups of her in her hidden control room—hand, back of head, lips: important foreshadowing. Interestingly, the first full look we get of Mia is a fabrication; the painting on the wall Vincent studies, "Portrait of Mia" (painted by Tarantino's childhood friend Steven Martinez), depicts a barefoot Mia curled up on a couch. Tarantino is teasing out his star here, giving the viewer and Vincent scraps of her as the seductive Dusty Springfield track "Son of a Preacher Man" plays diegetically over all. The finale of this sequence lingers on a close-up of Mia's bare sole, her toes bent and on display, an Ingres painting of nude splendor. At this early stage in Tarantino's career, it's revealing that this is intended as our first full look at Mia: you don't need to see her face or body to know she is in charge.

This brief moment is accompanied by Mia commanding, "Let's go," at once putting her in control and heightening the sexual tension with playfully suggestive language. Because Tarantino is inviting us—maybe forcing us—to accept that merely watching Mia's bare soles is the final word in sensuality, he has finally answered the earlier question: touching them isn't just sexual, it *is* sex.

Later, in what is arguably *Pulp Fiction*'s most famous sequence, Mia bullies Vincent into entering (and winning) the Jack Rabbit Slim's twist contest. It's no mistake that while Vincent remains in socks, Mia—now aggressive—dances barefoot. (Can this be read as Vincent wearing protection?) We move here from any sexual or sensual trappings, indicating Tarantino's first move completely away from erotic connotations with bare feet. Mia stripping her shoes off is an act of power here—seductive, maybe, but in the service of winning her the trophy she wants. During the twist contest, we are allowed only one close-up of her gyrating feet. Any more, Tarantino seems to say, would be to rob the sequence of its power, degenerating it to something like pornography.

That Mia's power move comes before her fall—her accidental overdose—is not incidental. Here again, Tarantino singles out a single body part meant to symbolize the whole, in this case, Mia's heart, which Vincent pierces with an adrenaline shot to bring her back to life. After an evening of Mia's foot-focused seduction and power trips, Vincent is able (in gruesome terms) to finally reach her heart, putting them both on more even turf.

In the final scene of this sequence, Mia—exhausted and sallow from her near-death experience—carries her shoes back into her home. We are privy to but not focused on her bare feet in these moments, and Tarantino's intent here has shifted. Mia's feet have gone from engaging the male gaze sexually to being utilized for power and control, and now, ultimately, as symbols of vulnerability. She stands before Vincent, more naked than naked, her masks and barriers cast off as readily as her shoes. Even in this early film, Tarantino displays his actress's feet in ways that transcend the commonly held notion that they are mere fetish objects for him.

Of course, fetish is very much on the roster in *From Dusk Till Dawn* (1996). Though not directed by Tarantino, it was written by him and stars him and offers an intriguing evolutionary step in this aspect of Tarantino's development. In one scene, Salma Hayek, as erotic dancer Satanico Pandemonium, moves seductively across a table toward Tarantino's Richie Gecko. Bikini-clad and wearing a writhing snake around her shoulders, Pandemonium lifts her foot to Gecko's face, pouring alcohol down her thigh and inviting Gecko to lap it off her toes. That Pandemonium is revealed to be a vampire recontextualizes this scene, echoing Jonathan

Harker's seduction by Dracula's concubines. The theme of consumption mixed with sexuality is key in vampire stories, and it is no mistake that later, Pandemonium drinks more literally from Richie Gecko, transforming him into a vampire. This classic horror movie trope of sex (again, here the arched woman's foot *is* sex, not standing in for intercourse but intercourse itself) leading to death will be explored in far more detail in Tarantino's later *Death Proof.*

The image of alcohol and feet re-emerges in *Jackie Brown* (2007), a movie concerned above all things, with age. When Bridget Fonda's Melanie first appears, several shots focus on the soles of her bare feet, prettied up with toe rings; as it is later suggested that she is "past her prime," the toe rings—along with her skimpy outfits and garish fake tan—serve to accentuate her desire to cling to her youth. The first close-ups of her feet frame them next to a glass of alcohol sipped intermittently by Robert DeNiro's Louis Gara—seen here grizzled and old. The proximity of girlish feet next to this man's alcohol underlines their drab *Lolita* relationship and foreshadows its violent conclusion. Whereas Salma Hayek's bare foot—dripping with alcohol—symbolized her power over Tarantino's character, the power dynamic is reversed here. Following a brief and blunt sex scene (recalling—and perhaps exploiting—DeNiro's boudoir scene with Jodie Foster's child prostitute in the 1976 film *Taxi Driver*), Gara shoots Melanie in broad daylight. It's a moment of shocking, unexpected violence, reminding one of the ear-slicing scene in *Reservoir Dogs.* The viewer is conditioned to be edgy and aware of more shocking reversals, of which *Jackie Brown* has several.

Tarantino's framing of lead Pam Grier's feet is far more subtle and less provocative. At first, she appears in her stewardess uniform, tight and revealing, when gun-runner Ordell Robbie pays her a visit. *Sans* shoes, she explains to Ordell about her brief incarceration, attempting to convince him that she didn't rat on him. Tarantino's misdirection here is key; while the lights are on and her feet are in plain sight, she seems hesitant, almost girlish in her fear. This is another misdirection; baring her feet, she is essentially naked before Ordell—vulnerable and transparent. Only when the lights go out does she reveal her power, saving her own life and threatening Ordell's. We understand that the power was there all along, in spite of (or because of) her symbolic nudity.

Immediately following this scene, Robert Forster's Max Cherry arrives the following morning to collect the gun Brown had liberated from him. Jackie is in a robe and again barefoot, but the intention of her feet has changed. Again, Jackie attempts a sort of overwhelmed coquettishness at first, a mirror image of Bridget Fonda's youth pretending to be older. Does she sense already that Cherry is growing infatuated with her? Everything is suggestion, but Jackie Brown seems to drop the act when she plays her record (the choice of the song "Didn't I Blow Your Mind This Time" is about the least subtle aspect of this scene). When she crouches down before her record player, the camera follows her movement, her bare feet on full display. If the prior sequence played her symbolic nudity as a mixture of perceived naiveté and strength, here it feels somewhat unguarded, vulnerable. Because Cherry is fascinated with her, this scene invites a sensual gaze; as with Mia and the seductive "Son of a Preacher Man," Tarantino's choice of the Delfonics' smooth soul song works to layer on a healthy sense of eroticism, not to mention tenderness. Whether Jackie is playing Max as she had played Ordell is almost beside the point here. This scene is about trust, and Jackie allowing herself to appear to this relative stranger as exposed—in several connotations of the word—implies that, on some level, she trusts him not only not to hurt her but to help her.

In these early Tarantino films, sexuality is the often undercurrent of his focus on feet, though suggesting themes of more symbolic importance. Sex is either presaged or entirely subverted by the fetishization of feet.

However, by the time of *Kill Bill: Volume One* (2003), the focus shifts. Early on, Uma Thurman's Bride character awakens from a coma partially paralyzed. Before she can embark on her "roaring rampage of revenge," she must first get her feet moving. A close-up of Thurman's bare feet fill the screen as she commands herself to "wiggle her big toe." Epic importance is attached to this moment; this is the Bride's first major act of independence since being shot in the head by Bill years prior. In this context, a woman's feet are as much symbolic of her power and strength as her swordplay. It is important that Lucy Liu's O-Ren Ishii removes her shoes before her climactic battle with the Bride—her bare feet in the snow put her, no pun intended, on equal footing with her opponent.

In *Kill Bill: Volume 2* (2004), we again see The Bride's feet in a flashback before her later violent retribution. During her talk with David Carradine's Bill—before his attempt on her life—we see her in sandals, the tops and sides of her feet exposed. Bill appears in loafers, and there are several shots of both pairs of feet approaching one another. Scenes like this underscore how Tarantino's fascination with feet is flexible, malleable, and able to convey as many different emotions as an actor's eyes. If, in *Volume One*, bare feet were a sign of strength and power, here they feel like symbols of vulnerability. The dynamic in this sequence is clear: Bill has caught The Bride unaware, putting him in control ... though his control is not total. Though he shoots her, she lives, suggesting that her covered soles are a symbol of things even Bill is not allowed to see—her hidden strengths.

One of the most powerful moments in the film, echoing the ear-severing in *Reservoir Dogs*, is the climax of the fight scene in Budd's trailer between Elle Driver and The Bride (whose real name, Beatrix Kiddo, is revealed here; the stripping away of both code names and aliases not only works as Kiddo's real self slowly coming to the fore but as immediate foreshadowing). Just as Driver's and Kiddo's mentor, Pei Mei, had plucked out one of Driver's eyes, Kiddo now finishes the job, yanking Driver's other eye out and tossing it to the floor. In a final display of how strong she has grown since "wiggle your big toe," Kiddo crushes Driver's eye under her bare foot, not needing to kill her to reduce her.

With the exception of *From Dusk Till Dawn*, Tarantino has proven that his interest in women's feet is not merely prurient, not merely fetishization. But that exception is important; horror has always had inextricable ties to sex and sexuality, from the vampiric orgy in *Dracula* (1897) and the telekinetic awakening of *Carrie* (1974) to the sexually-transmitted supernatural stalker of *It Follows* (2014) and the homoerotic nightmare of *The Lighthouse* (2019). The subgenre that arguably trucks in sexuality most potently is the slasher film, where sex (particularly teenage sex) is punishable by death. Slasher franchises like *A Nightmare on Elm Street*, *Halloween*, *Scream*, and especially *Friday the 13th* bonded sex and death together so powerfully that a TV show like *Stranger Things* that posited that teenage sex didn't have to automatically warrant murder was surprising and refreshing.

In *Death Proof*, Tarantino's half of the *Grindhouse* experiment, the tropes of the slasher film are upfront and obvious if subverted slightly through Tarantino's particular lens. Frank sexuality is indeed a major part of the film—sort of. In the theatrical release, momentum builds toward a sexy lap dance performed by Vanessa Ferlito's Butterfly, only to have the entire sequence cut, replaced by a MISSING REEL card. Tarantino's knowing use of the grindhouse "tradition" of explicit reels being secreted away by pervy projectionists makes for a great laugh, even though it subverts our expectations. In the later DVD release, the sequence is reinstated, and it is every bit as sensual and titillating as implied by the MISSING REEL card.

Butterfly's highly erotic dance for the seated Stuntman Mike—performed in sandals, showcasing fiery-red toenails—lingers on a shot of Ferlito's foot planted on the chair agonizingly close to Kurt Russell's crotch. In context, this feels like nothing less than a quick shot of bare breasts in more traditional grindhouse films, a moment where the director seems to be giving in to baser, suggestive instincts. But even in the theatrical release, women's feet symbolize this most simplistic read of Tarantino's interest. Feet here *are* fetish. They *are* sex.

The film opens with a bright shot of feet crossed at the ankle resting on a dashboard; this is meant to be as sexual (and iconic) an image as a scantily-clad woman writhing on the hood of a car. Our first glimpse of one of the film's sexy leads, Sidney Poitier, as radio personality Jungle Julia, is of her walking barefoot through her apartment, with many shots tracking her at foot level. Later, she appears with her feet dangling off a porch during a rainstorm, the water sluicing sensually between her toes, bringing to mind similar skinny-dipping scenes in earlier slasher movies. Immediately before she is murdered, we see Julia's foot dangling out of the window of a car: bare feet equal sex, and sex equals death.

In the second segment of *Death Proof*, a sleeping Abbie Ross (Rosario Dawson) is spotted by the slasher-killer Stuntman Mike; her feet, too, are dangling out a car's window. While she dozes, Stuntman Mike runs a finger over the heels of her feet. This act is the height of repugnance, implying sexual aggression, even attempted rape.

Stuntman Mike's twisted mentality sees this accidental sensuality as reason to murder. It is no accident that Dawson and her friends later take their revenge on Stuntman Mike by stomping him to death. The shoe, truly, is on the other foot.

Inglourious Basterds (2009) is a tricky, intricately plotted foreign film hiding inside a brash Tarantino genre-bender. Over the course of the film, we learn that Diane Kruger's actress Bridget von Hammersmark is working as a double agent for the Americans within the Nazi ranks. During a climactic scene, she is nearly killed and just manages to escape with her life. Christoph Waltz's Hans Landa, a brutal Nazi officer who has uncovered her high-heel shoe amidst the wreckage she escaped, tracks her down and, in an unbearably tense perversion of the Cinderella story, matches the shoe to her foot. One foot is already broken, symbolic of her suddenly diminished usefulness; her other, exposed by Landa, literally and figuratively explicates where her loyalties lie. Far from being a sexual symbol— though there is an element of dark sexuality in this scene, as there was in the similar scene in *Death Proof*—here, Diane Kruger's bare foot reveals her secrets and makes her vulnerable. Her feet broken and exposed, von Hammersmark is powerless.

Powerlessness is one of Tarantino's central themes in his "Southern," *Django Unchained* (2012). Is power defined by birthright? Is it only given, or can it be taken? In an antebellum milieu defined by people owning other people, Black people's power is at a premium. During most of the movie's runtime, Black power and liberation can only be given by whites: Django's real freedom by King Schultz and Stephen's illusion of freedom by Calvin Candie. Only during the film's violent third act is Black power achieved and maintained by Black people, most powerfully in Django's rescue of his wife, Kerry Washington's Broomhilda von Shaft. Following the climactic sequence in which Django's bloody battle through Candieland, Broomhilda is seen cowering in bed, helplessly awaiting whatever fate will come to her. Her face contorts in abject terror, and in a quick shot, we see her from behind, her bare feet helplessly rubbing against one another, perhaps for warmth, perhaps for comfort. Once again, Tarantino asks us to accept his actress's feet as a synecdoche of her entire body; the nakedness of Broom-hilda's feet stand in for the nakedness of her soul, body, and predicament.

The shot is quick yet powerful, underscoring Broomhilda's ongoing torment without itself becoming exploitative. It's followed by another shot of her face, still scared, and then the shot tracks down her body, punctuated by a glance at the *top* of her feet, subtly indicating a change in fortune for Broomhilda. Indeed, as the camera pans past her feet to the door of the room in which she's locked, music swells as we realize that Django is back, here to rescue her for good this time.

Tarantino's following film, arguably an adaptation of Agatha Christie's *And Then There Were None* (1939), up to and including the grisly hanging of a woman as the denouement, features no bare feet. It's set in deep Wyoming winter, and bare feet would make little sense, though there are long and contextually disturbing shots of a nude man walking for his life in the bitter cold. It's tempting to draw an analogue to this and Tarantino's favorite motif: men must be fully nude in order to be completely vulnerable, while women need only be barefoot, their soles—and, not accidentally, souls—exposed. But that's a thorny argument, especially in the context of *The Hateful Eight* (2015); one of our last shots of Daisy Domergue is off her feet kicking in the throes of death … but her feet are clad in chunky black shoes, despite the fact that her true motives are finally out in the open and she is in her final extremity. Perhaps this is Tarantino saying that, even in death, even after the violence done to and by her, Domergue reserved some dignity for herself.

The relative lack of bare feet in *Django* and *Hateful* might have masked a wire burning steadily in the background, exploding into the powder keg of Tarantino's most recent film, *Once Upon a Time in Hollywood* (2019).

In his acceptance speech at the Screen Actors Guild Awards for his role as stuntman Cliff Booth (a role which would later garner him his first Oscar) in *Once Upon a Time in Hollywood*, Brad Pitt announced, "I want to thank my costars, Leo [DiCaprio], Margot Robbie, Margot Robbie's feet, Margaret Qualley's feet, Dakota Fanning's feet." It's a good joke; on the heels of relatively barefoot-free films *Django Unchained* and *The Hateful Eight*, *Once Upon a Time* teems with barefoot youth. So many of *Once Upon a Time*'s themes are about old-guard Hollywood giving way to an influx of youth culture and new ideas threatening the core of long-held traditions and beliefs, as well as the actors who hold them. It's where vintage American concepts of traditional, somewhat toxic masculinity (witness DiCaprio's Rick Dalton playing to macho Western archetypes in film, and the hubris and menace of Cliff Booth, not to mention a lingering shot of Brad Pitt's chiseled abs) and old-school stardom are challenged by a freewheeling hippie culture with a menace of its own. One could argue that the multiple shots of women's bare feet represent innocence with an expiration date, but it's not that simple. As we've seen time and again, the vision Tarantino has for his actress's feet rarely are.

Take Margot Robbie's Sharon Tate. In our reality, Tate was murdered by the Manson Family cult—a tragic end to the life of a promising young film star. In the movie's reality, Tate lives, having avoided her fate via the intervention of Dalton and Booth. In a pivotal scene in the middle of the film, Tate spends an afternoon watching one of her own movies on the big screen, *The Wrecking Crew* (1968), with a small but appreciative audience. While Tarantino focuses on her hip vinyl boots on her journey to the theater, underscoring Tate's good taste and stylish nature, during the watching of the movie, Tate removes her boots and props her bare feet up on the chair in front of her.

She's also wearing enormous glasses and a giddy, unpretentious smile throughout the scene, silently overjoyed to see herself on the silver screen among people who are also enrapt by her performance. This is the "real" Tate, unadorned and unassuming. But this is also the "fake" Tate, one of Tarantino's clever bits of meta-commentary. Where the movie screen is showing Tate to the world, this scene is showing Tate to *us*, in our real world. The fact that Tarantino opts to show the real Tate in *The Wrecking Crew* while Margot Robbie's interpretation of her watches, barefoot and ebullient, is Tarantino foreshadowing and blurring the line between fiction and reality. The movies are fake, and reality ends in murder and bloodshed. Only in the world of *Once Upon a Time in Hollywood*, movies *are* the reality, a fairy tale come to life. Anything can happen, just as in *Inglourious Basterds'* machine-gun slaughter of Adolf Hitler. This unreality, symbolized in Tate's dual exhibitions of herself in this scene, allows her to not only live to the end of the film but to share her fortune with Rick Dalton, bridging the gap between generations of movie stars.

Where for Tate, bare feet represent delight and a Hollywood sort of innocence, for the Manson cult members, they symbolize something entirely different. When Pitt's Cliff Booth picks up a hitchhiker, Qualley's "Pussycat" (an echo of *Kill Bill*'s Pussy Wagon?), she attempts to seduce him in standard ways, crossing her bare legs suggestively on a bench, bending into his car wearing a woven top revealing her midriff, biting her lower lip. Tarantino, using the fact that the viewer knows about his interest in women's feet, has Pussycat press her bare feet against the glass of the windshield, putting them on display for Booth … and the viewer. That Booth and Pussycat's feet are occupying the same realm inside the car inverts the upsetting sequence in *Death Proof* in which Stuntman Mike fondles Abbie Ross's feet without consent. In this scene, both consent and intent are in play.

Cleverly (and not a little pruriently), Tarantino is very intent on drawing the male gaze toward each of these titillating moments, culminating in Pussycat asking Booth if he wants her to "suck your cock while driving." The blatant, traditional forms of sexiness spiral out from here. As Booth determines, Pussycat is young and playing mature, spouting dogma she barely understands about actors and Vietnam. Now, as he drives, she puts her head on his lap and her feet out the window, indicating that the promise of her sexuality is now out of reach. Despite her still talking about wanting to fuck him, those bare feet on the other side of the window indicate that she is now unattainable—another echo of *Death Proof.*

As we learn more about the cult staying at the Spahn Ranch, we see that most, if not all, the residents are also barefoot. This paints the thwarted sex between Booth and Pussycat in a new light; her playacting as a grownup is both sexy and dangerous, but the barefoot Manson family is just dangerous. Tarantino interprets them as children with children's ideals of good and evil, twisted by a sociopathic leader who wills them to murder for those ideals. Prefiguring the film's dénouement, Booth knocks a male cult member named Clem to the ground; for one of the first times in Tarantino's oeuvre, we focus on bare male feet, filthy, flying through the air as Clem is overtaken. In this one scene, we understand Tarantino's intent with feet in this film, utilizing them not only as symbolism but as thesis. Sharon Tate's feet are that of a grown woman experiencing a moment of childlike glee, whereas the cultists' feet represent the exact opposite, children experiencing an extended period of adult misery and ennui. As Clem's feet fill the screen, Tarantino illustrates that this brand of performative callousness and misguided righteousness has consequences.

However Tarantino's "quirky, personal stuff" first emerged onscreen, it is evident that his passion for feet has evolved into something far more interesting than kink or fetish. As symbols of sexuality, power, of vulnerability, his actresses' (and occasionally actors') feet are as versatile as any other signature at Tarantino's disposal. One can't help but be intrigued as to what his next step will be.

Notes

1. "Brad Pitt Joked about Jolie, Aniston and Tarantino's Foot Fetish in His Hilarious SAG Awards Speech," *Esquire,* January 22, 2020, https://www.esquire.com/uk/culture/film/a30592238/brad-pitt-sag-award-speech-jennifer-aniston-angelina-jolie/.

2. M. Graham, "Okay Okay, Quentin Tarantino Has a Foot Fetish, We Get It!" *Vulture*, May 4, 2009, https://www.vulture.com/2009/05/okay_okay_quentin_tarantinos_g.html.

3. R.J. Smith, "Faster, Pussy Wagon! Kill! Kill!" *The Village Voice*, September 30, 2003, https://www.villagevoice.com/2003/09/30/faster-pussy-wagon-kill-kill/.

Not a Straight Line

Kill Bill, *Three Ways*

Katharine Coldiron

This is a long piece of work, and it's messy, but it does have a point and I intended it to bring you satisfaction. I wrote that sentence about the essay that follows, but I would also put these words in Tarantino's mouth[1] when he presented us with *Kill Bill*, his fourth film, divided into two volumes and released a year apart in 2003 and 2004. The central foci of this essay are threefold, which is itself a bad start, as Tarantino most often works with pairs, not trios. Nevertheless, they are:

> 1. *Kill Bill* is a creative hinge for Tarantino, dividing his films into two distinct types/phases: mixtapes and Westerns.
> 2. *Kill Bill* is a rape-revenge film, or is usefully interpreted as one.
> 3. Tarantino's work may be properly considered only by investigating it in light of both high *and* low art, through fandom *and* scholarship, by men *and* women.

Genre is a knotty problem, not a simple label, in all of Tarantino's work. Attempts to classify his early films have resulted in an umbrella diagnosis of "crime film," but anyone who has seen *Pulp Fiction* (1994) will be dissatisfied with that. These films are *concerned* with crime, but perhaps more essentially, they are ensemble character pieces. The latter half of his career has ranged across multiple genres, including war film, hangout movie, and slave narrative. *Kill Bill* neatly distinguishes these two career halves, in that the first volume has a hybrid genre and the second volume is, without doubt, a Western.

At the hinge of *Kill Bill*, Tarantino turned his attention to America thematically rather than geographically. Most of his later films are Westerns,[2] a useful vehicle for such a journey. Through this most American of genres, he has explored race relations, masculinity, violence (of course), revenge, power, and many other abstract ideas.

60

Other connoisseurs of the Western have delved into these same concepts since the early 20th century. That is, Tarantino's choice to use the Western to spread out his ideas is not a novel one among directors, nor is it a surprise to anyone who has studied the genre seriously. However, few critics would have predicted that the frenetic mixtape artist of *Pulp Fiction* would turn to the broad landscapes and slow movements of the Western.

Yet he did, and the proof is right there, between *Kill Bill Vol. 1* and *Kill Bill Vol. 2*. What happened to Tarantino personally at that time, I don't know. But finding artistic evidence of the shift—well, that's what I'm here to do.

Chapter 1: Mixtape

One challenging aspect of studying Tarantino is the way exceptions plague his oeuvre. Make a pronouncement about the patterns of his work, and an exception will immediately spring to mind. For example: his films all play with story sequencing—except *Death Proof* (2007). His films are all, in some fashion, revenge stories—except *Once Upon a Time in Hollywood* (2019). His films include strong, intriguing female characters—except *Reservoir Dogs* (1992). This doesn't mean his body of work is inconsistent, but that its consistencies overlap, shift, or disappear, depending on what interests Tarantino about the particular story he's telling. There is almost no "always" in Tarantino's cinema, which is itself worthy of study, but which makes writing about him a little bit infuriating, because the *except, except, except* of his films weakens any critic's sentences.

So when I say that I believe *Kill Bill* to be a creative hinge, closing one half of his career and opening the other, I recognize that the evidence I'm going to use to delineate this idea will have exceptions. Tarantino didn't only make Westerns after *Kill Bill*, and he didn't only make mixtapes before it. But if I look at his work as a long freeway, for most of the trip up through *Kill Bill Vol. 1*, he drove in the left lane, and for most of the trip from *Vol. 2* forward, he drove in the right lane. Occasionally he'd change lanes to pass.

Overall, it's a single journey.

When I say "mixtape," I mean a work that is stronger, on the whole, due to its being composed of elements from disparate contexts. A mixtape is pleasurable because of how its songs collide and contrast. A true artist of the mixtape form will engineer your emotional state from the beginning of side A to the end of side B, giving you ups, downs, and passages of bliss. The mixtape, as a form, also gathers up the best and leaves aside the worst: hits only, no misses.

Seeing Tarantino as a mixtape artist, through at least the first half of his career, is only natural. He creates literal mixtapes with music in his films, the soundtracks of which have been outrageously successful. But he also makes the visual equivalent of mixtapes, using snap zooms from kung fu movies, camera moves from Max Ophuls, costume and character ideas from exploitationist Jack Hill, scene structure from Jean-Luc Godard. He trades on the personas of his actors, on the established significance of colors and objects, on the way a snatch of music from 1970s drive-ins can make a neuron fire in a viewer's brain.

The way he blends all these bits and pieces, and the meaning and significance he intends to evoke with each fragment, varies wildly from one project to another. The theme from the television show *Ironside* (1967–75) is the musical cue used when Beatrix flashes on memories of what was done to her (the synthesized siren, percussion, and six big brassy notes), and the content of the show has nothing apparent to do with the content of *Kill Bill*. However, the music from *Death Rides a Horse* (1967) is also used frequently across *Kill Bill*, and Tarantino borrowed a great deal from that film: open landscapes, colored overlay for certain subjective shots, and a kind of thematic irresolution of revenge. With the *Ironside* theme, Tarantino chose a cool piece of music to use as a leitmotif, and did not draw on the meaning of that music's source, whereas with the *Death Rides a Horse* score, the cool piece of music has additional resonance due to where it came from.

Guessing whether a repurposed bit of music, a line of dialogue, a cinematic technique drags its context along with it into the Tarantino film, or whether it is just a cool thing, can lead those of us who analyze Tarantino into big trouble. Is Elle's eyepatch a reference to Madeline in *Thriller: A Cruel Picture* (1973), a semi-arty rape-revenge film from Sweden? Or is it a reference to Patch in *Switchblade Sisters* (1975), a grimy but entertaining exploitation film? A critic could unpack either meaning, relating either reference to other aspects of *Kill Bill*. But it's also possible that Tarantino just liked the look of the girl in the eyepatch, in either film or both of them, and there's no thematic relationship at all. When a boy makes you a mixtape, he might mean you're gonna be the one who saves him, or he might just like Oasis.

So, when Tarantino moves on from the mixtape, it matters. It changes the way we interpret his films, the guesses we have about what he's saying in his native language.[3] The move makes it apparent that Tarantino is grappling with big ideas, particularly about America, not just chopping and screwing six decades of cinema for aesthetic kicks.

There's a postmodern aspect to the mixtape form, a sense that can only be made by considering play and interplay. In Tarantino's later films, he moves from play to work. Other critics have described Tarantino as a magpie, stealing and storing the shiniest objects he encounters and embedding them in the choicest parts of his nest. This is accurate, too. But the idea of the mixtape leads to fruitful questions about what is left *in* his films. If *Pulp Fiction* is a collection of all hits, no misses, why does it include conversations of no consequence, bits and pieces that would be cut out of the first draft of any other screenplay? Why is there such duration in certain scenes, like Butch preparing to ambush Maynard and Marsellus talking to Butch about throwing the fight? These choices are deliberate, and they lead to a question audiences rarely ask of American films: what is the purpose of *this* scene, *this* moment, *this* shot? What does it contribute to the overall effect of the film on me?

Tarantino's films have offered different answers to these questions over the years.

Initially, he was working more with characterization and relationships. Marsellus takes his time talking to Butch because he's the boss of him and wants to make that clear, and Butch takes his time approaching Maynard because he's not in a hurry to rescue Marsellus. (These scenes also have an element of Tarantino showing us something cool: Marsellus' Band-Aid and Bruce Willis tautly holding a katana.) Over time, though, Tarantino has come to work with duration and payoff in ways that few American directors have ever bothered with. He has often written scenes with no predictable direction, in which the characters are calm but the audience is tense. The most famous example is the Jules/Brett encounter in *Pulp Fiction*, which ends in a violent murder, but other examples include Stuntman Mike's conversation with Arlene on the porch in *Death Proof*, the masterful opening scene of *Inglourious Basterds* (2009), and Bill and Beatrix outside the chapel in *Kill Bill Vol. 2*.[4] In these scenes, the characters talk almost mundanely, the conversation winding here and there, and we in the audience have no idea where they're going with this. There's clearly a conflict, and on one side of the conversation there's clearly an agenda—a murderous one—but that is all subtext, and we must wait for quite a length of time before we learn how the encounter will shake out for the characters.

I note this because duration is the most significant difference between the volumes of *Kill Bill*. There are where-is-this-going scenes in *Vol. 1* (in Hattori Hanzō's sushi restaurant, between Buck and his customer over Beatrix's hospital bed), but there are more of them, and longer ones, in *Vol. 2* (between Budd and his boss in the My Oh My bar, between Budd and Elle over margaritas, and several times between Bill and Beatrix). The predominant style of Tarantino's scenes changed pretty radically at the hinge of *Kill Bill*: from scenes with quick-fire dialogue to scenes with repetition and empty space, from scenes with showy camera movements to scenes with wider angles and slower takes. All this is visible in comparing the volumes of *Kill Bill* to one another.

Vol. 1 calls back to everything Tarantino has done before. This is apparent in the broadest characteristics of the film (conspicuously repurposed music, genre mixing, and over-the-top violence) and in the smallest ones as well, right down to Uma Thurman drawing a partial rectangle in the air, echoing her character in *Pulp Fiction*. *Vol. 2* presages everything Tarantino is going to do. He will turn toward the Western, he will use more orchestral music and fewer songs, and he will use duration skillfully to tug the audience from near-boredom to peak emotion. His worlds will still be his own—there will still be Red Apple cigarettes and Samuel L. Jackson monologues—but those worlds will exist in a meaningfully real context.

Chapter 2: East to West

The two most prominent genres in *Kill Bill Vol. 1* are the samurai film and the Spaghetti Western. Patrick McGee and Edward Gallafent have argued for the influence of each of these genres on *Kill Bill* individually without reckoning with their inherent similarities. Both genres copiously depend upon revenge; both involve loners, cartoonishly evil antagonists, and violence; and both often shunt women into secondary roles. Stories have crossed over between the two genres into remakes and reimaginings across the history of world cinema. Mid–20th century, Akira Kurosawa's *Seven Samurai* (1954) was adapted by John Sturges into *The Magnificent Seven* (1960). Only a few years later, another of Kurosawa's films, *Yojimbo* (1961), was so closely copied by Sergio Leone for *A Fistful of Dollars* (1964) that it resulted in legal action. Further down the art ladder (and closer to Tarantino's natural habitat), *Harakiri* (1962) was remade as *Requiem for a Gringo* (1968), and *Django* (1966) borrowed elements from both *Fistful* and from its progenitor, *Yojimbo*.

There's a great deal more to say about the cross-pollination between these two genres, but it's a point that doesn't especially need me to prove it. Even David Carradine was aware of this: "The pace, the style [of *Kill Bill Vol. 1*], point out the huge similarity between Japanese samurai and Italian Western—all the beauty and all the violence of both genres."[5] In sum, then, *Kill Bill*'s blend of samurai lore with Spaghetti Western influence is not at all strange or even new to anyone familiar with both genres. But the film *refers* to them, draws on them, to create something rather new. *Kill Bill Vol. 1* repeatedly fuses East with West visually, musically, and thematically to create an impression of duality: elements in the film that cause the viewer to consider two cultures at once, rather than primarily one or the other.

Examples in *Vol. 1* abound, particularly in the House of Blue Leaves. The proprietor wears an obi, an Eastern garment, colored exactly the same way as the shirt of Charlie Brown, an icon in American pop culture. The performing band, the 5.6.7.8's, women of plainly Asian descent, perform rockabilly music and style their hair in 1960s bouffants, both American in inception. More generally, in the second half of the film, a recurring song is "The Lonely Shepherd," which has a slight swing in its accompaniment similar to the style of "Goodbye Yellow Brick Road." It sounds very much like it belongs with 1970s American light rock, but its main melody is performed, by the Romanian musician Zamfir,[6] with a pan flute—a European instrument, but one which recalls typically Eastern flute music (like that played by Bill in two scenes of *Kill Bill Vol. 2*).

Two of the film's main characters also represent the duality of East and West. Beatrix, a California blonde who can kill you with a wide variety of Asian martial arts, wears a version of Bruce Lee's *Game of Death* costume while using breakdancing moves to amputate the limbs of her enemies. And Bill.

It's nearly impossible to consider Bill apart from David Carradine, the actor who portrays him, and all the resonance that actor has for cinephiles. One of his best-known roles, and perhaps the one most relevant to *Kill Bill*, is as the race-bending Kwai Chang Caine on *Kung Fu*, a television show that ran from 1972 to 1975. That character is pretty uncomfortable today (he is meant to be half Chinese, although Carradine is fully Caucasian), but Tarantino nevertheless capitalizes on its fame and implications. It's not quite true that Bill is copied from Caine's personality or from Carradine's own, but Tarantino certainly spent some of those riches when building Bill on the page and on the screen. Although they exist in two different time periods, with opposing morals, Caine, like Bill, is a man making his way through the American West with Eastern martial arts training.

Before *Kill Bill*, Carradine had a long and complex history as an actor and a human being. He often played characters with stereotypically Asian knowledge, tastes, and philosophies, and he himself had a lot of interest and knowledge of the East, including martial arts training and even knowledge of how to carve and maintain bamboo flutes. A good deal of this history seeped into *Kill Bill* under Tarantino's guidance.[7] If Beatrix, the "yellow-haired warrior," is a figure of dual hemispheres, Bill is, too, both textually and contextually.

All this is to say: *Kill Bill Vol. 1* offers many indications of being a multi-genred film. It swerves between two often-associated genres (samurai and Western) but also makes stops in crime film, action film, anime, and music video. Some of these are new to Tarantino, while others had been his milieu for a decade by now. *Vol. 1* sews its sequences together from these genres with grace and an almost overdetermined style—also Tarantino's milieu.

Kill Bill Vol. 2, however, does something completely different: it sticks to one thing at a time as it moves through its chapters. It does not create evident dualities as *Vol. 1* does, but instead displays scenes and situations that adhere to single genres. Aside from the main characters, East/West duality is hardly present in *Vol. 2*, further dividing the films' atmospheres.

The primary genre *Vol. 2* evokes is the Western. This begins in the first chapter of the film, when Beatrix exits the Two Pines Wedding Chapel in a shot precisely copied from *The Searchers* (1956), a John Ford Western.[8] The sequence of Beatrix walking through the desert after digging herself out of a grave is visually similar to any number of traveling scenes in Westerns both American and Italo-Spanish. In focusing briefly on Budd, showing bits of his sad life, the film joins neo–Westerns like *Breaking Bad* (2008–13) and *No Country for Old Men* (2007) in evoking dread and sorrow over the empty modern life of the West.

To say "the primary genre *Vol. 2* evokes is the Western" is to say something different than "the primary genre *Vol. 1* evokes is the samurai film." If a coroner were to totally deconstruct *Kill Bill Vol. 1* and put all of its costumes, dialogue, actions, props, and camera angles into genre buckets, the fullest bucket would be the one labeled "samurai," probably.[9] But you wouldn't have a film at the end of this process, nor even complete scenes. You'd just have scraps, nuts and bolts, and it would take Dr. Frankenstein to reassemble the project. If you did this same action to *Vol. 2*, you would definitely have complete scenes in the buckets, whole recognizable parts. *Kill Bill Vol. 2* is not a film in which threads of different genres have been woven together inseparably; it is a quilt made from recognizable patches. Much of it is a Western, "a film about America,"[10] with a few passages of samurai or Hong Kong action (the Pai Mei chapter, mainly) and some crime scenes. It also includes a lot of scenes recognizable as Tarantino but not, as with past work, scenes in which Tarantino allows the work of others to run through the coffee filter of his own sensibilities.

This shift represents a step toward America. Gallafent writes at length about geographical and fantastical locations in both films, "departure from the ordinary world" in *Vol. 1* and the return to it in *Vol. 2*.[11] David Roche points out that "the Tokyo and Japan of *Kill Bill* are clearly marked as inventions"[12] via Beatrix's travel scenes (on a map of Okinawa, over a miniature Tokyo). Thus, the transition to *Vol. 2* is a move out of the fantastical and into the real world: America. What happens in America is not exactly realistic, in that Beatrix survives attempted murder in scenarios in which she probably should have died. But the style of *Vol. 2*, its long takes and wide shots, is less busy, less ostentatious, allowing the emotional journey greater prominence and resonance.

Tarantino has chosen, in *Vol. 2* and the films that follow, to examine America in a way that's close to political but closer to historical. *Django Unchained* (2012) is the film of Tarantino's that most scathingly examines American attitudes and ideas (historical or present-day), and it's also the film that's most obviously, fetishistically a Western.[13] Yet Tarantino's interest in exploring American violence, race relations, and cinema specifically through the Western begins in *Kill Bill Vol. 2*, and it has continued across the latter half of his career.

The critic can measure Tarantino's artistic growth by comparing the two volumes of *Kill Bill*, by stretching backward to see how his early career culminates in *Vol. 1* and stretching forward to see how the seeds of his later films were sown in *Vol. 2*. Although the two films are one work, their midpoint represents the midpoint, too, of Tarantino's career.

Chapter 3: Duration

Prior to *Kill Bill Vol. 1*, Tarantino was no less thoughtful or meticulous a filmmaker, but his style intruded on his thematic interests. The flourishes of his mixtape sensibility dazzled the viewer (and the filmmaker) and set him in search of intertextual references, rather than engaging him to think for himself. After settling on the Western as the proper vehicle, Tarantino's films became slower, longer, more challenging, and more consequential. Individual scenes may move slowly in the mixtape films, but on the whole the films go fast; this is not true for the later films. Over time, Tarantino has written fewer references into his movies, has transformed revenge from a vehicle for pleasure into a vehicle for political satisfaction,[14] and has expanded his interest in landscapes, culminating with the use of Ultra Panavision 70 in *The Hateful Eight* (2015). These tendencies align, if imperfectly, with how Westerns deepened across the 20th century—how the genre transformed from a celebration of imaginary American spaces to an excoriation of their underlying principles. Another trend of Tarantino's later films aligns even more closely with this deepening: his use of duration.

Let me explain this with the non–Tarantino example of Joanna Newsom. A singer and harpist, Newsom writes odd, lengthy songs. Her 2006 record *Ys* includes the song "Only Skin," which is 17 minutes long, and which for most of its length is Newsom's voice, her harp, and a few violins.

In the final four minutes a male vocalist joins her, as does a background chorus and bass percussion. The tempo speeds up, the song gains a new structure, and the experience swells into something completely different. The effect on the listener is almost euphoric. I tried fast-forwarding to that part of the song and listening just to it; it's not that I didn't enjoy the first 13 minutes, but they were so much less robust, less satisfying, than the conclusion. But when I listened to the end without hearing the beginning and middle, it wasn't as good. I never skipped through the song again.

Eventually I figured out that this was a trick of duration. Without getting accustomed to the simplicity, the poetry, the halting one-woman show of the first 13 minutes of the song, the final four minutes can't have the same emotional effect. Newsom used the same trick in *Have One on Me* (2010) with "Baby Birch," a spare 10-minute grief lullaby with an intense conclusion. Skipping to the end lessens the impact. I don't have an explanation for this, but I know it to be true.

Tarantino has become an expert on duration across the second half of his career.

Again, the Jules/Brett scene in *Pulp Fiction* is an early example: how remarkable the shooting feels to the viewer after such a long scene of dialogue that barely has a trajectory. All of the major where-is-this-going scenes in Tarantino's oeuvre resolve with some kind of flashy conclusion, and he ratchets up the emotional intensity of that conclusion with excruciating duration. Examples include the dinner scene in *Django*, the monologue about oral sexual assault in *The Hateful Eight*, and (again) the opening of *Basterds*. The entirety of *Once Upon a Time in Hollywood* uses this technique: we know the film is about the Tate murders, and we know what Tarantino's famous for, so we are waiting, the whole movie, for the violent night of August 8, 1969. When that night comes, it's more satisfying than we ever dreamed, and such is the case because we waited for more than two hours.[15]

In the old West, there's nothing but time, but everything that happens with a gun happens instantly. There's irony there, and pleasurable tension—the long slowness of the American West (and of Spaghetti Westerns, many of which run well over two hours), and the prize of speed that gunslingers seek. This is the model for Tarantino's later work: quick-draw endings to porch-snoozing days. The Western is the most useful genre for meditation on the American experiment, and Tarantino realized this in the early '00s, as he transitioned from one part of *Kill Bill* to another. In both volumes, he tells revenge stories, because revenge has stamped every one of his films in one way or another. But the sources of those stories are both obvious (the Western, the samurai film) and largely unexplored (the rape-revenge film).

Chapter 4: Rape-Revenge

Kill Bill is certainly, obviously a revenge story, and critics and scholars have discussed it as such in fruitful ways. But as part of the general trend of scholars overlooking the more distasteful genres that influence Tarantino, little writing has considered *Kill Bill* as a rape-revenge film. This is a useful, underexplored lens for the film. The ways in which typical genre codes of rape-revenge films shape *Kill Bill* are worthy of study.

There are two parts to a revenge story: the harm done, and the revenge for that harm. Some examples of the genre omit the first part, for sound or unsound reasons, and go directly to the revenge. *Kill Bill* does not omit the harm entirely, and in fact both volumes open with the scene of Bill's attempted *coup de grâce* on the Bride. But only a few scenes of context exist for what the Bride's life was like before the harm: the Pai Mei sequence, the hotel scene with Karen Kim, and the chapel scene. And all of these describe extraordinary circumstances. Although their details are telling (Beatrix owns a Rolex, her El Paso friends giggle like girls), nothing about these scenes is normal. Their extraordinariness means they merely sketch the outlines of the Bride's life before the Massacre at Two Pines rather than lending us significant insight on that life.

In order to gauge the harm that triggers revenge, a viewer usually needs fuller context—what exactly was ripped away from the subject such that she seeks revenge. In some stories, this can be self-evident; tales of proxy revenge on behalf of a child don't need much in the way of proof that the child deserves avenging, and when one's entire family is killed, as in *Death Rides a Horse*, one scene will suffice to explain what was lost. *The Searchers*, on the other hand, spends 20 minutes setting up the family to be killed/kidnapped, only moving on to revenge later. *Kill Bill* might have benefited from a scene or two that explored Beatrix's ordinary life with Bill and/or the Deadly Vipers. As it stands, the only scenes that perform this function are the long conversations between Bill and Beatrix on the chapel porch and by the fire near Pai Mei's home, both of which occur in *Vol. 2*. Revenge stories can be told asynchronously—that is, the harm can be related in flashback, later, rather than in the early part of the story. But only Tarantino has elected to tell a revenge story in such a squirrelly way, with minimal, out-of-sequence context for the harm done to the subject and most of the emphasis on the details of her revenge.

Although revenge plots in many Westerns are bound up with rape, rape-revenge movies are distinct from Westerns. In fact, they exist within multiple genres: horror films, melodramas, thrillers, and others. Rape-revenge movies are usually very simple in structure: first there is the rape, and then there is the revenge. The movie is a diptych in style, storytelling, and often pacing. The most fundamental rape-revenge movie is *I Spit on Your Grave* (1978), which divides almost cleanly down the middle where the hyphen goes in terms of screen time. The closest Tarantino can come to such straightforwardness is *Death Proof*, which also divides cleanly at the hyphen between rape and revenge (if metaphorically),[16] but *Kill Bill* does not even try to follow a linear chronology. Gallafent usefully applies a Jean-Paul Sartre quote about William Faulkner to Tarantino: he "did not first conceive this orderly plot so as to shuffle it afterwards like a pack of cards; he could not tell it in any other way."[17] Roche, too, finds *Kill Bill*'s a chronology elemental: "Forcing the classical Hollywood structure onto the film is misunderstanding it."[18] Yet this lack of linearity does not eliminate *Kill Bill* from the genre of rape-revenge. Claire Henry considers the film "an interesting variation on the rape-revenge flick,"[19] while Alexandra Heller-Nicholas claims it "may not be a rape-revenge movie as such ... but it references them heavily."[20]

Nor does the lesser emphasis on actual rape disqualify *Kill Bill* from the genre.

Heller-Nicholas again: "Not all rape-revenge films must explicitly contain rape."[21] While in a coma, Beatrix is raped (repeatedly, we presume) via nonconsensual pimping by Buck, a hospital orderly. She kills one of the men—an immediate threat—and she kills Buck. In the normal line of rape-revenge films, she would then track down all the other men who paid Buck to rape her and kill them. However, this series of violations is not the main focus of her revenge. It is, instead, Bill, who has not raped her, but who has shot her in the head and stolen her baby.

Rape-revenge is an elastic genre. Some critics, in fact, see it as a structure or a cycle rather than a genuine genre. Carol J. Clover, the first theorist to write about rape-revenge at length, decreed it a subgenre of slasher films, while Jacinda Read described it as a kind of thematic cycle that only gels around certain cultural contexts. Recent work by Heller-Nicholas and Henry has argued convincingly that rape-revenge is a full-on genre, one with distinct phases: exploitation films in the 1970s, mainstream Hollywood films in the early 1990s, and an explosion of women-made films in the 21st century. Such flexibility makes the genre a bit slippery, but it also allows for reconsiderations and novel analyses of films with some, but not all, of rape-revenge's characteristics.

For example, usually the rape is literal, but sometimes it is metaphorical. Read discusses *Sleeping with the Enemy* (1991) and *Batman Returns* (1992) as having characteristics of rape-revenge, although these films translate rape to domestic violence or simply murder. Sometimes the rape is sexual but unspecified, as in *Thelma and Louise* (1991), and often it occurs to a person who is then proxied for revenge, as when a daughter is raped and a parent takes revenge. Henry theorizes that certain films portray "collective revenge," using as examples *Sleepers* (1996), *Mystic River* (2003), and … *Death Proof*. *Lady Snowblood* (1973), a strong influence on *Kill Bill*, is a proxy rape-revenge film of a rare kind: the raped mother trains the daughter to avenge her. She imbues the daughter with tremendous rage, even though the daughter's body has not been violated.

Beatrix's experiences easily fall into the category of metaphorical rape. She has had everything taken from her. Her body has been destroyed, pushed as close to death as possible, and then violated by strange men. She spends the remainder of the story seeking revenge on those who harmed her, and that revenge is largely a satisfying experience for the audience; her subjectivity is an important aspect of the film, as is the victim's subjectivity in rape-revenge films.

Why, then, do a number of Tarantino critics fail to consider rape-revenge when reading *Kill Bill*? What I've noticed, in researching both topics, is that almost all critics working on Tarantino are male, while the definitive texts about rape-revenge were written by women. I've also noticed that Tarantino *scholars* (i.e., writers from academia) tend to write more about the French New Wave than they write about exploitation cinema, the category into which early rape-revenge films fall. It's unfortunate, because readings of Tarantino that encompass feminist film theory or analyze his work thoroughly in light of its exploitation influences are, I'd argue, a necessary addition to the body of critical work on him. But where will we find scholars who can, and want to, do such work?

Chapter 5: Missing Pieces

It is impossible to deny the influence of both high and low art on Tarantino, and no scholars really do. But I'd wager that a lot of academic writers have barely dipped their toes into the various streams of exploitation cinema in which Tarantino's been swimming like a seal for most of his life. Such films aren't "important" to cinema studies on the whole[22]; even Roche declares that Spaghetti Westerns are "lesser cinematic genres" which use "crude images."[23] Rape-revenge films of the 1970s, while very plainly influential on *Kill Bill* and *Death Proof* at least, have been relegated to the same category of "lesser" cinema. Rape-revenge has only been studied since 1993, and within that short lifespan, only by a small handful of mostly women scholars.

In sum, these worlds don't collide much: exploitation cinema's mostly unscholarly fans; academic writers who, intentionally or not, minimize the influence of "lesser" cinema on Tarantino's sensibility; and terminally degreed feminist film scholars. However, in schoolyard terms, it takes one to know one. Scholars do Tarantino a significant disservice when they downplay or deride the "low" influences that make his films what they are. No scholar has formulated theories that cover everything Tarantino is and does as a filmmaker. This is partially a problem of scope, as no theory can ever be totally comprehensive without being a library. But it's also a problem of blinders, whether deliberate or not.

For instance, Patrick McGee's study of the Western, *From Shane to Kill Bill* (2007), barely mentions the influence of samurai films on *Kill Bill* (nor on the Western generally), and even refers to Hattori Hanzō as "a Shane figure."[24] The Hanzō depicted in *Kill Bill* is a riff on a character played by the same actor, Sonny Chiba, in a Japanese television show, *Kage no Gundan* (1980–85). Further, this character is a fictionalized version of a real 16th-century samurai. To erase all this context and replace it with "a Shane figure" is to ignore crucial referents in *Kill Bill*—to make it much smaller, less international, less delightfully intertextual, than it really is.

Other examples abound in critical studies. Aaron Barlow's book on Tarantino positions *Kill Bill* almost solely as a fairy tale, attaching its characteristics to each of Vladimir Propp's 31 "functions" of fairy tale narratives in an agonizingly off-target chapter. Gallafent's book, although uniquely insightful about many aspects of the film, does not even concern itself with genre in *Kill Bill*. Even Roche's study, far and away the best of all work on Tarantino, only briefly acknowledges rape-revenge as an influence and organizing principle on *Death Proof* and *Kill Bill*, misnaming the main character of *Thriller: A Cruel Picture* and quickly turning to other genres (exploitation, car movies) to explore the films further.[25]

Meanwhile, popular books on Tarantino only reheat the same stories and obvious influences over and over, acting as promotional vehicles for the films or explaining references without analyzing them. DK Holm's casebooks, more obsessive and useful than the rest, come from compiling information posted on internet fan boards by hundreds of users. Many heads are better than a few when it comes to Tarantino's references. These books have a wealth of information about what informs *Kill Bill*, some of which does not appear elsewhere. For instance, Holm quotes another writer in pointing out that O-Ren's death includes a scalping, a stereotypical threat in American Westerns, and he is the only writer I've read who notes how often scenes occur in doorways and on porches. The first observation connects a very samurai-esque scene of *Kill Bill* to the Western (which McGee, given a whole chapter, did rather weakly), and the second idea could be a chapter of its own. Holm gives each idea a portion of a page.

This little constellation of problems—who studies Tarantino and the angles they use to approach him—has significantly limited the work on this filmmaker. No women have written full-length studies on Tarantino, despite his supposedly feminist characters and ideas.[26] Few scholars cite the work of pop books on him, like the Holm books or David Carradine's production diary. Pop writers reinvent the wheel on him by not reading the scholarly work. It goes around in circles, everybody missing something because no one researches him with more than one or two angles in mind.

Few filmmakers work at so many levels that criticism about them can revolve around multiple, perfectly valid ideas and yet never collide in single theories. He's like a popular person with several totally discrete social circles: he winds up with a lot of confused guests at his parties. "Tarantino is a cultural omnivore, rejecting categorization, ingesting all he finds with equal fervor and delight—or seeing each as simply a first course for whatever larger meal he wishes to create and dig into."[27]

We need multidisciplinary scholars and studies of Tarantino. Feminists, exploitation junkies, literary theorists, obsessive fans, avant-garde experts—bring them all in for a conference and publish the results. Only by taking an encyclopedic approach to Tarantino do we begin to understand his work with *all* its intended resonance. Fans cannot be the ultimate arbiter for Tarantino's films. But neither can critics. Everyone is missing a piece.

Last Chapter: Mystery

The people who are smartest about Tarantino are not scholars at all, nor are they quite fans. They're the people who have met and worked with him. David Carradine wrote that an early conversation with Tarantino was "about all kinds of things, but all of it had to do with movies. Quentin doesn't care about anything else."[28] Ethan Hawke, who was married to Uma Thurman during her experiences in *Kill Bill*, said, "The thing that's remarkable about Quentin is that he's as true to his art as anybody. It's just that his taste is very commercial.... Most art house directors aren't interested in blowing somebody's head off."[29] These quotes explain the artist a great deal better than any of the books about him. I can write about duration, about how his films map onto various genre structures, about how some references signify and others signify less. But I don't think any of that is as interesting as considering what he *does*, which is make films intended to be pleasurable.

At first, he made films by arranging the work of others into pleasing sequences, making an art film that felt like an exploitation film or vice versa. Crossing the streams. Over time, he has developed a rhythm for scenes and for whole films entirely unique to him, and has publicly unpacked his racial concerns in ways few filmmakers ever dare to. He has leaned less and less on the work of others (even as the rest of culture has become more and more imitative), until his films require only a little bit of explanatory context. Holm's minute-by-minute casebooks, if written for his other films, would shorten a great deal over the years.[30]

In seeing *Kill Bill* as a creative hinge for Tarantino, we understand both movies, and both halves of his career, better. In considering the traditions of rape-revenge when looking at *Kill Bill*, we come to understand more about how he positions the film's main character and what drives her. In opening our viewing habits to include "low art" films in exploitation subgenres, we understand his influences much better than if we only watch "high art" films. Yet those are just three arguments for understanding Tarantino better, and even if they're correct, there's a lot more to be unraveled. Why has he chosen the Western to explore American issues rather than the noir? Why are there so many exceptions to the rules of his work? Why is revenge such a keystone of his films?

We can only work with what we have, and as Tarantino knows better than anyone, it takes multiple kinds of knowledge to unravel a mystery. In true cinematic fashion, the greatest mystery of all about Tarantino is what he's going to do next, and we have to wait as long as he wants us to in order to solve it.

Notes

1. Here is an important note for the rest of this essay: in my research, I did not read or watch any interviews with Tarantino. The main reason is that there are so many it would have easily doubled the time I spent researching, but a secondary reason is how, philosophically, an artist's own opinions on his work tend to close the work to the interpretations of others. Tarantino is an interesting case, as he's unusually insightful (and perhaps rarely dishonest) about what he's up to, but the philosophy holds.

2. Aside from *Inglourious Basterds* and *Death Proof*, sort of. *Basterds* grapples with American force and masculinity, but not markedly as a Western. Critics disagree on *Death Proof*'s genre, but in its stew are some ingredients of the Western—open spaces, saloons, revenge. The others are obvious Westerns (*The Hateful Eight*) or mixed-genre Westerns/neo–Westerns (*Django Unchained, Once Upon a Time in Hollywood, Kill Bill Vol. 2*).

3. As Aaron Barlow writes: "Tarantino never simply makes movies about movies and never has. What he does, instead, is *speak* 'movies,' speaking movies via film" (p. 4).

4. It's a surprise how many scenes like this take place on porches. The porch is a particularly key location in *Django Unchained*, but that follows for the role of porches in Southern life. Yet important scenes happen on porches in *Once Upon a Time in Hollywood*, too. For Tarantino, porches are a crucial liminal space, much like doorways, about which DK Holm has written convincingly (*Kill Bill Casebook, Vol. 1*, pp. 33–34).

5. *Diary*, pp. 259–60.

6. Holm refers to Zamfir as a "joke musician" (*Kill Bill Casebook Vol. 1*, p. 82). I believe his place in American pop culture differs for *Kill Bill* viewers depending on the year of one's birth, but commercials for his music were a staple on American TV for a time. His

stuff is as earnest and cheesy as Kenny G's, and both have been the butt of nationwide jokes and have laughed all the way to the bank.

7. In *The* Kill Bill *Diary*, Carradine notes that costume designers and set decorators plumbed his own collections to devise Bill's onscreen look and the objects he owns.

8. There is too much to say about this shot for a footnote. It may be the most influential single shot in all of classical Hollywood cinema. Tarantino has copied the shot in multiple films; see Roche, pp. 185–87, although my interpretation of what Tarantino intends to evoke by copying the shot differs from Roche's.

9. The film owes so much to *Lady Snowblood* (1973), in so many ways, that I feel confident saying this.

10. Gallafent, p. 111.

11. Gallafent, p. 107; chapter 7 generally.

12. Gallafent, p. 167.

13. You might be able to convince me that *The Hateful Eight* is slightly more of a Western than *Django*, but it's a near thing.

14. Particularly in *Inglourious Basterds* (Jewish revenge) and *Django Unchained* (Black revenge). The latter should be relatively obvious, but for further arguments on the former, see Barlow, chapter 5.

15. Compare this to his segment of *Four Rooms*, 14 years earlier, which tries to use duration in the same macro way as *Hollywood*. He had not mastered the technique, or even become very good at it, so artistically the segment is a failure.

16. As Claire Henry posits in chapter 5 of *Revisionist Rape-Revenge*, although the second set of "girls" in *Death Proof* are unaware of the murder of the first set, the film is designed and executed *as if* they are avenging the first set.

17. Gallafent, p. 4.

18. Roche, p. 145.

19. Henry, "Maternal Revenge," p. 106.

20. Heller-Nicholas, *Rape-Revenge Films*, p. 80.

21. *Ibid.*

22. Barlow understands that this is nonsense in general, but also in particular for this filmmaker: "The hierarchy of cultural values, the idea of distinct high and low arts with intrinsic difference in value, doesn't exist in his universe" (p. 6).

23. Roche, p. 235.

24. McGee, p. 236. He is referring to the title character of *Shane* (George Stevens, 1953), whose traits influenced Western heroes for decades. Coincidentally enough, David Carradine starred as Shane in a TV spinoff (1966).

25. Roche also joins the pool of incorrect critics who designate *Death Proof* a slasher.

26. I'm not convinced about Tarantino as a feminist, but that's a completely different essay.

27. Barlow, p. 5.

28. Carradine, p. 1.

29. Biskind, p. 192.

30. In fact, the *Vol. 2* casebook is fully 20 pages shorter than *Vol. 1*.

Works Cited

Barlow, Aaron. *Quentin Tarantino: Life at the Extremes.* Santa Barbara: Praeger/ABC-CLIO, 2010.

Biskind, Peter. *Down and Dirty Pictures: Miramax, Sundance, and the Rise of Independent Film.* New York: Simon & Schuster, 2004.

Carradine, David. *The Kill Bill Diary: The Making of a Tarantino Classic as Seen Through the Eyes of a Screen Legend.* New York: Harper, 2006.

Clover, Carol J. *Men, Women, and Chain Saws: Gender in the Modern Horror Film.* Princeton: Princeton University Press, 2015.

Gallafent, Edward. *Quentin Tarantino*. Harlow: Pearson Education Limited, 2006.
Heller-Nicholas, Alexandra. *Rape-Revenge Films: A Critical Study*, 2nd ed. Jefferson, NC: McFarland, 2011.
Henry, Claire. "Maternal Revenge and Redemption in Postfeminist Rape-Revenge Cinema." *Best Served Cold: Studies on Revenge*, ed. Sheila C. Bibb and Daniel Escandell Montiel. Oxford: Inter-Disciplinary Press, 2010.
_____. *Revisionist Rape-Revenge: Redefining a Film Genre*. New York: Palgrave Macmillan, 2014.
Holm, DK. Kill Bill: *An Unofficial Casebook, Volume One*. Glitter Books, 2012.
_____. Kill Bill: *An Unofficial Casebook, Volume Two*. Glitter Books, 2012.
Kenworthy, Christopher. *Shoot Like Tarantino: The Visual Secrets of Dangerous Storytelling*. Studio City, CA: Michael Wiese Productions, 2015.
McGee, Patrick. *From Shane to Kill Bill: Rethinking the Western*. Malden, MA: Blackwell, 2007.
Roche, David. *Quentin Tarantino: Poetics and Politics of Cinematic Metafiction*. Jackson: University Press of Mississippi, 2018.

Whose Truth? Race
and Quentin Tarantino

Troy D. Smith

Quentin Tarantino burst into the national consciousness in 1992 with his debut film, *Reservoir Dogs*. It was immediately evident that the 29-year-old video-clerk-turned-director was something different, but critical opinions varied as to exactly what that something was. Siskel and Ebert gave the heist film two thumbs down, saying that the director was promising but that his movie was all style with little substance.[1] I remember being immediately drawn in by the first clips I saw from the film, and the aforementioned style had a lot to do with that: the music, the coolness of the skinny ties and sunglasses, the boldness, the swagger. I loved the movie, and when it was released on video I made all my closest friends watch it, believing they would appreciate the treasure I was bringing them. Almost all of them hated it. It was, they asserted, too violent, too profane, and most of all, too confusing. For my part, I enjoyed the nonlinear storytelling technique (it was structured more like a novel than a movie). Many critics and moviegoers felt the same, and Tarantino would demonstrate the same techniques in his highly successful follow-up, *Pulp Fiction*.

There was one element almost no one was talking about in reference to Quentin Tarantino in 1992: race. The only non-white character in *Reservoir Dogs* was Detective Holdaway, superior officer to the undercover operative Mister Orange (Tim Roth). There were six instances of the "n-word," which seemed to be more a marker of the speech patterns and racial attitudes of the working-class white bank robbers, inserted for authenticity. The same tack was taken by Francis Ford Coppola with the mobsters in his *Godfather* movies.

Throughout the rest of Tarantino's career, though, race has loomed large as a controversy, sometimes to the point of almost eclipsing the films themselves. While, on the one hand, Tarantino's films have often heavily

77

featured characters of color in a positive, empowered fashion (in fact, making them the principal protagonists of one-third of his films), some cultural critics and scholars have pointed to the stereotyped behavior of those characters, and accused Tarantino of inappropriate cultural appropriation in his handling of characters of color.

In most cases, the criticism is directed at the dialogue and actions of the films themselves. As Derrick Clifton said in a 2016 NBC op-ed, "Even when you're a white person who demonstrates some level of appreciation or affinity for Black people and Black culture—you're still white. You don't get a free pass to play around with the words, phrases, and experiences that reinforce the marginalization of Black people."[2] In other cases, Tarantino's critics have pointed, not just to his work, but to his defenses of it as evidence of personal racism and/or reinforcement of the institutional racism that undergirds white supremacy. Tarantino has taken exception to both approaches, and if anything has doubled down on publicly defending his own art. "Social critics don't mean a thing to me," he has said. "It's really easy to ignore them, because I believe in what I'm doing 100 percent. So any naysayers for the public good can just fuck off. They might be a drag for a moment, but after that moment is over, it always ends up being gasoline to my fire."[3]

Tarantino's most prominent detractor has been Spike Lee, an African American fellow director. The two filmmakers have engaged in a very public, often very contentious, exchange on the subject for a quarter of a century. It started when Lee took exception to the fact that, in Tarantino's 1997 film *Jackie Brown*, the n-word appeared 38 times. "I'm not against the word," Lee said, "and I use it, but not excessively. And some people speak that way. But, Quentin is infatuated with that word. What does he want to be made—an honorary Black man?" In the same *Variety* interview, Lee said, "I want Quentin to know that all African-Americans do not think that word is trendy or slick…. If I had used the word 'kike' 38 times in *Mo' Better Blues*, it would have been my last picture."[4]

For context, Spike Lee's *Mo' Better Blues* (1990) featured three uses of the n-word.[5] *Do the Right Thing* (1989) had seven, and *Jungle Fever* (1991) had 15. For further context, Tarantino cast 1970s Blaxploitation star Pam Grier as the lead in *Jackie Brown*. Grier gained her Blaxploitation Queen identity as a result of such films as *Foxy Brown* (1974), which featured five uses of the n-word. Of the most successful Blaxploitation or proto–Blaxploitation movies of the early 1970s, *Sweet Sweetback's Baadasssss Song* (1971) used the word four times; *Superfly* (1972) used it 18 times; and, believe it or not, *Shaft* (1971) did not use it at all. Those three movies, incidentally, all had Black directors; most of the less-successful Blaxploitation films that would imitate them in ensuing years, including *Foxy Brown*, would be helmed by white directors. With those facts at hand, it is clearly not an exaggeration to say that *Jackie Brown* featured an extremely high tally of n-words (most of them by actor Samuel L. Jackson). Tarantino's *Hateful Eight* (2015) would use the word 58 times, and *Django Unchained* (2012) would use it 110 times.

When asked by a *Playboy* interviewer in 2003 whether he thought Spike Lee's 1997 complaints had any merit, Tarantino called Lee "self-serving" and deflected the question.

> It's funny, because he talks in these grandiose terms, but as much of a loudmouth as he can be, the press doesn't really listen to what he says. They print his tone. If you boiled down what he was saying, it wasn't that I didn't have the right to say "n-----r" as many times as I did. It was why do I have the right to say "n-----r" 37 times, but he doesn't have the right to say "kike" 37 times? That is what he was really saying.[6]

In 2012, Tarantino declared victory over Lee where *Jackie Brown* was concerned. "Fifteen years has proven the case," he said. "That movie's beloved."[7] While Lee and many others might disagree with that assessment, the point was almost moot; 2012 would bring a whole new round of controversies, this time more layered, over *Django Unchained*. Since *Jackie Brown*'s debut, Tarantino has also been accused of Orientalism and cultural appropriation due to his kung fu couplet *Kill Bill* and his portrayal of Bruce Lee in *Once Upon a Time in Hollywood* (2019).

It would be unfair, though, to focus on the racial indictments of Tarantino without giving due consideration to his own defense of his artistic vision (beyond his penchant for aggressive defensiveness). Tarantino has often expressed a firm belief in the right, he might say the duty, of a writer to deal in truths without watering them down. This frequently leads the filmmaker to stress the need for verisimilitude. Movie dialogue should reflect, as much as possible, how people really talk and what they really talk about. He has also expressed a need for integrity in a writer following the story, and the characters, wherever they go. In the aforementioned *Playboy* article, he stated, "I am working with The English language. I am not just a film director who shoots movies. I'm an artist, and good, bad, or indifferent, I'm coming from that place. All my choices, the way I live my life, are about that."[8]

In 2013, at the backstage press conference after he won the best screenplay Golden Globe for *Django Unchained*, Tarantino addressed both those principles—verisimilitude and artistic integrity—when asked about the prevalence of the n-word in his script. "If someone is out there actually saying that when it comes to the word n----r that the fact that I was using it … more that it was used back in the antebellum south, in Mississippi 1858, then feel free to make that case. But no one is actually making that case, so in other words what they're actually saying is I should soften it, they're saying I should lie, that I should whitewash, they're saying I should massage and I never do that when it comes to my characters." Of course, the writer probably hurt his own argument by articulating it in his typically intemperate style—one report sported the headline "Quentin Tarantino Drops the N-Word Less Than a Minute into Press Conference."[9] Conversely, one could argue that—if Tarantino's oeuvre stresses spectacle over message, which he concedes himself—his press conferences and interviews are performance art which does the same thing. He expressed a similar idea more effectively in an interview with Henry Louis Gates, in which he said that when making a movie about slavery "you're going to hear some things that are going to be ugly, and you're going see some things that are going be ugly. That's just part and parcel of dealing truthfully with this story, with this environment, with this land … [you're saying] I should be watering it down. I should be making it easier to digest. No, I don't want it to be easy to digest. I want it to be a big, gigantic boulder, a jagged pill and you have no water."[10]

Essentially, then, any discussion of Quentin Tarantino and race must come down to three questions. First, as discussed briefly above, which carries more weight: the effect racial representations in Tarantino movies have on people of color, or the right of the artist to follow his vision without self-censorship? Second, are the social rules different for white writers dealing with nonwhite characters (and, if not, should they be)? Third, should the oeuvre of Tarantino—or anyone else, for that matter—be examined solely as a text, divorced from authorial intent, to be interpreted by the audience, or should it be colored by the opinions/views of the author as expressed outside their medium, and judged accordingly?

That third question, relative to Tarantino, has been engaged in academia by two scholars in particular. Adilifu Nama teaches on the intersections of pop culture and race at Loyola Marymount University. His 2015 book *Quentin Tarantino: Race on the QT* won the Best Reference/Primary Source Work from the Pop Culture Association. He is also known for his 2011 book *SuperBlack: American Pop Culture and Black Superheroes*.

Sean M. Tierney is a university film lecturer in Hong Kong. He wrote about Tarantino and Orientalism in a 2006 *Journal of Communication* article, "Themes of Whiteness in *Bulletproof Monk, Kill Bill,* and The *Last Samurai*," and wrote a chapter called "Quentin Tarantino in Black and White" in the 2011 anthology *Critical Rhetorics of Race*, edited by Michael G. Lacy and Kent A. Ono. We will discuss their oppositional views on Tarantino in detail, as well as define "whiteness" in a theoretical framework.

But first, now that we have laid out those questions, let us examine them in order and in more detail, beginning with the one about the effect of Tarantino's racial representations to people of color as opposed to the execution of his artistic vision. It is no great secret that a big part of that artistic vision consists of pastiches, homages, and reimaginings of popular low-budget genres of the early 1970s, when Tarantino was a child: Spaghetti Westerns, kung fu movies, exploitation crime and prison movies … and Blaxploitation films. As Tarantino recalled in an interview, "[My mother's] boyfriends would come over, and they'd … take me to blaxploitation movies, trying to, you know, get me to like them and buy me footballs and stuff, and … my mom and her friends would take me to cool bars and stuff, where they'd be playing cool, live rhythm-and-blues music … while Jimmy Soul and a cool band would be, you know, playing in some lava lounge-y kind of '70s cocktail lounge. It was really cool."[11]

For much of his career, Tarantino seems to have focused primarily on recapturing the coolness factor of those early 1970s films—with a significant degree of success, as my description of my own initial response to *Reservoir Dogs* demonstrates. Colorful characters, dynamic action, creative dialogue—with no conscious attempt to moralize or attach underlying themes. "Any time you try to get across a big idea, you're shooting yourself in the foot," he said in 1994. "First, you need to make a good movie." If something else develops along the way and comes across in the movie, "that's great." However, it should not "be this big idea. It should be a small idea, from which everyone can get something different."[12]

The filmmaker seems to have made some adjustments to that approach later in his career, with the cathartic revenge fantasies against evil portrayed in *Inglourious Basterds, Django Unchained,* and *Once Upon a Time in Hollywood.* In many of his statements after *Django* was released, describing his hopes for the movie, Tarantino implied he was finally looking for an overt message. "There's the brutal reality that slaves lived under for … 245 years, and then there's the violence of Django's retribution," he said in an NPR interview. "And that's movie violence, and that's fun and that's cool, and that's really enjoyable and kind of what you're waiting for."[13] He told *GQ*'s Zach Baron in 2015 that, with *Django*, he was "trying to show America itself," specifically, "America's culpability in its past." He told Baron that *Django* "was definitely the beginning of my political side." He expressed hope that Black teens would view Django as their cowboy hero, and watching the movie with their dads would become a rite of passage.[14]

Of course, those 1970s Blaxploitation movies—in varying degrees, depending on the film—all had a subtext that was far more potent than simple action sequences or engaging plots. Their very existence was a message. Whether the protagonists were detectives, gangsters, pushers, Old West bounty hunters, or female vigilantes, they walked through their cinematic world with poise, confidence, and swagger, deferring to no one. They stood up to The Man … and not only survived, but often emerged victorious. They were celluloid reifications of Black Power, living the three tenets of that movement: self-defense, self-determination, and self-respect. While Django may have made a transition on his hero's journey from helpless slave to a living embodiment of the Black Power tenets, it seems that it took Tarantino until his seventh movie (and the year 2012) to make the best elements of Blaxploitation more than window dressing. It is sheer speculation to wonder whether it took the director's approaching his 50th birthday to reframe how he looked at the movie genres that inspired him as a child, and move beyond the aesthetic trappings and tones that had first grabbed his attention to a more mature examination of their thematic potential. Even if that were true, though, *Django* still included plenty of the spectacle Tarantino's movies are known for.

Both Tarantino's most vocal Black critic, Spike Lee, and his most vocal Black defender, Samuel L. Jackson, have spoken to his history with 1970s Black cinema and its possible influence on him. "His whole deal with African Americans is through Black exploitation films. His knowledge of Black people is based on Black exploitation films from the early '70s," Lee said in 2000.[15] On another occasion he said, "It's just the n-word, the n-word, the n-word. He says he grew up on Blaxploitation films and that they were his favorite films but he has to realize that those films do not speak to the breadth of the entire African-American experience. I mean the guy's just stupid."[16]

Samuel L. Jackson defended *Jackie Brown* in 1998, calling it "a wonderful homage to Black exploitation films," and adding, "This is a good film. And Spike hasn't made one of those in a few years." For a while, the Lee/Tarantino feud became a Lee/Jackson feud, with Lee calling Jackson (who had appeared in movies by both directors) a "House Negro" who "kisses [Tarantino's] butt."[17] Jackson, when told that Spike Lee was a "voice for African Americans," responded, "I didn't get a chance to vote in that election."[18]

The previous year, Jackson had told *Entertainment Weekly* that "Quentin wants to be Black. He watched a lot of Black-exploitation films growing up. He has a lot of Black friends. He has an affinity for Black characters. He's like my daughter's little hip-hop friends. They're basically Black kids with white skin."[19]

Derrick Clifton, in his aforementioned MSNBC op-ed, threaded the needle between the oppositional assertions of Lee and Jackson.

> There's nothing wrong with being fascinated with Black culture as a white person. But when there's not enough respect for the everyday racial slights experienced by Black people, and how that connects with the larger system of white power and privilege in America, any sense of maintaining a respectful

boundary gets lost. Black people aren't asking for white folks to walk on egg-shells around them. Black people are asking to be respected and under-stood. And when people like Tarantino disregard the constructive criticisms of Black people, they're not really interested in using their power to help the community—they're instead reveling in tacit validations of their own racial privilege.[20]

Following Clifton's reasoning, a white author or director's apprecia-tion for Black culture does not validate their use of that culture without at least a subtextual acknowledgment of white power and privilege. Doing so, in fact, whether consciously or intentionally or not, is actually an expres-sion of that white power and privilege.

Tarantino has countered this accusation, down through the years, in two discreet ways. First, by stressing the artist's right to create without censorship, and secondly, by claiming an indirect right to represent Black culture by implying a close personal relationship to it. The first argument has many valid elements, and is a legitimate framework through which to examine Tarantino's work in relation to many Black people's reaction his films. The second argument is an unfortunate one. It is a classic expression of appropriation—a white person insisting on an inherent right, not just to describe or write about, but to personally claim the identity of a non-white population.

Regarding the first argument, Tarantino described his writing pro-cess to Henry Louis Gates. "I follow the characters wherever they want to go," he said. While he might have a vague outline for the first half of a film, to set things up, the second half is more organic, almost stream-of-con-sciousness. "Now everything's different. I'm now those people. I've learned more about them. I am them. They are going their own way. And I might have some places I want them to go. Usually they take their time about getting there. But sometimes they get there. And if they don't want to go there, if they want to go their own way, that's them telling me it's bulls—t. So I follow their way. For better or for worse. So the characters really dic-tate and really decide. All my characters are coming from me."[21] Having to self-censor or tailor speech patterns to appease others would impede his flow and his own mental connection to the characters.

Responding to a comment about the flood of n-words in *Django*, Taran-tino said, "In each situation I've ever done it, it's just been the truth of the characters. And here it's also the truth of the characters and the truth of the time period." For people who said he "should have cleaned it up," his response was, "Well that's just not what I do. I don't clean it up." No amount of criticism, he said, had ever changed one scene or even "one word" of any of his scripts. "It's my job to ignore them … because I believe in what I'm doing wholeheartedly and passionately, and it's my job to just get on with it."

Or, as he told Roger Ebert in 1994, "So the bottom line is, my No. 1 responsibility is not to society at large; it's to my characters. And to be true to them."[22]

Let us take a moment to unpack those quotes. Tarantino has repeatedly said he is not interested in historical accuracy, which he considers to often be dry, yet at the same time he is insistent on presenting "the truth of the characters and the truth of the time period." This is an approach I have taken personally in my own fiction, adhering to the words of novelist Oakley Hall: "The pursuit of truth, not of facts, is the business of fiction." On the other hand, Tarantino told Gates that "all my characters are coming from me." This is so obviously true of fiction writers in general that on the surface it seems like a truism. It is easy, therefore, to miss the deeper implications of such a statement. If all my characters come from within me, then those characters' truths come from within me, as well, making them subjective, not objective, truths. While it is objectively true that the n-word was used freely in the antebellum South, the liberality with which Tarantino's characters use them—remaining "true" to the author's internal vision of those characters and their setting—is not an indicator of how (and how often) they might have been used. And it fails to take into account its effect on African American audiences. As anthropologist Yarimar Bonilla put it, "must representations of slavery strike a certain mood? Can they be 'wrong' not just in their facts, but in their effect?"[23]

Tarantino's version of the "truth" about slavery or Black culture—like my own, or any other white author's—is a white person's imperfectly understood, unlived truth. This is not to say that a writer, or any other kind of artist, should not strive to understand those topics the best they can, and seek the universalities of human experience ... but doing so in such a manner as to ignore the lived experience of members of that community is a different story.

Tarantino addressed the issue on Howard Stern's radio program in 1997:

> It's simply about me being a writer. All right? And they cannot say I can't write another character. They can't say I can't write Black characters, I can't live my Black characters, I can't be my Black characters, I can't be my Filipino characters.... Spike Lee can do the Johnny Cash story if he wants to. I am not saying that he can't. Not gonna say that. But the thing about it is, as a writer, I am God. As a writer. And all these characters are mine and they're me and I'm telling the truth. And you know what? He might not like it, but there's a hell of a lot of Black guys in Compton saying "n----r" all the goddamn time.... You know, in Carson, in Inglewood, that's where I'm from. Not everybody, but there's a hell of a lot of guys....[24]

In that exchange with Stern, Tarantino conflates his argument of artistic integrity with his claim of special qualification to use the n-word and to write about Black culture because of where he lives and people he knows. Samuel L. Jackson's off-hand observation that "Quentin wants to be Black" extends to an insistence on "whitesplaining" Blackness. For example, he once said that Black people respond well to his movies because they are the only group of people who can "laugh off" violence; "they don't let violence affect them at all."[25] Tarantino is casually presenting a personal opinion as definitive fact, applying it authoritatively to an entire group of people.

More to the point, in a 1994 *Vibe* interview, Tarantino self-identified as a "n----r":

When I was growing up in the '60s, "n----r" was a fighting word. It never was to me because I always said, Okay, I can be identified as that, because it speaks volumes about who I am. It's somebody who's not to be fucked with, it's somebody who grew up a certain kind of way, who has certain kinds of traits that will get your ass fucked up if you step to them the wrong way. I'm one of those kind of people, yeah.[26]

The context of Tarantino's story seems to be that white kids in Los Angeles would call each other the n-word as an insult, but that he took it as a compliment—or at least an accurate assessment—instead. This definition of the n-word, though, is one that is internal to Tarantino and disregards the history of that word and its effect on actual African Americans. Like the white friends of Jackson's daughter, he took identification with Blackness as a badge of honor, like the white youths in the classic Dave Chappelle "Black White Supremacist" skit.

In his 1997 interview with Stern, Tarantino expounded on the theme of his own self-perceived Blackness. "I was like the white kid that went to an all–Black school that hung around all the Black guys, and everything, and just had this Black thing going." Rich Juzwiak points out, by the way, that Narbonne High School is mostly Latino; this does not mean, however, that Tarantino could not have "hung around all the Black guys." Juzwiak compares Tarantino's attitude in these quotes to someone saying, "It's OK.

I'm *really down*, not like those other white people. I can say recklessly racial things, including the word 'n----r.'"[27] Tom Carson, in the *New Republic,* called it "a white boy's impudent and corkscrewed take on African-Americaness."[28] As Derrick Clifton put it, "It's as if Tarantino believes his cinematic depictions of Black experiences, his hiring of Black performers like Foxx, and his outspoken support of #BlackLivesMatter means he's entitled to act a lot more flagrantly than other white people on matters of race. But that's not quite how this works."[29]

We have segued into the second of the three questions I posed earlier, to wit: are the social rules different for white writers dealing with non-white characters (and, if not, should they be)? Several of the points made, and sourced quoted, in the preceding paragraphs already point to the answer. Most of Tarantino's critics are not saying, despite his protests to the contrary, that he as a white artist should not write about, or tell stories featuring, non-white characters. As Clifton said, "Black people aren't asking for white folks to walk on eggshells around them. Black people are asking to be respected and understood."[30] It is how the stories are told that matter to people like Clifton and Lee.

African American screenwriter John Ridley, who won an Oscar for *12 Years a Slave* (2013), complained that Tarantino "luxuriates" in the n-word, using it "just to be used." Nonetheless, Ridley said, "It's painful and it's infuriating. But at the same time, I wouldn't sit and say, 'OK, you can never use that word.'"[31] Even Spike Lee, near the beginning of his long-running feud with Tarantino, was making a similar point. "I will say it again and again. I have a definite problem with Quentin Tarantino's excessive use of the n-word. And let the record show that I never said that he can not use that word—I've used that word in many of my films—but I think something is wrong with him."[32]

The very history of the expression "n-word" as a substitute for "nr" helps to frame the issue. Although almost never heard on television before the 1970s, "nr" became commonplace in that decade … if spoken by a Black actor in sitcoms, or by anyone in historical dramas such as *Roots* (1977). The first notable example was a 1971 episode of *All in the Family*, wherein Archie Bunker—the epitome of bigotry—meets entertainer Sammy Davis, Jr. Davis expresses surprise that Bunker called him "colored" instead of "n----r." The word wound up being used occasionally on series with principally Black casts, such as *Sanford and Son, The Jeffersons*, and *Good Times*. One notable example is the January 11, 1974, episode of *Sanford and Son*, titled "Fred Sanford, Legal Eagle." When a policeman says under oath that he does not practice racial profiling, Sanford says, "Take a look at this courtroom, you got enough n----rs in here to make a Tarzan movie."[33]

Another prominent example from that decade is the December 13, 1975, episode of *Saturday Night Live*, which included a skit that featured Richard Pryor as a job applicant and Chevy Chase as the person conducting the interview. Chase's character does a word association exercise; the white interviewer ends up saying anti–Black racial epithets, to which the Black applicant responds with anti-white ones. When Chase says "spearchucker," Pryor replies "honky." When Chase says the n-word, Pryor responds, "dead honky." The scene demonstrated, through satire, that the n-word was the one racial insult that evokes the most anger in African Americans.[34]

How and when did the word become banished from television (though not movies) and be supplanted in polite discourse with the term "the n-word"? There is a concrete answer to that question: during the O.J. Simpson trial in 1995. LAPD detective Mark Fuhrman had discovered the infamous bloody glove on Simpson's estate and was called to testify about it; Simpson's lawyers contended that Fuhrman had a long history of racism and had planted the evidence. They wanted to introduce into testimony recordings of Fuhrman from the previous decade when he had expressed highly bigoted opinions about African Americans and said "n----r" 41 times on tape. Christopher Darden, a Black lawyer who was on the prosecution team, contended that the recordings would prejudice the jury, some of whom were Black. *The New York Times* described Darden's statement:

> Christopher Darden, a deputy district attorney who is Black, said that what he called the "N-word" was so pejorative that it would inevitably prejudice the mostly Black jury against Mr. Fuhrman, and perhaps other white police officers who were expected to testify at trial.
> "If you allow Mr. Cochran to use this word and play the race card," he said, "the direction and focus of the case changes: it is a race case now."
> "It becomes an issue of color" and "it becomes a question of who is the Blackest man up here," Mr. Darden said, referring to himself and Mr. Cochran, who is also Black.
> The prosecutor, his voice trembling, added that the "N-word" was so vile that he would not utter it.[35]

CNN and other news outlets began, in their reports on the trial, to refer to the slur as "the n-word" rather than saying it aloud. In a short period of time it had become *de rigeur*. After all, quoting from the Fuhrman statements that *were* allowed to be presented would have meant a torrent of the pejorative in every news segment for months. Not long afterwards I was surprised to find that, when the classic 1977 slavery-centered miniseries *Roots* was re-run on television, every instance of "n----r" was bleeped out. Bear in mind, this all took place only one year after the release of *Pulp Fiction* and its infamous "Jimmie" n-word scene, which we will soon discuss. Incidentally, the Simpson trial was also the origin of the term "the race card."[36]

> I said that the origin of the term "n-word" helps to frame the issue. The word n----r was essentially expunged from public use due to the sheer number of times one white man said it during a racially charged era—at around the same time Tarantino started to use it heavily in his films.

Whereas 1992's *Reservoir Dogs* had featured six uses of the n-word, 1994's *Pulp Fiction* used the epithet 14 times. Nine were uttered by Black actors Samuel L. Jackson or Ving Rhames, and one by a white drug dealer played by Eric Stoltz. What had people upset, though, were the four n-words dropped by Tarantino himself, and the context in which they were used.

In the film, hitmen Jules Winnfield and Vincent "Vinnie" Vega (Samuel

L. Jackson and John Travolta) accidentally shoot a captive in the back seat of their car, leaving a bloody mess. Needing a place to hide the car and the body until they can (literally and figuratively) get the situation cleaned up, Jules goes to the home of the only friend he knows in that part of town, a white man named Jimmie (played by Tarantino). Jimmie is upset that the body has been brought to his property and insists that it be removed before his wife (who, incidentally, is Black) gets home. Jimmie embarks on an angry tirade, cutting Jules off every time he tries to speak. Even the white hitman, Vinnie, calls Jimmie's manner "abusive."

When Jules compliments Jimmie's choice of coffee, Jimmie responds furiously, "What's on my mind at this moment isn't the coffee in my kitchen, it's the dead n----r in my garage." When Jules attempts a reply, Jimmie continues, "I'm talking. Now let me ask you a question, Jules. When you drove in here, did you notice a sign out front that said, 'Dead n r storage'?"

Jules tries to speak again, and is again interrupted. "Answer to question. Did you see a sign out in front of my house that said, 'Dead n----r storage'?"

"Naw man," Jules says contritely. "I didn't." "You know why you didn't see that sign?" "Why?"

"'Cause storing dead n----rs ain't my fucking business!"

The scene has Tarantino's character condescendingly saying the n-word four times in less than a minute. Moreover, he does so while brow-beating Samuel L. Jackson's character, who has been established as a strong, competent Black man—in fact, one of the most well-rounded Black characters in a Tarantino movie. Eric Deggans, in a 2012 *Salon* article primarily about *Django Unchained*, describes Jimmie's behavior as "hectoring him like he's scolding a kid."[37] That very apt assessment reminds me of a scene from Disney's 1946 *Song of the South*, in which Uncle Remus—portrayed in that movie as essentially the wisest slave on that or any nearby plantation—is scolded alongside a white child as if he, too, were a child. I sometimes show that scene in class to demonstrate the paternalism of slave owners. The fact that the behavior by Jimmie is accompanied by a stream of n-words only serves to compound the discomfort.

"I think I know why Tarantino went there," Deggans wrote. "He seems to delight in scenes where the power dynamic shifts, and seeing Jules kowtow to this geeky white guy throws off the audience … it felt a bit gratuitous; we already know this guy somehow has the power to make Jules fall in line—we didn't really need to see him get smacked with the n-word to confirm it all."[38]

That scene was the beginning of Tarantino's contentious public interaction with the n-word. Mario Van Peebles—whose father Melvin Van

Peebles was the director of the film some historians say started, or at least presaged, Blaxploitation, *Sweet Sweetback's Baadaaaass Song*—weighed in on the subject in 1995. "Now you know that there is no way ever in his life Tarantino would say that to someone who looks like Samuel Jackson. No way! He's just thinking, 'I can finally say n----r to a black person—I must be cool."[39]

That same year, on the set of *Crimson Tide*—for which Tarantino had rewritten some dialogue—actor Denzel Washington called Tarantino out in person, in front of the cast and crew. "How come you use 'n----r' so much, huh? I mean, do you know what you're doing with that word?" Tarantino reportedly did not reply. "Well, I just told the guy what I thought, I was just being honest," Washington recalled later. "But perhaps I shouldn't have done it in front of so many people. I mean, I like the guy." Washington later apologized, and has said that Tarantino was very gracious.[40]

One of the earliest—perhaps the first—occasions Tarantino discussed the n-word controversy and the Jimmie scene in public was in a 1994 interview in The *Toronto Star*. "It's like, when you say a n----r joke," he said, "you gotta use the word 'n----r' or it's not funny. It's only the dirtiness of it, the nastiness of it, that makes it funny. So I don't want you to censor the way my characters talk." A few years later, though, in a 1998 article in *The Australian*, he seems to indicate that it is not only verisimilitude or truth that motivates his use of the word, but a recognition of its potency (and the implication that the use of it can decrease its negative strength). "When you're talking about the word 'n----r,' you're talking about probably the most volatile word there is in the English language. The N-word is a word we can't even say out loud. It has that much power."[41]

This and other statements—such as the admission that recreating the brutality of slavery in *Django* drained him emotionally and led to a bout of depression—show that he does, in fact, recognize the racial weight of his subject matter and dialogue—when he is not being directly challenged on it, and responding defensively.[42] They also indicate that such recognitions are trumped by his devotion to truth in art as he sees it. It is worth pointing out that several of his films—*Kill Bill 1 & 2I Inglourious Basterds*, and *Once Upon a Time in Hollywood*—feature no use of the n-word at all, doubtless because the settings of those films did not compel Tarantino to depict his versions of Black culture or small-time racist white criminals.

Even Tarantino's frequent defender Samuel L. Jackson, though, had cautioned him against the dialogue in the Jimmie scene. "When we did *Pulp*, I warned Quentin about the whole 'n----r storage.' I was like, 'Don't say 'n' r storage.' He's like, 'No, I'm going to say it like that.' And we tried to soften it by making his wife Black, because that wasn't originally written.

But you can't just tell a writer he can't talk, write the words, put the words in the mouths of the people from their ethnicities, the way that they use their words. You cannot do that, because then it becomes an untruth; it's not honest. It's just not honest. And half the time, too, there are other ways. And I generally add like at least five n---as to what Quentin has already written, just because I'm talking."[43] Jamie Foxx also reiterated Tarantino's views on verisimilitude: "Then when *Django* came around, I understood the text. The N-word was said 100 times, but I understood the text—that's the way it was back in that time."[44]

Sometimes, in his frustration, Tarantino seems to feel that the majority of his critics are questioning his right to write about Black characters and themes. "The bad taste that was left in my mouth had to do with this: it's been a long time since the subject of a writer's skin was mentioned as often as mine. You wouldn't think the color of a writer's skin should have any effect on the words themselves. In a lot of the more ugly pieces, my motives were really brought to bear in the most negative way. It's like I'm some supervillain coming up with this stuff."[45] He has also said, "As a writer, I demand the right to write any character in the world that I want to write. And to say that I can't do that because I'm white … that is racist."[46] As Steve Rose of the *Guardian* pointed out, while "the first half of that statement is honorable," the second half—the claim of reverse racism—is not, and he does himself no honors by making it.[47]

The Black community, like any other community, is not monolithic. Tarantino has both fans and detractors in Black America; some Black viewers cheered the exploits of Django while others were disturbed by the language and imagery. Very few, though, have said that white artists should not be allowed to engage Blackness. What it comes down to, ultimately, with Tarantino or any other white artist, is whether he tells stories structured around Black characters and Black history with respect for the Black community. He apparently feels that his admiration for Black culture and desire to center Black characters (and thereby actors and actresses) in leading, even heroic roles, is the full expression of that respect. On a personal level, he has engaged in anti-racist activities, especially near the beginning of the Black Lives Matter movement—not only speaking out, but participating in protests on the ground.[48] Surely, he might think, that shows where he stands on racism, making accusations of racist ideas from Black intellectuals grate ever harder.

For many African Americans, though, true respect means listening to, acknowledging, and acting on the suggestions that are made from their lived experience. It also means engaging with institutional racism, and recognizing the ways it influences you as a white artist (or white person in general), rather than digging in with the intent of absolving yourself of all traces, or implications, of personal racism. Such digging in misses the point. White privilege and white fragility are usually not consciously intentional—that is part of what makes it privilege, you do not have to think about it. Criticism of your role in institutional racism is not a blanket statement about your worth, or morality, as an individual. It asks you to see beyond yourself, to perceive the overall structure, to truly empathize with those who are excluded from it, and ultimately to look for ways to "abdicate your whiteness" as best you can.

Part of my own scholarship involves comic books, and this discussion of Tarantino reminds me of a couple of situations in that genre. First, it calls to mind several liberal white comics writers from the 1950s and 1960s, such as Harvey Kurtzman and Stan Lee, who wrote powerful stories critical of racism and segregation—yet did so within the confines of their own whiteness, often missing important elements of the very stories they were trying to tell, and often centering white characters.[49] It also calls to mind my research on kung-fu-and-Blaxploitation-inspired comics of the 1970s, in which fans of color wrote in the letters columns to criticize the (almost always white) writers' and artists' representations of African American or Asian/Asian-American characters. The writers and editors were usually very defensive, sometimes accusing the fans of reverse-racism (though the actual term did not exist at the time). Gradually, though, some of the fans got through and racial representations in the industry started to shed longstanding stereotypes.

In 2015, amid the renewed cycle of public discussion on Tarantino's use of the n-word due to the release of *The Hateful Eight*, he made the following statement: "when the Black critics came out with savage think pieces about *Django*, I couldn't have cared less. If people don't like my movies, they don't like my movies, and if they don't get it, it doesn't matter." On the one hand, at least at the time of that conversation, Tarantino was letting go of the defensive-combative posture on the subject he had exhibited for two decades. On the other hand, though, while he no longer cared whether Black critics "got" his perspective, he still seemed to have no impulse to try to "get" theirs. It is my hope that, like those 1970s comics writers, he will eventually "get" it after all.

This brings us to our third and final question: should we even be talking about Quentin Tarantino the man, or should we confine our critiques to the texts—his screenplays and films—and what they tell us about race in and of themselves? We have already examined the words of several people—journalists, actors, directors, and academics—who make their judgments of Tarantino's oeuvre through the lens of the man himself. We will now augment that with a look at the scholarship of Sean Tierney, who has written one influential article about Tarantino and representations of

Blackness, and another about Tarantino and representations of Asianness. Both, then, were really about Tarantino and whiteness.

In "Quentin Tarantino in Black and White," Tierney highlights even more Tarantino quotes about growing up around Black people than I have. For example, Tarantino has stated that "whenever I get violent I turn into a Black male ... when I get mad or when I get in a fight I talk with a Black dialect." Tierney quotes a story in which the filmmaker bragged about how, unlike other white people, he did not back down from big Black men. In another quote, Tarantino said "we all have a lot of people inside of us, and one of the ones inside me is Black. Don't let the pigmentation fool you; it is a state of mind." On another occasion, Tarantino expressed the belief he had been "a Black slave in America. Maybe even like three lives."

Tierney posited that the sort of "ethnic detachment" Tarantino described, in which he deferred to his own state of mind over phenotypical and physiological fact to determine his own ethnicity, is in fact "one significant aspect of the construction of white identity ... an interpretive framework that privileges individualism and racial neutrality." Furthermore, in Tierney's view, Tarantino's musings about reincarnation were "a significantly troublesome, insensitive, and to many outrageous act that implicates both the speaker and those who accept such statements."

Tierney does not take at face value Tarantino's claims that "he possesses an ability to transcend his own ethnicity and to take on those of his characters," or the director's assertion that he wants to decrease the "division between Black and white." Claims of wishing to bridge racial differences are instead, according to Tierney, based "on the self-flattering presumption of initial benevolence." Tarantino's very insistence that he is not racist, speaking in "arrogance and resentment," is, in fact, a common tactic among white people "most often used to deflect accusations of racism while in fact maintaining and/or re-inscribing racist assumptions, which implicitly suggest that there are rational reasons for said racism."

In other words, Tarantino is asking the world to believe he is not racist simply because he says so, despite any opinions to the contrary from nonwhite people. Tierney calls that "an arrogant device of white privilege: An opinion has no truth and means nothing unless the (white) individual deigns to validate it by adopting it as his/her own." Tierney describes Tarantino's use of the n-word as a form of "hooliganism"—"a gleeful, willfully adolescent revelry in negative behavior for nothing more then the sake of shocking others, self-amusement, and a vain display of the privilege of engaging in such behavior." Tierney concludes that, even if we *could* accept at face value Tarantino's stated desire to help promote racial unity, the practical effect of his methods is that he encourages other white people to use the same sort of racist language.[50]

In his 2006 *Journal of Communication* article, Tierney examined three movies that debuted in 2003: *Kill Bill, The Last Samurai,* and *Bulletproof Monk,* and traced the common themes of Orientalism that run through them. Orientalism, for the uninitiated, does not mean a study of Asia; as explained by Edward Said in his classic 1978 work of the same name (*Orientalism*), it is the Western tendency to "other" the East, and to present Asians (and other peoples not from Europe) as inferior, strange, and mysterious.

These are the four markers of Orientalism that Tierney identified in *Kill Bill* and the other films he examined, which can be found in most Western works about Asia: "The supraethnic viability of whiteness, the necessary defeat of Asians, the disallowance of anti–White sentiment, and the presence of at least one helpful and/or generous Asian cohort."[51] The Bride, the white female protagonist of *Kill Bill*, trains in Asian martial arts and quickly exceeds the skills of her Asian allies and opponents; she proves her superior skill by killing the female Japanese antagonist O-Ren; her Chinese trainer, Pai Mei, does not reject her for being white, but teaches her things he has not taught his previous (Asian) students.

Kill Bill is obviously an homage to 1970s kung fu movies, to the extent that the martial arts expert "Bill" is played by David Carradine, star of the 1970s TV series *Kung Fu*. In what was almost certainly unintentional irony, the American actor Carradine had been cast in that TV series— despite having no martial arts training—in place of Bruce Lee, whom producers deemed "too Asian" for white audiences to identify with. In another bit of irony, the white hero The Bride fought through most of the movie dressed in an outfit clearly modeled on the one worn by Bruce Lee in his biggest hit, *Enter the Dragon* (1973). Unlike in his 2011 essay about Tarantino and whiteness, in this article Tierney hewed mostly to the film itself and the Orientalist tropes implicit in it rather than speculating about the director's intentions. He did, however, criticize what he considered Tarantino's limited and shallow knowledge of Asian culture, and the fact he conflated Chinese and Japanese elements as if all Asians are the same.

The same has generally held true for journalists and public intellectuals since the release of the *Kill Bill* movies in 2003 and 2004. While frequently criticized for Orientalism, *Kill Bill* is usually cited as simply one work out of many that constitute a racist trend endemic in Western culture, rather than singling out Tarantino as an especially pernicious perpetrator of it. One recent example is India Roby in March 2021, using O-Ren (Lucy Liu) as an example of the hypersexualized Dragon Lady stereotype that has contributed to a wave of violence against Asian women.[52] Tarantino has come under personal fire, though, for his portrayal of Bruce Lee in 2019's *Once Upon a Time in Hollywood*, especially by the late martial artist's daughter Shannon Lee. She, and many others, took exception to Bruce

Lee's depiction as arrogant and cocky, and used as a vehicle to show how tough the movie's protagonist (played by Brad Pitt) was.[53] As Clayburn Griffin at *Chowder Bucket* put it, "Tarantino participated in that timeless tradition of Hollywood denying Asian men their masculinity."[54]

Tarantino's response, given on the Joe Rogan podcast: "I can understand his daughter having a problem with it, it's her fucking father! I get that. But anybody else? Go suck a dick."[55]

Of course, speculating on Tarantino's unconscious motives, as Tierney did (and, admittedly, as I have done), or engaging him directly in a public argument, as *many* have done, "makes it easy to fall into intentional fallacy," as Chris Vognar said in a 2013 issue of *Transition*, the journal of the Hutchins Center for African and African American Research at Harvard University. Vognar supplies the *Encyclopedia Britannica* definition of intentional fallacy: "the problem inherent in trying to judge a work of art by assuming the intent or purpose of the artist who created it." Vognar continues, "It is fruitless to look at a film as a full representation of the maker's psyche. You can, however, draw some conclusions from the films themselves." The conclusions that Vognar draws from Tarantino's body of work is that the director is not afraid to address race in his movies, even when he knows it will create controversy. "He's testing us," Vognar says. "He's provoking us. He's making us think. And he's making us ask still more questions. It's hard to fault an artist for that."[56] *New York Times* critic A.O. Scott proclaimed the inherent value of *Django Unchained* because it broke a major taboo—"regenerative violence" that was directed at white people from Black people, instead of the other way around, something that had previously "been almost literally unthinkable" in popular culture.[57]

Joi Carr came to a similar conclusion in a 2016 article in the Black film studies journal *Black Camera*. Carr wrote that, by defying the expectations of realism in a historical film with Django and instead blending history with western-themed fantasy, Tarantino "creates a paradigm shift for slave narratives." Audiences are thus forced to forego any preconceived perceptions of the topic and open themselves to going beyond stereotypes and tired tropes, seeing the subject with new eyes. Carr said, "I would argue Tarantino's project is to challenge the pernicious imagery of Black inferiority."[58]

Eric Deggans, in his previously quoted 2012 *Salon* article, concluded that—while the Jimmie scene in *Pulp Fiction* was overkill—Tarantino's use of language and Black culture was usually appropriate in context, and lent his works more authenticity and power than that of many other filmmakers who tread more lightly in their filmic representations of Blackness.

> That's really all I ask: that a filmmaker prove, when deploying the n-word, that there's a reason for going there that makes artistic sense. As much as Lee and others want to complain about how Tarantino's characters sling around

that epithet, most of the time, in most of his movies, it makes creative sense.... Tarantino's Black characters may be flawed, but they are also very powerful, smart, human and effective without the approval or enabling of white characters, a rarity for big Hollywood films. That's really why The Help went over with some Black folks like a lead soufflé; the Black victims in that story were saved by a white girl instead of saving themselves.[59]

Adilifu Nama, author of the book *Race on the QT*, concurs with Deggans. He calls Tarantino "a white director who makes race a sharp cornerstone in all his films…. In other words, Tarantino films are very much about race" even though they do not follow the "paint-by-numbers" racial template used by some Black directors, such as Spike Lee or Lee Daniels (*Precious, the Butler*), whose work Nama calls "garish racial sociology" and "contrived and squeaky melodrama."[60]

Nama believes it is unfair, and inaccurate, to merely say that the racial components of Tarantino's work is a simple homage to Blaxploitation, and therefore just an expression of Tarantino's own personal tastes, or to say that the movies are proof of "some warped racial prejudice lurking deep in Tarantino's subconscious." Rather, Nama stresses, Tarantino's choices are very conscious and very intentional, and rooted in the tradition—not just of Blaxploitation or grindhouse movies—of 1970s New Cinema, which at its root challenged and reframed social taboos. The filmmaker's sense of spectacle—including extreme violence, profanity, and racially charged dialogue—tends to distract from what he is actually doing. "When it comes to the body of Tarantino's films, the radical racial politics coursing through them is hidden in plain sight." His body of work "ideologically engages the cultural politics of race in America…. Accordingly, Tarantino's films are not merely movies that entertain; they symbolize racial anxieties circulating throughout American society."

Nama directly engages the scholarship of Sean M. Tierney, identifying him as a critic who "views Tarantino through the prism of white studies" and who asserts that the filmmaker is "an active advocate of the very racism Tarantino is a critic of." Nama posits that Tierney's approach is flawed, because by exclusively analyzing Tarantino on a personal level, "Tierney for the most part bypasses the body of work for which Tarantino became famous in the first place." From Nama's perspective, "examining Tarantino for his racist tendencies is too reductive an analysis and too easy a solution for not engaging the cinematic representations of race in America that are his films." Nama reasons that "deconstructing why and how Tarantino's films resonate with established and emerging discourses concerning race in America" is "a more challenging approach … more concerned with engaging the cultural work his films represent."

It has become evident by this point in our discussion that examining race and the movies of Quentin Tarantino is a complicated endeavor. There are multiple points-of-view, with varying degrees of validity but most with at least some. I have expended significant energy in presenting the words and thoughts of several people who have waded into the issue, Tarantino himself foremost. What should our conclusion be? Is there a single conclusion?

I am going to step outside the bounds of how I usually approach an academic work and interject some personal perspective. The act of writing this essay has caused me to reflect on my own pedagogy and authorial intent. You see, Quentin Tarantino and I have several things in common beyond being white men in their 50s. We share a Tennessee connection (as does Samuel L. Jackson, who grew up in Chattanooga)—Tarantino's grandparents lived in the Knoxville area, and he spent a lot of time there while growing up. I have always appreciated the fact that he makes some sort of Tennessee reference in almost all of his films, and I watch for them. I also share a deep love for the cinema of the early to middle 1970s, and have devoted quite a bit of scholarly work to the kung fu and Blaxploitation genres. None of those things, though, led to my personal introspection.

That was motivated by the fact that, in addition to being a history professor, I am also an author of fiction who has written several African American–centered works in both the western and crime genres. One of those novels, *Bound for the Promise-Land* (2000), won a Spur Award from Western Writers of America—another distinction I share with Tarantino. Another, *Cross Road Blues* (2011), deals with small-time criminals and musicians in the Black neighborhoods of 1950s Nashville. I empathize with Tarantino's desire to protect his artistic integrity in the universes he creates, and with his devotion to verisimilitude and "truth."

And I used the n-word in both of those books. I was motivated, while writing this piece, to do a search and find out exactly how often I did so. The crime novel, which is 55,000 words long, had an n-word count of seven. The other book, though—which traced the life of a Black man from slavery to fighting in the Union Army to Reconstruction to a long career in the West as a Buffalo Soldier, and is about 120,000 words long—has that word in it 117 times. I had already decided in recent years to avoid that word in my future works, unless the context absolutely called for it, and then as sparingly as possible. I have come to understand more fully the power of that term, and the pain it inflicts. This has carried through to the classroom. I used to spell the word out in quotes—like the infamous Lee Atwater dog-whistle interview—projected on power point presentations. I felt, at the time, that it was important for students to be confronted with the word and truly feel the grievous, ugly effects of it. I stopped doing that a long time ago. Still, seeing the sheer number of times I used it in the work I consider my single greatest professional achievement is unsettling. If I had it to do over I would only have used it a handful of times, if any at all—the makers of the 2021 Black-centered western film *The Harder They Fall* consciously chose not to use the word, and it did not detract from the effect of the movie. I still do not want to water down my work—but I don't want to set it on fire anymore, either.

It seems appropriate at this point to talk a little more about whiteness theory, as a vehicle to explain why I made the decisions I did about my own art and to give some more perspective to that of Tarantino. Whiteness as a theoretical academic approach started with a series of important works in the early 1990s, starting with David Roediger's *The Wages of Whiteness* in 1991, followed by works from Toni Morrison, Ruth Frankenberg, Noel Ignatiev, and others (full disclosure—Roediger was one of my mentors and served on my dissertation committee). The true starting points, though, which influenced those scholars, were the works of W.E.B. Du Bois and James Baldwin.[61] Both Du Bois and Baldwin asserted that there is no true "white" identity, but that whiteness has always been defined, not by what it is, but by what it is not—"non-white" identities, primarily Black. Whiteness, then—as developed in the colonial period—is not truly a matter of pigmentation or melanin, but rather the privileged point of a racialized power structure. Various groups that have been considered "non-white" in the past can, gradually, work their way toward whiteness by joining in the majority's philosophy of anti–Blackness. Black people are the only ones, in this structure, who cannot move up the racialized ladder toward whiteness, because they have been chosen (via the racism that developed to facilitate slavery) to be the defining factor, the perpetual oppositional "other."

Critical race theory, which has recently become a conservative bugaboo, also deals with institutional racism—the difference being that CRT focuses on the ways the legal system has augmented and solidified that racial structure, while whiteness theory looks at the way culture has done the same thing. Both have white privilege as a foundational element. Where many people misunderstand these approaches, including perhaps Tarantino (based on his defenses), is that the problem is a racialized structure that is designed to protect white supremacy, and not a personal indictment of every white individual. Every white individual benefits from the system, whether they want to or not; but each white individual, once they understand the structure, can choose to work toward dismantling it from within, using their own white privilege to do so. This should be done in solidarity with people of color, with empathy, and with humility—using white privilege to amplify one's own voice when educating fellow white people, who may be more inclined to listen to "one of their own," but without drowning out or superseding the voices of people of color themselves, which would be a demonstration of white privilege promoting white supremacy, even if not intentionally so.

How can a white artist do this? Not by refraining from addressing Black (or other non-white) characters, culture, or experience in his or her art. This is not what Tarantino's critics (for the most part) are asking him to do. Rather, such an artist should create their art, but with respect—and respect in this case would mean listening to the criticisms and suggestions of people of color, and weighing them honestly. If enough people tell you something is offensive, you have to admit the possibility that, to them, it really is—whether it is to you, or not. Does this mean you should water down your art and your truth? I do not think so. I think it is possible to let your characters and their dialogue flow as they will, from your own unconscious, but then as the artist edit—not censor, but edit—the results to make them most effective. And insulting a large portion of the people whose culture and experience you are honestly trying to promote is not effective.

Just as importantly, as a white artist one should—in the process of using their privilege to expose the unjust racial structure of American society—at the same time go to great lengths to promote the voices of artists of color, so that you are speaking *with* them instead of *for* them. So, then: continue creating art that exposes the racial truths of America; do so honestly but respectfully to communities of color; and promote the voices of Black artists who are, after all, telling their own stories.

Relative to that first point, David Sirota said this on the release of *Django Unchained*: "Tarantino has performed something of a civic service by using his considerable entertainment platform to effectively expose right-wing bigotry (as seen in conservatives' ugly reaction) and also help force serious racial questions into the national debate (as seen in some African Americans' substantive critique)."[62]

To follow that with the second point, I am going to restate (and expand) the quote from Derrick Clifton that I used near the beginning of this essay: "Black people aren't asking for white folks to walk on eggshells around them. Black people are asking to be respected and understood. And when people like Tarantino disregard the constructive criticisms of Black people, they're not really interested in using their power to help the community—they're instead reveling in tacit validations of their own racial privilege."[63]

Finally, Deggans pointed out in his article, "If anything, I would say Tarantino's success means it is time for him to help more Black filmmakers get to the hallowed place where he now resides. Spike Lee has a tough enough time getting his own films made; time for Q.T. to bring more vibrant Black storytellers to Hollywood."[64]

Regarding the question of whether Tierney is right, and Tarantino the individual is hampered by racist assumptions that corrupt his work and it is appropriate to judge that work based on the author's worldview, or whether Nama's assertion that the work should be analyzed solely on its own merit without looking at authorial intent…. I think the answer lies somewhere in the middle. Ultimately, I do not think either question is the right one to ask, let alone try to answer. I think the most appropriate consideration—or at least the one that interests me the most—is what Tarantino the auteur, and what his work, *could be* where race is concerned—and whether it can evolve into a more effective way of working toward dismantling whiteness, rather than unintentionally supporting it. In fact, that's a question all us white folk should ask about ourselves.

Notes

1. *Siskel & Ebert*, October 23, 1992. https://www.youtube.com/watch?v=5MO-HHJJ64Rw. Accessed January 1, 2022.

2. Derrick Clifton, "Quentin Tarantino Does Not Have a 'Black Card' and Never Will," NBC News Op-Ed, January 11, 2016. https://www.nbcnews.com/news/nbcblk/oped-quentin-tarantino-does-not-have-Black-card-never-will-n493981. Accessed December 26, 2021.

3. Lane Brown, "In Conversation: Quentin Tarantino," *The New York Magazine*, August 24, 2015. Reprinted at https://www.vulture.com/2015/08/quentin-tarantino-lane-brown-in-conversation.html. Accessed December 23, 2021.

4. Amy Archerd, "Lee Has Choice Words for Tarantino," *Daily Variety*, December 16, 1997. https://variety.com/1997/voices/columns/lee-has-choice-words-for-tarantino-111779698/#!o. Accessed December 23, 2021.

5. I have decided that, in this work, I will use the term "the n-word" when talking about the word itself, and "n----r" when using a direct quote.

6. The Quentin Tarantino Archives, https://wiki.tarantino.info/index.php/Playboy_Interview_1994. Accessed January 1, 2022.

7. Rich Juzwiak, "The Complete History of Quentin Tarantino Saying 'N----r,'" *Gawker*, December 21, 2015. https://www.gawker.com/the-complete-history-of-quentin-tarantino-saying-nigge-1748731193. Accessed December 26, 2021.

8. The Quentin Tarantino Archives, https://wiki.tarantino.info/index.php/Playboy_Interview_1994. Accessed January 1, 2022.

9. Jorie Rivas, "Quentin Tarantino Drops N-Word Less Than a Minute into Press Conference," *Color Lines*, January 14, 2013. https://www.colorlines.com/articles/quentin-tarantino-drops-n-word-less-minute-press-conference. Accessed December 22, 2021.

10. Henry Louis Gates, Jr., "An Unfathomable Place," *Transition* 112 (2013): 54.

11. *Fresh Air*, "Quentin Tarantino, 'Unchained' and Unruly," NPR, January 2, 2013. https://www.npr.org/2013/01/02/168200139/quentin-tarantino-unchained-and-unruly. Accessed December 22, 2021.

12. The Quentin Tarantino Archives, https://wiki.tarantino.info/index.php/Playboy_Interview_1994. Accessed January 1, 2022.

13. *Fresh Air*, "Quentin Tarantino, 'Unchained' and Unruly," NPR, January 2, 2013. https://www.npr.org/2013/01/02/168200139/quentin-tarantino-unchained-and-unruly. Accessed December 22, 2021.

14. Zach Baron, "Quentin Tarantino Explains the Link Between His *Hateful Eight* and #BlackLivesMatter," *GQ*, December 8, 2015. https://www.gq.com/story/quentin-tarantino-hateful-eight-Black-lives-matter. Accessed January 2, 2022.

15. Rich Juzwiak, "The Complete History of Quentin Tarantino Saying 'N----r,'" *Gawker*, December 21, 2015. https://www.gawker.com/the-complete-history-of-quentin-tarantino-saying-nigge-1748731193. Accessed December 26, 2021.

16. Cited in Adam Howard, "Spike Lee-Quentin Tarantino *'Jackie Brown'* N-Word Battle Revisited Fifteen Years Later," *The Grio,* June 14, 2012. https://thegrio.com/2012/06/14/spike-lee-quentin-tarantino-jackie-brown-n-word-battle-revisted-15-years-later/. Accessed December 23, 2021.

17. Cynthia Fuchs, ed., *Spike Lee: Interviews* (Jackson: University Press of Mississippi, 2002), 152; Howard.

18. Howard.

19. Juzwiak.

20. Clifton.

21. Gates.

22. Robert Ebert, "Quentin Tarantino, a 'Pulp' Hero," rogerebert.com, October 9, 1994. https://. Accessed January 2, 2022.

23. Yarimar Bonilla, "History Unchained," *Transitions* 112 (2013): 69.

24. Quoted in Juzwiak.

25. Quoted in Peter Verstraten, *Humour and Irony in Dutch Post-War Fiction Film* (Amsterdam: Amsterdam University Press, 2016). https://www.jstor.org/stable/j.ctt1d8hb79.13. Accessed December 28, 2021.

26. Quoted in Juzwiak.

27. Ibid.

28. Tom Carson, "Tarantino, Chained," *The New Republic*, January 1, 2013. https://newrepublic.com/article/111501/tarantino-chained. Accessed December 22, 2021.

29. Clifton.

30. Ibid.

31. Keiran Southern, "Oscar-Winning Screenwriter John Ridley Criticizes Tarantino's Use of the N- Word," *Yahoo Entertainment*, June 12, 2020. https://www.yahoo.com/entertainment/oscar-winning-screenwriter-john-ridley-021108161.html. Accessed January 3, 2022.

32. Howard.

33. Billy Ingram, "How a Forbidden Word Re-Entered Our Vocabulary Via Television," tvparty.com, no date. http://tvparty.com/70-n-word-on-tv.html. Accessed January 3, 2022.

34. *Saturday Night Live*, Season 1, Episode 7, December 13, 1975.

35. Kenneth B. Noble, "Issue of Racism Erupts in Simpson Trial," *New York Times*, January 14, 1995.

36. Anne McDermott, "Ito Ruling on 'N-Word' Seen as Setback for Defense as Tourtelot Cuts Fuhrman Loose," CNN.com, August 31, 1995. http://www.cnn.com/US/OJ/daily/8-31/tape_ruling/indexold.html. Accessed January 3, 2022.

37. Eric Deggans, "Tarantino Is the Baddest Black Filmmaker Working Today," *Salon*, December 27, 2012. https://www.salon.com/2012/12/27/tarantino_is_the_baddest_Black_filmmaker_working_today/. Accessed December 27, 2021.

38. Ibid.

39. Quoted in Juzwiak.

40. Juzwiak; Michael Hainey, "The GQA: Denzel Washington," *GQ*, September 18, 2012.

41. Quoted in Juzwiak.

42. NPR; Gates; Baron.

43. Carvell Wallace, "Samuel L. Jackson Operates Like He Owns the Place (He Does)," *Esquire*, March 12, 2019.

44. Nick Schager, "Role Recall: Jamie Foxx on living the high life for 'Any Given Sunday,' earning Ray Charles's respect, and landing his 'badass' *Spawn* reboot," *HuffPost*, July 18, 2018. https://www.huffpost.com/entry/role-recall-jamie-foxx-on-living-the-high-life_n_5b4f8cbbe4b0fd5c73c1aa87. Accessed January 2, 2022.

45. Quoted in Steve Rose, "Quentin Tarantino Tells 'Black Critics' His Race Is Irrelevant," *The Guardian*, October 13, 2015. https://www.theguardian.com/film/2015/oct/13/quentin-tarantino-on-race-and-Black-critics-the-hateful-eight. Accessed December 23, 2021.

46. Quoted in Steve Rose, "The Quentin Tarantino Race Debate Isn't Black and White," *The Guardian*, October 13, 2015. https://www.theguardian.com/film/2015/oct/13/tarantino-race-debate-isnt-Black-and-white. Accessed December 23, 2021.

47. Ibid.

48. Steve Pond, "Quentin Tarantino Lets Loose on Race, Violence, and 'The Hateful Eight,'" *The Wrap*, December 24, 2015. https://www.thewrap.com/quentin-tarantino-lets-loose-on-race-violence-and-the-hateful-eight/. Accessed December 21, 2021.

49. On this topic I strongly recommend the book *EC Comics: Race, Shock, and Social Protest* by Quianna Whitted (New Brunswick: Rutgers University Press, 2019).

50. Sean M. Tierney, "Quentin Tarantino in Black and White," *Critical Rhetorics of Race*, Kent A. Ono and Michael G. Lacy, eds. (New York: NYU Press, 2011), 81–97.

51. Sean M. Tierney, "Themes of Whiteness in *Bulletproof Monk, Kill Bill*, and *The Last Samurai*," *Journal of Communication* 56 (2006): 607.

52. India Roby, "Hollywood Played a Role in Hypersexualizing Asian Women," *Teen Vogue*, March 24, 2021.

53. Hannah Frishberg, "Bruce Lee's daughter fires off racial response to Tarantino: 'I'm really f**king tired of white men ...'" *New York Post*, July 2, 2021.

54. Clayburn Griffen, "The Inexcusable Racism in Tarantino's Once Upon a Time in Hollywood," *Chowder Bucket*, August 10, 2019. https://www.chowderbucket.com/entertainment/racism-in-once-upon-a-time-in-hollywood/. Accessed January 1, 2022.

55. Zack Sharf, "Tarantino Tells Critics of Bruce Lee Scene to 'Suck a D*ck': He 'Had No Respect for American Stuntmen,'" *IndieWire*, June 30, 2021. https://www.indiewire.com/2021/06/tarantino-bruce-lee-hollywood-scene-critics-1234647709/#!. Accessed January 3, 2022.

56. Chris Vognar, "He Can't Say That, Can He? Black, White, and Shades of Gray in the Films of Tarantino," *Transition* 112)2013): 24, 31.

57. A.O. Scott, "The Black, the White, and the Angry," *New York Times*, December 25, 2012; David Sirota, "Could a Black Director Have Made Django'?" *Salon*, December 28, 2012. https://www.salon.com/2012/12/28/could_a_Black_director_have_made_django/#:~:text=In%20the% 20case%20of%20%22Django%20Unchained%2C%22%20as%20evidenced,have%20even%20been%2 0green-lighted%20by%20a%20major%20studio%29. Accessed December 21, 2021.

58. Joi Carr, "*Django Unchained*—Disrupting Classical Hollywood Historical Realism?" *Black Camera* 7, no. 2 (Spring 2016): 37.

59. Deggans.

60. Adilifu Nama, *Race on the QT: Blackness and the Films of Quentin Tarantino* (Austin: University of Texas Press, 2015).

61. The primary examples are essays by each writer: "The Souls of White Folk" by DuBois (1917) and "The Price of the Ticket" by Baldwin (1985).

62. Sirota.

63. Clifton.

64. Deggans.

Works Cited

Archerd, Army. "Lee Has Choice Words for Tarantino." *Daily Variety*, December 16, 1997. https://variety.com/1997/voices/columns/lee-has-choice-words-for-tarantino-111779698/#!o. Accessed December 23, 2021.

Baron, Zach. "Quentin Tarantino Explains the Link Between His *Hateful Eight* and #Black LivesMatter." *GQ*, December 8, 2015. https://www.gq.com/story/quentin-tarantino-hateful-eight-Black-lives-matter. Accessed January 2, 2022.

Bonilla, Yarimar. "History Unchained." *Transitions* 112 (2013): 68–77.

Brown, Lane. "In Conversation: Quentin Tarantino." *The New York Magazine,* August 24, 2015. Reprinted at https://www.vulture.com/2015/08/quentin-tarantino-lane-brown-in-conversation.html. Accessed December 23, 2021.

Carr, Joi. "Django Unchained—Disrupting Classical Hollywood Historical Realism?" *Black Camera* 7, no. 2 (Spring 2016), 37.

Carson, Tom. "Tarantino, Chained." *The New Republic,* January 1, 2013. https://newrepublic.com/article/111501/tarantino-chained. Accessed December 22, 2021.

Clifton, Derrick. "Quentin Tarantino Does Not Have a 'Black Card' and Never Will." NBC News Op-Ed, January 11, 2016. https://www.nbcnews.com/news/nbcblk/oped-quentin-tarantino-does-not-have-Black-card-never-will-n493981. Accessed December 26, 2021.

Deggans, Eric. "Tarantino Is the Baddest Black Filmmaker Working Today." *Salon,* December 27, 2012. https://www.salon.com/2012/12/27/tarantino_is_the_baddest_Black_filmmaker_working_today/. Accessed December 27, 2021.

Ebert, Roger. "Quentin Tarantino, a 'Pulp' Hero." rogerebert.com, October 9, 1994. https://www.rogerebert.com/interviews/quentin-tarantino-a-pulp-hero. Accessed January 2, 2022.

Fresh Air. "Quentin Tarantino, 'Unchained' and Unruly." NPR, January 2, 2013. https://www.npr.org/2013/01/02/168200139/quentin-tarantino-unchained-and-unruly. Accessed December 22, 2021.

Frishberg, Hannah. "Bruce Lee's daughter fires off racial response to Tarantino: 'I'm really f**king tired of white men …'" *New York Post,* July 2, 2021.

Fuchs, Cynthia, ed. *Spike Lee: Interviews.* Jackson: University Press of Mississippi, 2002.

Gates, Henry Louis, Jr. "An Unfathomable Place." *Transition* 112 (2013): 46–66.

Griffen, Clayburn. "The Inexcusable Racism in Tarantino's *Once Upon a Time in Hollywood.*" *Chowder Bucket,* August 10, 2019. https://www.chowderbucket.com/entertainment/racism-in- once-upon-a-time-in-hollywood/. Accessed January 1, 2022.

Hainey, Michael. "The GQA: Denzel Washington." *GQ,* September 18, 2012.

Howard, Adam. "Spike Lee-Quentin Tarantino 'Jackie Brown' N-Word Battle Revisited Fifteen Years Later." *The Grio,* June 14, 2012. https://thegrio.com/2012/06/14/spike-lee-quentin-tarantino-jackie-brown-n-word-battle-revisited-15-years-later/. Accessed December 23, 2021.

Ingram, Billy. "How a Forbidden Word Re-Entered Our Vocabulary Via Television." tvparty.com, no date. http://tvparty.com/70-n-word-on-tv.html. Accessed January 3, 2022.

Juzwiak, Rich. "The Complete History of Quentin Tarantino Saying 'N----r.'" *Gawker,* December 21, 2015. https://www.gawker.com/the-complete-history-of-quentin-tarantino-saying-nigge-1748731193. Accessed December 26, 2021.

McDermott, Ann. "Ito Ruling on 'N-Word' Seen as Setback for Defense as Tourtelot Cuts Fuhrman Loose." CNN.com, August 31, 1995. http://www.cnn.com/US/OJ/daily/831/tape_ruling/indexold.html. Accessed January 3, 2022.

Nama, Adilifu. *Race on the QT: Blackness and the Films of Quentin Tarantino.* Austin: University of Texas Press, 2015.

Noble, Kenneth B. "Issue of Racism Erupts in Simpson Trial." *New York Times,* January 14, 1995.

Pond, Steve. "Quentin Tarantino Lets Loose on Race, Violence, and '*The Hateful Eight.*'" *The Wrap,* December 24, 2015. https://www.thewrap.com/quentin-tarantino-lets-loose-on-race-violence-and-the-hateful-eight/. Accessed December 21, 2021.

The Quentin Tarantino Archives. https://wiki.tarantino.info/index.php/Playboy_Interview_1994. Accessed January 1, 2022.

Rivas, Jorje. "Quentin Tarantino Drops N-Word Less Than a Minute into Press Conference." *Color Lines,* January 14, 2013. https://www.colorlines.com/articles/quentin-tarantino-drops-n-word-less-minute-press-conference. Accessed December 22, 2021.

Roby, India. "Hollywood Played a Role in Hypersexualizing Asian Women." *Teen Vogue,* March 24, 2021.

Rose, Steve. "The Quentin Tarantino Race Debate Isn't Black and White." *The Guardian,*

October 13, 2015. https://www.theguardian.com/film/2015/oct/13/tarantino-race-de-bate-isnt-Black-and-white> Accessed Dec. 23, 2021.

_____. "Quentin Tarantino Tells 'Black Critics' His Race Is Irrelevant." *The Guardian*, October 13, 2015. https://www.theguardian.com/film/2015/oct/13/quentin-tarantino-on- race-and-Black-critics-the-hateful-eight. Accessed December 23, 2021.

Rose, Steve. "Quentin Tarantino Tells 'Black Critics' His Race Is Irrelevant." *The Guardian*, October 13, 2015. https://www.theguardian.com/film/2015/oct/13/quentin-taranti-no-on- race-and-Black-critics-the-hateful-eight. Accessed December 23, 2021.

Saturday Night Live, Season 1, Episode 7. December 13, 1975.

Schager, Nick. "Role Recall: Jamie Foxx on living the high life for 'Any Given Sunday,' earning Ray Charles's respect, and landing his 'badass' 'Spawn' reboot." *HuffPost*, July 18, 2018. https://www.huffpost.com/entry/role-recall-jamie-foxx-on-living-the-high-life_n_5b4f8cbbe4b0fd5c73c1aa87. Accessed January 2, 2022.

Scott, A.O. "The Black, the White, and the Angry." *New York Times*, December 25, 2012.

Sharf, Zack. "Tarantino Tells Critics of Bruce Lee Scene to 'Suck a D*ck': He 'Had No Respect for American Stuntmen.'" *IndieWire*, June 30, 2021. https://www.indiewire.com/2021/06/tarantino-bruce-lee-hollywood-scene-critics-1234647709/#!. Accessed January 3, 2022.

Sirota, David. "Could a Black Director Have Made Django'?" *Salon*, December 28, 2012. https://www.salon.com/2012/12/28/could_a_Black_director_have_made_django/. Accessed December 21, 2021.

Siskel & Ebert, October 23, 1992. https://www.youtube.com/watch?v=5MOHHJJ64Rw. Accessed January 1, 2022.

Southern, Keiran. "Oscar-Winning Screenwriter John Ridley Criticizes Tarantino's Use of the N-Word." *Yahoo Entertainment*, June 12, 2020. https://www.yahoo.com/enter-tainment/oscar-winning-screenwriter-john-ridley-021108161.html. Accessed January 3, 2022.

Tierney, Sean M. "Quentin Tarantino in Black and White." *Critical Rhetorics of Race*, Kent A. Ono and Michael G. Lacy, eds. New York: NYU Press, 2011, 81–97.

_____. "Themes of Whiteness in *Bulletproof Monk, Kill Bill*, and *The Last Samurai*." *Journal of Communication* 56 (2006): 607–624.

Verstraten, Peter. *Humour and Irony in Dutch Post-War Fiction Film*. Amsterdam: Amsterdam University Press, 2016. https://www.jstor.org/stable/j.ctt1d8hb79.13. Accessed December 28, 2021.

Vognar, Chris. "He Can't Say That, Can He? Black, White, and Shades of Gray in the Films of Tarantino." *Transition* 112 (2013): 22–31.

Wallace, Carvell. "Samuel L. Jackson Operates Like He Owns the Place (He Does)." *Esquire*, March 12, 2019. https://www.esquire.com/entertainment/movies/a26454543/samuel-l-jackson-captain-marvel-interview-2019/. Accessed December 20, 2021.

Whitted, Qianna. *Comics: Race, Shock, and Social Protest*. New Brunswick: Rutgers University Press, 2019.

Form Over Content in *The Hateful Eight*

Tarantino's Acousmektos

VLAD DIMA

Overture

While not an entirely novel development, the mainstream cinema of the 21st century seems to live more than ever before in the space beyond the screen and the theater. Paratextual and extradiegetic narratives accompany most productions, to the point that the narrative content of the films themselves almost becomes an afterthought.

Quentin Tarantino's eighth film, *The Hateful Eight* (2015), may be an extreme example of this practice, as the marketing for the format (shot in 70mm) and the decorum of the theater visit (featuring an oversized program, an extended musical prelude, and an intermission) dominated the popular discourse surrounding the film. However, this supposedly innovative format was in fact a return to previous ways of shooting Hollywood movies, and is there a director better at using nostalgia as a paradoxical springboard into the future, into the "new," than Tarantino? If a few years later, *Once Upon a Time in Hollywood* (2019) showed considerable interest in plot and careful narrative construction (while once again looking back in order to look forward),[1] in 2015 *The Hateful Eight* was mostly concerned with aesthetics. In *Hateful*, it is form and aesthetics that fill the empty space of the narrative, a practice which represents a manifestation of the wider abandonment of meaningful content in contemporary cinema. As a matter of fact, emptiness is indeed the point! In this essay, I explore the cinematic artifices of *The Hateful Eight*—intertextuality, acoustic effects (*acousmêtre* in particular), and details of the *mise-en-scène*—to show that they more than make up for its inherent narrative emptiness. In the process, one may discover that Tarantino's voice makes itself heard, seen, and felt across his entire body of work. Ultimately, this voice, which I call *acousmektos*, also helps to paper over the cracks and gaps of the narrative, filling up the emptiness of *The Hateful Eight* with bits of narrative from elsewhere in the Tarantino canon.

Prologue

The Hateful Eight begins with a couple of establishing shots, then quickly settles on close-up of a wooden Jesus on the cross, covered in snow. As the opening credits appear, the camera smoothly moves ever so slightly to the right, on the crane dolly, as if caressing the Lord's motionless face. Initially obscured by wooden Jesus, a stagecoach is finally revealed as a speck in the whiteout, far away in the background. The opening credits keep rolling as the stagecoach approaches and the camera waits patiently for it to pass behind the cross and arrive to the foreground. It is a beginning ripe with heavy-handed symbolism, but that hardly matters—what matters is the pure aesthetics of it.

Sure, Jesus has symbolically turned his back on the passengers of this stagecoach. Sure, Tarantino has a God-complex that he unabashedly flaunts, as the objective point-of-view (but really *his* point-of-view) floats thanks to the crane. In other words, he is making films in his own image. And sure, the plot of the film turns out to be as irrelevant as the initial speck of the stagecoach, almost impossible to identify in the whiteout. The only thing that matters is the entertainment, and this is pure divertissement. It is a masturbatory (Tarantino inserts himself into the fabric of the narrative), incestuous (many of the Tarantino usual suspects appear), gloriously violent, three-hour-long *gorgeous* vortex of 70mm images.

The stagecoach is headed to Red Rock, a town in post–Civil War Wyoming where bounty hunter John Ruth (Kurt Russell) intends to deliver his captive, Daisy Domergue (Jennifer Jason Leigh). On the way, they are joined by another bounty hunter, Major Marquis Warren (Samuel L. Jackson), who is dressed in a Union cavalry uniform, a detail which becomes relevant when newly appointed sheriff of Red Rock, the Southerner Chris Mannix (Walton Goggins), comes into the fold. Together, racial tensions and all, they seek shelter from a blizzard at Minnie's Haberdashery, a saloon where the band of "hatefuls" is completed: retired Confederate commander (Sandy Smithers, played by Bruce Dern), a hangman (Oswaldo Mobray, played by Tim Roth), a Mexican (Bob, played by Demián Bichir), and a quiet, suspicious cowboy (Joe Gage, played by Michael Madsen). As other characters emerge throughout the film, it remains rather unclear who the "hateful eight" are supposed to be. Perhaps the title simply refers to Tarantino's filmography—all his movies are, after all, full of hate. As an avid connoisseur of cinema, Tarantino is surely aware of Federico Fellini's 8½ (1963), which refers to the Italian director's number of films. Moreover, in another intertextual connection to Fellini, the latter's *La Dolce Vita* (1960) also famously features a large statue of Jesus, although that one is flown over Rome in a helicopter (so the same God-complex principle applies here, too). At any rate, the Italian culture of the 1960s seems to feature prominently in *Hateful*, especially given Ennio Morricone's involvement in scoring the film and the film's unavoidable links to the Spaghetti Westerns. Tarantino's reliance on nostalgia (i.e., the homage to the Spaghetti Western) turns out to be an intertextual double return, because Morricone's haunting music harks back to Sergio Leone's films, which he also scored, and were themselves adaptations of Akira Kurosawa's samurai films. Title and Jesus aside, this film amounts to a visceral *experience* of cinema because of the addition of several aforementioned paratextual elements: Morricone's sinister, tone-setting eight-minute overture, the intermission, the colorful program, and perhaps most importantly, the lulling whir of the 70mm projector in the back of the theater. To reiterate, it had been well advertised that Tarantino decided to shoot with antique lenses and to project the film in widescreen 70mm Panavision at several theaters around the country. Using these lenses, though, might come off as gimmicky. One could speculate that Tarantino may have grown paranoid that the film was not going to be a box office hit after his script had been leaked long before going into production (extradiegetic drama!), and so he came up with yet another "trick," a publicity stunt meant to reanimate the project. However, the end product may have accomplished more than simply convincing spectators to see the film in theaters. It may have proved that form can successfully supplant content, that form suffices to entertain, and that it can also turn into the dominant *modus operandi* of the director.

In spite of presenting the film in chapters (which I maladroitly mimic myself in this essay), Tarantino is clearly aware of the lack of narrative, and he does not even pretend to hide his intentions of covering up the emptiness with various visual and aural artifices. The clearest indication of his self-awareness and its acknowledgment to us, the audience, is the repeated debate over John Ruth's choice to transport Daisy to Red Rock alive, instead of killing her and receiving the same payout (a query posed to John by both the Major and Oswaldo). The reasoning behind his choice essentially comes down to the fact that that John Ruth must stay true to his nature, best described by his nickname, the Hangman, which dictates that he must see to it that Daisy hangs in Red Rock. Narratively speaking, this explanation is unsatisfactory. Indeed, it would be much easier and less messy to bring a dead Daisy to Red Rock, but then there would be no drama, no film.

Therefore, John Ruth's choice turns out to be the perfect metaphor for the film's mission, which has Tarantino choosing the most complicated, needless really, option, in order to stay true to his cinematic nature.

Chapter 1: Auteurs, Akousma, *Inter/Intratextuality, Acousmektos*

Quentin Tarantino is certainly one of the premier directors of his generation, and perhaps even of film history in general. His attitude toward filmmaking is modeled in the vein of mid-20th-century French *auteur* theory, which François Truffaut laid out in his influential essay, *A Certain Tendency of French Cinema* (1954), and which gives the director unlimited power over the creative process. A veritable *auteur* crafts a personal, unique style that can be easily recognized by audiences. Tarantino's aesthetic tendencies rely on prolix dialogue (often punctuated by spurts of incredibly graphic violence), *mise-en-abyme* effects, and multiple intertextual references. Interestingly, his intertextual references often dialogue with other Tarantino films (i.e., *intra*textuality) in addition to the wider cinematic universe, which can be as surprising as a link with *Animal House* (1978)—John Belushi's Bluto and Kurt Russell's John Ruth from *The Hateful Eight* both (hilariously) destroy guitars.

However, it is Tarantino's *intra*textuality that gives way to the creation of a distinctive voice that goes beyond the tenets of *auteur* theory. The masters of the French New Wave (Godard, Truffaut, Chabrol, Rivette, Rohmer)[2] and of the Left Bank Movement (Varda, Marker, Resnais) often opted for diegetic references to their peers (i.e., intertextuality), while Tarantino's penchant for intratextuality leads to overly transparent dialogues with the audience about his films, *while* we find ourselves inside a specific work. His authorial voice is not only obvious, but also "loud." In essence, this is a voice one "hears" across the entire body made up of all his films, as all the films become one incredibly lengthy, perhaps incoherent text. The existence of this extended, authorial voice happens to be matched by the use of his actual voice in *The Hateful Eight*, as Tarantino inserts himself aurally into the movie[3] and creates a unique *mise-en-abyme* sonic effect. By way of French composer Pierre Schaeffer, sound theorist Michel Chion often invoked the Greek word *akousma*, meaning "thing heard" (*The Voice in Cinema* 18), in his writings, to refer to sounds and voices coming from off screen.[4] I will return to the literal acousmatic voice(s) in my analysis of the film, but I propose a slight adjustment to this term by adding to it another Greek word, "ektós" (outside of). The result, "acous-mektos," could then figuratively apply to Tarantino's voice from the outside (of the film) and to his blatantly recognizable style of directing, an authorial style that "screams" at us from off screen and that blows across his entire body of work. In other words, in *Hateful* one can identify both a literal voice from off screen (i.e., voice-over) and a more diffused voice from other Tarantino films (i.e., an *acousmektosmiektos*5).

Let us look back at a few selective examples of intratextuality. The aforementioned objective point-of-view shot from a crane is one of the quintessential shots in all of Tarantino's films. Akin to the God's eye view camera angle, this shot underlines the director's authority and creates a sense of omniscient power. In *Inglourious Basterds* (2009), Tarantino often uses crane shots to track the characters from above, establishing a correlation not just with an authority from the beyond, but also with historical fact (although *Basterds* famously alters history). Moreover, the camera occasionally moves between rooms or floors in a continuous shot that reveals the top of the walls, emphasizing that same omniscient quality. In *Kill Bill* (2003–2004), there are three such instances: at Vernita's house, in the bathroom at the Japanese club, and at Budd's trailer. *The Hateful Eight* features this staple shot, too: as Major Marquis walks over to John Gage, the camera glides over the ceiling beams of the chalet. Of course, this omniscience is ironically misguided because bad guy Jody is hiding *under* the floor—the Devil's eye view—at this very time.

To take one more example, Western-style standoffs[6] occur in sword fighting in *Kill Bill* (more on this shortly) and in the *Inglourious Basterds* bar shooting sequence. For the latter, the scene takes place in an underground tavern where two officers, one British and one German, face off with their revolvers pointed at each other's groins. This might be a bit of a running motif in Tarantino's films: Major Marquis has his testicles blown off in *Hateful*; Django (Jamie Foxx) from *Django Unchained* (2012) almost has his cut off and shoots off another man's; Marsellus (Ving Rhames) from *Pulp Fiction* (1994) takes a shotgun to his aggressor's groin; *Jackie Brown* (1997) features the colorful line "gun pressed up against my dick" uttered by Samuel Jackson's character, which turns out to be a bit of foreshadowing, fulfilled in Jackson's appearance in *Hateful*. (On a related note, perhaps Tarantino's overpublicized foot fetish is just a classic manifestation of Freudian castration fear....) Tarantino himself admits an intratextual connection, characterizing the face off scene from *Basterds* as a miniature *Reservoir Dogs* (1992) in an extended interview with the renowned French publication, *Cahiers du cinéma* (in yet another link with French cinema) from 2009. The 30-minute-long scene, shot in a small, confined space, epitomizes the entire film: meandering and seemingly never-ending dialogue climaxes into a short, violent burst, which leads to everyone's death. Sound familiar? The main difference lies in the fact that *Hateful* extends that scene by another two and half hours.

Chapter 2: Acousmêtre

Beyond his visual talents, Tarantino's use of sound is also in line with the *auteur* approach to making films, meaning that he must always remain clearly in charge while simultaneously showing off his cinematic knowledge and talent. Tarantino also adds a new level of omniscient power through a sound technique that Chion calls the *acousmêtre*. The *acousmêtre* refers to a sound or voice whose origin on screen is not immediately obvious, "neither inside nor outside the image … [but] forever on the verge of appearing in it" (*Audio-Vision* 129). The disembodied and placeless voice seems to come from everywhere, and carries four intrinsic qualities: ubiquity, panopticism, omniscience, and omnipotence (*Audio-Vision* 129–130; *The Voice in Cinema* 23–24). In other words, the *acousmêtre* has a divine quality, aurally matching the visual purpose of the God's-eye-view angle. Furthermore, in Chion's opinion, the greatest *acousmêtre* is in fact God, and "even farther back, for every one of us, the Mother" (*The Voice in Cinema* 27). The mother constitutes an *acousmêtre* because during the earliest stages of life, the voice of the mother is everything that a child hears, ever-present, like an umbilical web (*The Voice in Cinema* 61).

It is fascinating to think in these terms about the two main characters in *Kill Bill*.

Evidently, Beatrix (Uma Thurman) is an actual mother, and therefore a possible *acousmêtre*. In the case of Bill (David Carradine), things are slightly more complicated. Visually, Bill never appears fully throughout the first part of the series, though his voice is often heard. Nevertheless, he appears to control everything, see all, and be everywhere. In short, he is God, and on screen, he supplants the persona of the director. On two occasions we see his hands, and the first time, he is playing with his sword. This is a typical, impish Tarantino joke: the Man is stroking his sword— the obvious phallic symbol—so he is fully in charge of his manhood. Bill actually calls himself "the Man," but the association with God is clearest when Beatrix gets her sword from Hattori Hanzo (Sonny Chiba). The latter claims that his sword will cut even God, which is the exact purpose of that particular weapon, to lacerate Bill/God.

To return to sound, one of the quintessential scenes in *Kill Bill* that exemplifies Tarantino's interest in the aural and in what one may call "sonic markers"—sounds that punctuate and dictate the pace of the visual narrative—is the fight sequence between Beatrix and O-Ren (Lucy Liu). As soon as Beatrix steps out in the snow where O-Ren waits for her, the first thing we hear is the clicking noise of a bamboo clacker fountain, which we do not see right away. We return to this noise throughout the scene, and it never superimposes over the dialogue. It always makes itself heard during moments of silence and inaction. This is a classic standoff, like in the Spaghetti Western or in *Basterds*, and also an intertextual reference because of the more obvious connection with Kurosawa's samurai films.

Every time the fighting pauses, we hear the clicking noise of the fountain.

Eventually, the camera pans out, and we see the source of the noise, the fountain, while the two women are in the far background. Sound theorists label this moment as "deacousmatization"—the moment when the magical powers of the sound/noise/voice should disappear, because we have found its logical diegetic source (Chion, *Audio-Vision* 130–131). However, to me, such sound always maintains a degree of magic, and it carries the potential to regain some measure of those powers when it disappears again from the screen. The placement of the camera, which focuses on the fountain in the foreground rather than on the clash between the two women, *visually* emphasizes the significance of the clacker. It is impossible to ignore its presence both aurally and visually. Moreover, the metronomic noise resembles the intermittent motion of a Geneva drive, or a Maltese cross, which is a mechanism that allows film to move at the normal rate of 24 frames per second. In other words, the noise of the fountain aurally creates an image of the cinematic apparatus—how is this not magical? So, the Maltese cross is an essential part needed for the reel in the film projector to continue moving. The resemblance between the two—cross and fountain—cannot be missed. Just as the Maltese cross makes the visual film move, the sound of the fountain allows this particular scene to advance, narratively speaking. The story and the fight go on because of the fountain, which supplies the necessary sonic marker. An entirely stunning visual scene hinges on the simple, repeated noise of the fountain, and the aural momentarily overshadows the visual.

In *The Hateful Eight*, there are several moments that seem to copy the same aural-drives-visual effect. From the first scene, as the stagecoach driver, O.B. (James Parks), yells at the horses while the audience tries to follow the history of the characters inside of the coach, the importance of the sonic interruptions from off screen becomes obvious.

Later on, when the Major tells a fantastical story meant to get a reaction out of the old Southern general, Bob's piano recital plays in the background to varying degrees of aptitude (how is he getting better at playing, as the Major's story gets more and more intense?). Finally, the noise of nailing the door shut, which is a clearer sonic marker in the same family as the *Kill Bill* fountain, features as both the dominant sound (when the arrival of the stagecoach is filmed from the indoors perspective in the *Last Chapter*, the voices we hear are in the aural background) and as the secondary aural cue while Daisy Domergue plays the guitar. I will return to this guitar before John Ruth smashes it against the cabin post.

Chapter 3: *Are We Not Entertained?* More Akousma (*from Elsewhere*)

Tarantino takes full advantage of the fancy Panavision lenses by underlining the two types of shots best suited for 70mm: close-ups and establishing shots. Just as in the beginning shot in which the camera shifts from a close-up of wooden Jesus to an extremely long shot of the stagecoach, the film continues to counterpoint the wide with the very narrow. If normally one establishing shot is sufficient to situate the spectators in the proper physical context of the film, Tarantino uses numerous shots and spends several minutes following the stagecoach from afar. Narratively, this is vastly unnecessary.

Aesthetically, though, it is so pleasing and so smooth that ultimately one does not care about cinematic dead time—it is all about entertainment value and to answer Russell Crowe's classic rhetorical bellow, "Are you not entertained?"—yes, yes, we are!

The close-ups also have added flair, as they are boosted by an inspired directorial choice: the characters generally raise their head up toward the camera and slowly emerge from underneath the brim of the cowboy hats, as is the case in the first shot of Major Warren. The result is that the facial details of the subject gradually fill up the wide screen as opposed to "dropping" the camera straight onto one's face. Daisy's first close-up is another perfect embodiment of this technique. Struck over the head with the butt of John Ruth's pistol, she slowly raises her head and the camera lingers on her face revealing every line, cut, and bruise. A gradual stream of blood begins to trickle from her forehead, onto a strand of hair, and finally onto her face in a foreshadowing act. It is just the beginning, like a small wound that will fester for hours and, of course, will end up literally exploding in everyone's faces (but mostly hers).

Tarantino's *acousmektos* is also quite present through directorial choices that amount to a kind of neurotic filmmaking. After *Django Unchained*, the director said that he had finally learned how to make Westerns, and therefore, he wanted to make another one. Practice (or repetition) makes perfect. The particular repetition of nailing the door of the haberdashery shut offers comic relief because the characters have to nail it shut every time it is opened, but it also doubles as a typical on-the-nose Tarantino suggestion: they are all inside a metaphorical coffin and they are nailing it shut (and unlike Beatrix in *Kill Bill: Vol. 2*, they will not kung-fu their way out). The first joke is that it is never the "last nail in the coffin"—instead, there are multiple last nails and yet the characters remain ironically unaware of their fate. The second joke is that, in spite of all the nail hitting, no one actually seems to hit the nail on the head—there is nothing completely true about any of these events. Tarantino also doubles up on the metaphor of the coffin by making the story inside of the haberdashery/coffin essentially a "dead" narrative, moving around in circles, never meant to get anywhere. The repetition of one particular line underscores the effect of this dead narrative: "You only need to hang mean bastards ... but mean bastards, you need to hang." This quasi-nonsensical line is first uttered by John Ruth at the beginning of the film, and then echoed by Chris Mannix, as he and the Major pass down the hanging sentence to Daisy. The placement of the repeated line—beginning and ending—neatly closes off the narrative, while the line itself is a type of chiasmus (an antimetabole, to be precise), which is a rhetorical device meant to bend back on itself, as it were.

Another example during which Tarantino's *acousmektos* is discernible is the dialogue between Warren and Bob in the barn, which is later reprised in the saloon. These two scenes exemplify Tarantino's penchant for prolixity that is inevitably followed by bursts of violence as in the first car murder in *Death Proof* (2007), or in practically the entirety of *Basterds*. In the first instance, framed in a medium shot, the two men are on opposite sides of the screen, and as they speak, their breath condenses and materializes into very clear clouds, which become the focal point of the scene. The under-exposure of the shot further emphasizes the misty shape of their breath that literally "shoots" out of their mouths. There are no guns taken out yet, and no firing except of words. The relevance of words, as opposed to the characters themselves, is further emphasized by the reverse shot, which is even further under-exposed to the point that the two men become silhouettes, shadows. It is a verbal Western-style standoff that features an actual Mexican man, which will culminate in the second instance of dialogue between the two, this time indoors. As the two characters come face to face again, this time in a close-up, their breath is once again visible. After Warren proves that Bob is a liar and shoots his head off, the guns are visible in a large close-up and the smoke coming from the guns, while initially not visible, finally appears when Marquis moves the guns up to his shoulders.

Smoking words can only go so far in supplanting actual smoking guns.

Chapter 4: The Rack Focus, or Half Emptiness

Furthermore, the film features repetitions not only of actual acts performed by the characters, but of cinematic techniques as well. When Daisy picks up a guitar to play a song about escaping to Mexico, the camera remains on her with John Ruth in the far background by the door. Every time she looks back toward him, from the right of the frame toward the left, the camera shifts focus, too, and this occurs repeatedly and conspicuously over the few minutes of the song. Because of the incredible aspect ratio of 2.76:1 of the 70mm film, the rack-focus effect here feels more jarring than normal. The loss of focus gives off the sensation that the entire screen shifts up or down, but in reality, it does not. Tarantino achieves movement without moving the camera or the characters, which cinematically matches what happens inside the claustrophobic saloon. In doing so, he also coalesces the two predominant types of visual narration—montage and *mise-en-scène*.[7]

Regarding montage, in the aesthetic tradition of mainstream cinema, the apparatus should remain invisible to the eye of the spectator. Mainstream cinema aims for continuity, to cover up the nuts of bolts of filmmaking in order to facilitate the spectators' identification with the story and with the heroes on screen. Regarding *mise-en-scène*, instead of the traditional theories of André Bazin and *Cahiers du cinéma* (i.e., that film best communicates through *mise-en-scène* or shot composition, through everything that fills out any particular frame), let us briefly consider Slavoj Žižek's notion of the parallax view. This view is generated by "the apparent displacement of an object (the shift of its position against a background), caused by a change in observational position that provides a new line of sight" (Žižek, *Parallax View* 17), which in turn exposes a parallax gap: "the confrontation of two closely linked perspectives between which no neutral ground is possible" (Žižek, *Parallax View* 4). The same parallax tension also emerges at a micro-level in the aforementioned cinematic technique of the rack-focus effect. This effect alternates foci between foreground and background (or right-left) to dictate what the audience should follow; in other words, it changes the observational position of the spectator. Moreover, the rack-focus effect is often used to mark the dialogue cue of two characters, who are both in the frame, without actual cutting, with no editing, thus maintaining the desired effect of the *mise-en-scène* (i.e., to give the spectator more time to interpret the meaning of the image).

The two characters in the shot alternate subject-object positions depending on who speaks, which means that the rack-focus effect horizontally or vertically "cuts" the frame. Therefore, a paradoxical effect ensues: on the one hand the audience is initially denied traditional suture—the process through which a spectator (unwillingly) becomes part of the narrative[8]—which occurs most naturally through montage; on the other hand, the audience is forced to follow the direction imposed by the rack-focus, by the "fake" cuts within each frame. In this particular scene where Daisy plays the guitar, thanks to the obstinate repetition and the exaggerated jarring effect, suture then innovatively occurs within the *mise-en-scène* rather than through traditional montage.

Whenever one sees a rack-focus effect on screen, one tends to follow the parts of the screen that are in focus. At the same time, the parts that lose focus do not go away entirely; they are still on the screen, and they still *matter*, despite their blurriness. In a way, this vertical rack focus effect only fills half of the frame at a time with meaning, while emptying the other half. This turns out to be the cinematic equivalent of the old glass-half-full expression. Italian physicist Carlo Rovelli often comments about blurriness in his studies about time and the nature of time. Rovelli theorizes that, while we may feel like we are able to experience everything about our world, in fact we are able to see, or perceive only a small fraction: "Our interaction with the world is partial, which is why we see it in a blurred way" (*The Order of Time* 196). In other words, there are plenty of material things that occur around us that we do not actually experience directly (that is, they happen regardless of our ability to experience them). The cinematic rack-focus effect then becomes a metaphor for the way we perceive and understand the world around us. We do not always see everything, yet things "happen," and we see just enough to make (limited) sense of the world. The key to arriving at (some) meaning of the world and of our being reveals itself in the rack focus effect. In the case of Tarantino and this particular scene, it just so happens that the vertical split, the chasm between what we experience and what we cannot is hyperbolized—the directorial choices scream at us yet again. To return to the main guiding thought of this essay, what happens narratively in this scene is much less relevant than the way in which it happens. As a matter of fact, nothing truly happens except that the cinematic apparatus reveals itself to us over and over again. In the process, Tarantino half fills the narrative glass with cinematic artifice, hoping to make us forget about the empty half.

Last Chapter

One more thought about the ending: Tarantino reprises an interest in Alfred Hitchcock's MacGuffin, with a twist. The letter from President Lincoln that Warren holds so dear, and that he eventually admits to be a fake, is a fascinating tidbit that provides the audience with something new in the world of Tarantino—the unveiling of the MacGuffin. It is never revealed, for example, what the briefcase from *Pulp Fiction* (1994) contains.

That is a true MacGuffin, the plot device meant to move the story forward without it ever being anything "real" (in other words, more emptiness). Warren's letter, while not actually advancing the plot, does emerge at key moments in the film, without having its content fully disclosed. During the very last scene, however, Chris Mannix reads it out loud as he and Major Warren hopelessly bleed on the sole bed of the saloon. The bed brings together the Black man and the racist Southerner in an optimistic projection, but it also indicates that they are about to die, lying in the bed they made, as it were. So, Mannix reads a bedtime story, an invented tale for children, just as the film itself is a fake story for the spectators (lest we forget that Tarantino clearly reads to us in voice-over). In spite of the full disclosure, though, the MacGuffin maintains its function of being "nothing," because it is a literal fake. Mannix's last words, "Nice touch," compliment Warren on the inclusion of one crucial detail in the letter (mentioning "ole" Mary Todd), which had rendered the letter a more convincing fake. Those words easily apply to Tarantino, too, who nails several such details in the making of a beautiful lie, a film that encapsulates Hollywood's 21st-century predilection for form, which matches our current society's valorization of the fake, of the empty, of communicating through symbols, emojis, acronyms, and fake news—everything seems to be losing meaning, void of actual content, where nothing will matter as long as we are entertained.

I am grateful to Lauren Surovi and her amazing editorial eye. —Vlad Dima

Notes

1. In June 2021, Tarantino released a 400-page novelization of this film, thus further extending the "life" of the film in popular consciousness.

2. One of Tarantino's first film production companies was called *Bande à part*, the title of a 1964 film by Godard. Although Tarantino has never admitted this, the plot of *Kill Bill* borrows liberally from François Truffaut's *The Bride Wore Black* (1968); the two films even feature the same over-the-shoulder shot of a vengeful woman crossing off names from her hit list.

3. The practice of a cameo voice-over is not original by any means: Orson Welles and Jean-Luc Godard are but two famous names, among several other *auteurs*, who did it.

4. It is from this word that Chion proposes "acousmètre," which combines the Greek

origin with the French "acousmate" (or "invisible" sounds) and adds the dimension of "maître" (master). See Chion, *The Voice in Cinema* for more, especially pages 18–20.

5. I am grateful to Irene Hatzopoulos for sharing her expertise in the Greek language in a personal communication from November 26, 2021. She pointed out that modern Greek drops the "m" from *mektós* (meaning, *apart from, outside of*) and that the combination "ektós skinís" (meaning, *off stage*) would be a close derivative of the proposed term, *acousmektos*.

6. I am purposely avoiding here the insensitive term "Mexican" standoff, even though Lieutenant Aldo actually tells a German soldier that they are in a "Mexican standoff."

7. This French term was originally applied to theater, and it is most appropriate for this film, whose setup is clearly theatrical, from having basically one stage (the haberdashery) to the overreliance on dialogue.

8. For more on the concept of suture, see Kaja Silverman's groundbreaking book, *Subject of Semiotics* (1983), pages 202–220 especially. Silverman posits that the shot/reverse-shot formation best exemplifies how suture is achieved in cinema.

Works Cited

Chion, Michel. *Audio-Vision: Sound on Screen.* New York: Columbia University Press, 1994.

———. *The Voice in Cinema.* New York: Columbia University Press, 1999.

Rovelli, Carlo. *The Order of Time.* Trans. Simon Carnell and Erica Segre. New York: Riverhead Books, 2018.

Silverman, Kaja. *Subject of Semiotics.* New York: Oxford University Press, 1983.

Žižek, Slavoj. *Parallax View.* Cambridge: MIT Press, 2009.

Tarantino as Adapter

Hateful Eight *(2015) as a Remake of John Carpenter's* The Thing *(1982)*

Andrew J. Rausch *and* Kieran Fisher

Quentin Tarantino's detractors are quick to point out similarities between his films and preexisting works by other filmmakers. Some believe he's a fraud; an emperor with no clothes. While it's true that Tarantino riffs on and lifts elements from various movies and genres, this is one of the writer/director's greatest talents. We would contend that Tarantino's reworking, remixing, and re-envisioning elements from preexisting films is a form of adaptation akin to adapting a literary work to film. If one accepts Tarantino's cinematic "thievery" as being a form of adaptation, then one must conclude that he is one of the most skilled adapters in the history of cinema. Tarantino biographer Wensley Clarkson asserts that Tarantino never believed he was stealing but rather recycling stories, and that he saw nothing wrong with it because he recognized early on that recycling was a common practice in Hollywood.[1]

To date, the only one of his films that has been an outright adaptation was *Jackie Brown* (1997), based on the novel *Rum Punch* (Elmore Leonard, 1992). However, there are other projects that can be seen as direct adaptations, even if they aren't labeled as such. The first of these is *From Dusk Till Dawn* (Robert Rodriguez, 1996). This project originated as a script written by Robert Kurtzman. Kurtzman then enlisted a then-unknown Tarantino to rewrite and rework ("adapt") the script, creating something new and fresh that still followed the framework and characters created by Kurtzman in his draft. This same claim of direct adaptation can be made regarding *Pulp Fiction* (1994), in which Tarantino adapted a preexisting screenplay by Roger Avary titled *Pandemonium Reigns*. (Nearly all of the story and dialogue from the pawn shop sequence in the *Pulp Fiction* chapter "The Gold Watch" originated in Avary's original screenplay.) While

117

Tarantino has never gone out of his way to acknowledge the contributions of Kurtzman and Avary (and, in fact, publicly downplayed Avary's role in the creation of *Pulp Fiction*), both writers received "story" credits on their respective films.

Beyond this, there are other obvious but less direct adaptations of previously existing works. One of the most notable examples of this is Tarantino's *Four Rooms* (1995) vignette, which is a blatant reworking of an episode from the *Alfred Hitchcock Presents* (1955–1962) television series. The episode in question is "The Man from the South" (1960). The episode, based on a story by Roald Dahl and starring iconic actors Peter Lorre and Steve McQueen, has essentially the same plot. (One man makes a macabre wager with another man, betting he can't light his new lighter 10 times consecutively.) If the man accomplishes this, the other man will hand over his new sports car. However, if the man fails to light the lighter 10 times in a row, he must forfeit one of his fingers. Of course Tarantino being Tarantino, he adds a lot of non-sequitur banter to the mix, but the stories are essentially the same. And while Tarantino doesn't give either Dahl or teleplay adapter William Fay a "story by" credit, he gives a wink and a nod to this artistic thievery by titling his vignette "The Man from Hollywood." Tarantino does this in clever fashion, having his characters first discuss the original *Hitchcock* episode and then deciding to reenact the wager based on their having seen it. By doing this, Tarantino essentially gets a pass by way of a semantic loophole; he's not *technically* lifting the plot, but instead having his characters decide on their own to mirror Lorre and McQueen's actions within his story.

We don't bring attention to these instances to discredit Tarantino's talent, imagination, or artistry in any way, but instead to highlight his penchant and skill in adapting the works of others, managing to resurrect and transform something old into something new. In this light, Tarantino must be seen as one of the most talented cinematic adapters in the history of the medium.

The first outcry of cinematic theft by Tarantino arose just after the release of his directorial debut, *Reservoir Dogs* (1992). The plot of the film is fairly simple. *Reservoir Dogs* begins with six professional thieves and the crime boss who hired them sitting down and having breakfast together before a jewel heist. Tarantino never shows the audience the heist itself (reminiscent of Stanley Kubrick's *The Killing*, 1955), instead picking up directly after the event. The viewer then learns that the police were at the jewelry store waiting for the robbers to show up. This led to a bloody shootout in the store and two of the robbers have been killed. Another robber, who is actually an undercover cop, has been gut-shot. The four remaining members of the group then hide out in a warehouse to await the impending arrival of their boss. The situation is tense and the anxious robbers begin to pick at one another, each accusing the others of being a mole. The crew's veteran robber unsuspectingly befriends the dying robber/cop, taking him under his wing. When the crime boss arrives and declares the robber/cop to be the mole, the veteran robber shoots the boss in defense of his new friend. At the end of the film, as the warehouse is being surrounded by a swarm of police officers, the dying cop comes clean and reveals his true identity to his robber savior. This leads to the robber killing the undercover cop just before being gunned down himself by police.

Critics and cineastes immediately zeroed in on *Reservoir Dogs'* hard-to-miss similarities to other films, including *The Taking of Pelham One Two Three* (1974), *A Better Tomorrow II* (John Woo, 1987), *Kansas City Confidential* (Phil Karlson, 1952), and *The Killing*. *Film Threat* then published an article illuminating the fact that Tarantino had lifted a number of key scenes and the basic plot structure for the film from a fairly obscure Chinese picture titled *City on Fire* (Ringo Lam, 1987). Following on the heels of the *Film Threat* article, Detroit film writer Mike White constructed a 20-minute video montage comparing the two films (*Who Do You Think You're Fooling?*, 1992).

When the two films are examined side by side, it is obvious that the plot of *Reservoir Dogs* originated with Lam's film. However, Tarantino approaches the material in a completely different manner. In *Reservoir Dogs*, the "robbers in the warehouse" material comprises the majority of the film's 99-minute running time. In *City on Fire*, however, this material makes up only a portion of the storyline. Despite Tarantino's obvious lifting of key elements, it cannot be disputed that he crafted something far better (and far more significant) than the source material. *City on Fire* is barely watchable and would now be forgotten were it not been for Tarantino's reworking. In contrast, *Reservoir Dogs* is widely recognized as a masterpiece and *Empire* magazine named it the "Greatest Independent Film of All Time."[2]

When pushed to comment on the similarities between the films at the Cannes Film Festival, Tarantino explained, "I love *City on Fire* and I have the poster for it framed in my house. It's a great movie. I steal from every single movie ever made. I love it—if my work has anything it's that I'm taking this from this and that from that and mixing them together. If people don't like that, then tough titty, don't go and see it, alright? I steal from everything. Great artists steal, they don't do homages."[3] Ironically, Tarantino's "great artists steal" line is itself borrowed from a Pablo Picasso quote, "Good artists copy and great artists steal." Taking this line of thought a step further, Picasso's original quote is believed to have been a riff on a similar quotation by poet T.S. Eliot.

In defense of Tarantino, we previously asserted that "great artists lift ideas from other works, but in truth this isn't stealing as much as reworking and re-appropriating familiar themes and scenarios. Great artists don't lift every aspect of their work, but they do borrow elements. All of them. Every single one." We went on to assert that these artists "update [earlier concepts] and put unique spins on them. This is what Quentin Tarantino does. And each time he lifts something, he dramatically improves it."[4] Italian cinema scholar Simona Brancati further dismisses Tarantino's reinterpreting and recycling genres as simply being a process of modernizing characters and situations and placing them into new and different contexts. In this revisiting and borrowing from genres, Brancati credits Tarantino with bringing new life and new audiences to marginalized genres.[5]

As anyone who is familiar with both Tarantino's work and his persona knows, he is an ardent cineaste and is knowledgeable about virtually every genre of film. As such, it's hardly a surprise that he is a fan of screenwriter/director John Carpenter's work. As a young man, he was enamored with Carpenter's *Assault on Precinct 13* (1976). In an early interview, Tarantino recalls following the film from theater to theater, watching it "wherever the hell it was playing."[6] In fact, Tarantino and his friends were such big fans of the film that in 1982 they made an (unfinished) *Assault on Precinct 13*-inspired video film titled *Warzone*.[7]

Despite his love for *Assault*, it was Carpenter's *The Thing* (1982) that Tarantino was most passionate about. Carpenter's film, written by Bill Lancaster, was based on John W. Campbell, Jr.'s (writing as Don A. Stuart) novella *Who Goes There?* (1938). The story had been previously adapted to film by Christian Nyby as *The Thing from Another World* (1955). Carpenter's film tells the story of a scientific research team in Antarctica who are trapped and hunted by an alien creature capable of shape-shifting itself to look like people, making it impossible for the researchers to ascertain which of their colleagues is an alien in disguise.

Tarantino referred to *The Thing* as "one of the great remakes ever made."[8] There were a number of aspects of the film that Tarantino admired, and he would later point out parallels between *Reservoir Dogs* and Carpenter's film. "[Y]ou need to feel the claustrophobia of these guys. You need to be locked in there with them. A film that actually did that was John Carpenter's *The Thing*. In some ways, it's exactly the same story as my movie. A bunch of guys trapped in one place that they can't leave. In *The Thing*, the tension and distrust and betrayal and paranoia those guys had going toward each other on that little outpost: it went right through the audience. I felt it, like a character in the movie, and it was freaking me out. That was what I was trying to achieve with *Reservoir Dogs*. I was hoping that lightning would strike twice and I could make an audience feel paranoid, creeped out, not knowing who to trust."[9] Tarantino would later directly credit Carpenter's film as being "a big influence on *Reservoir Dogs*."[10] So despite having aped much of *City on Fire*'s plot for the basic framework of *Reservoir Dogs*, Tarantino also drew inspiration from *The Thing* regarding its construction and how best he might create tension and create an affecting sense of claustrophobia.

With *Reservoir Dogs* being Tarantino's first film as director and *The Hateful Eight* being his eighth (his "hateful" eighth, if you will), almost the entirety of his body of work occurred in the years between their creations. Despite that passage of time, there is a distinct and undeniable connection between these films; where *Reservoir Dogs* owed a creative debt to Carpenter's *The Thing*, Tarantino's 2015 Western owes considerably more. While some will say the similarities between *The Thing* and *The Hateful Eight* are simply the filmmaker paying homage, I would contend it is far more substantial than that. Keeping in mind Tarantino's aforementioned assertion that great artists "don't do homages," I would contend that Tarantino crafted *The Hateful Eight* as a loose (and unofficial) remake of the Carpenter film. I would note that this type of remake was not a foreign concept to him as the late director Monte Hellman once shared a story about Tarantino suggesting that he remake *Ride in the Whirlwind* (Monte Hellman, 1969) as a 1930s gangster movie.[11]

Rather than being an alien film set in a remote Antarctic scientific research base, *The Hateful Eight* is a Western that takes place inside a remote Wyoming haberdashery. Just as in *The Thing*, the characters in Tarantino's film are trapped together, surrounded by snow. And like *The Thing*, the characters know that one of them is not who they claim to be. As the character John "The Hangman" Ruth proclaims, "One of them fellas ain't what he says he is."[12] As such, it becomes a *Ten Little Indians* (Agatha Christie, 1939)—style mystery with the characters doubting each other while simultaneously revealing clues about themselves and who they really are.

Interestingly, a few critics pointed out the similarities between *Reservoir Dogs* and *The Hateful Eight*, believing the filmmaker was simply rehashing his earlier film.[13,14] As mentioned previously, the similarities between these films are actually their similarity to Carpenter's film (and each other by proxy). *The Hateful Eight* was actually Tarantino taking his second stab at recycling the horror classic. Similar to the theoretical film he proposed to Hellman, he is just reworking a classic film and placing it in a different genre, creating a sort of hybrid. Film writer Kyle Anderson asserts that *The Hateful Eight* was poorly received by audiences because it wasn't what they were expecting to see. Since Tarantino's film takes place in the Old West and has all the trappings of a Western picture, they were expecting a traditional Western. However, what they got instead was a "paranoid, blood-stained horror movie."[15]

Tarantino told Christopher Nolan that the suspense was the most important element in his film. He believed if he failed to create and maintain that, the movie would bore audiences. Because of this, he sought to create a looming threat of impending violence that would have the audience on the edge of their seats waiting for it.[16] Elsewhere he has stated that *The Thing* is "the one movie that is most similar in its own way" to *The Hateful Eight* [17] and that both films are "studies in paranoia."[18] He also noted the similarities in plot: "None of the characters can trust the other characters, yet they're trapped together because they can't leave because of the harsh elements. It's basically what happens as they try to deal with each other."[19] In Tarantino's reworking, there is no literal monster like there is in Carpenter's film. But as Kyle Anderson observes, such a creature is unneeded because *The Hateful Eight* is a horror movie in which all the characters themselves are monsters.[20] Another critic, Adam Nayman, described the characters in the Western as being "already infected."[21]

In an effort to show the film's cast and crew the exact mood and atmosphere he was trying to duplicate, Tarantino screened *The Thing* for them.[22] It should be noted that it was the only film he screened for them.[23]

There are many similarities beyond the tone of the films. The most obvious connection is the casting of actor Kurt Russell, who had been the lead in Carpenter's film. It could also be asserted that Russell's *The Thing* character, MacReady, was himself a cowboy of sorts (complete with cowboy hat in some scenes). Beyond that, both films feature numerous nearly identical shots of snowy mountains. Carpenter had shot exteriors in Alaska and British Columbia to stand in for Antarctica in his film, and Tarantino shot exteriors in Colorado to substitute for Wyoming. Both films conclude with two dying characters—one white and one Black—bonding in their final, hopeless moments.

Aside from the casting of Russell, Tarantino also hired legendary composer Ennio Morricone, who had previously scored music for Carpenter's film. Tarantino had repurposed Morricone's pieces for other films, but this was the first time he actually worked directly with Morricone on new music. (This is significant because this was Morricone's first score for a horror film in four decades.) One might be tempted to conclude that Tarantino's using the same composer who had scored *The Thing* was a mere coincidence were it not for one tell-tale element: Tarantino actually used four tracks Morricone had written for *The Thing* and Carpenter had rejected. Strangely enough, where Morricone's score for *The Thing* had earned him a Razzie Award, his contribution to *The Hateful Eight* snagged him an Oscar.

Tarantino hasn't hidden the fact that *The Thing* was a direct influence on *The Hateful Eight*. However, while much has been said about Carpenter's horror classic inspiring the mood and premise of Tarantino's Western, similarities can be drawn from the way in which both films examine themes pertaining to race and prejudice in politically charged times.

Some critics and scholars have interpreted "Who Goes There?" as a commentary on America's fear of outside invaders such as Germany. However, as we'll discuss later, Campbell's story has much more insidious themes on display. Similarly, *The Thing from Another World* has been described as an allegory about the threat of communism during the McCarthy era. Unsurprisingly, then, *The Thing* also probes the real-world anxieties of its era, but the themes are more complex than the mere threat of foreign invaders and non-democratic political philosophies becoming the new norm. Carpenter's movie taps into humankind's distrust of those who live closer to home, inviting viewers to confront some uncomfortable truths as a result.

The Thing was critically lambasted upon release, but the film inherited new meaning and appreciation as society's fears evolved in the early 1980s. According to Kurt Russell, *The Thing* is a film about people experiencing paranoia in their daily lives, and one which taps into the darker recesses of the human condition. "You read a headline about a murder and, the next day, you begin looking at the person walking next to you a bit more carefully. This movie takes that underlying feeling and lets it grow."[24]

Carpenter's film is essentially about the fear of everyone and anything, and this extends to anxieties that stem from racial prejudice. This is typified by the antagonistic relationships between the white and black characters in the movie. As the Outpost 31 crew begins to perish at the hands of the titular thing, each member of the group is consumed by feelings of fear and paranoia. With the crisis worsening, two men volunteer to lead the group—MacReady (Russell), a white helicopter pilot, and Childs (Keith David), a black mechanic, which highlights the mistrust between the pair. Childs' attempt to assume power is rejected after he's deemed too hot-headed and temperamental by his peers, causing the group to rally behind MacReady.

Later in the film, the only other Black character, Nauls (T.K. Carter), leaves MacReady to fend for himself in the snow, under the assumption that the creature has invaded his body. In a subsequent scene, MacReady gets backed into a corner by his black colleagues, causing him to deliver the racially charged line, "You little sweethearts were about to have yourselves a little lynching party." While lynching is historically associated with white atrocities against black people, the line alludes to the characters in question harboring racially motivated fears.

According to author Robin R. Means Coleman, the characters in *The Thing* are divided into social hierarchies which are dictated by their race, education, and social status. The majority of the team is made up of white, educated, skilled professionals. Meanwhile, the only two black men in the group have menial roles and are positioned as lower than their colleagues, but the duo rejects being subjugated. Throughout the movie, Childs works to exert some power by challenging MacReady's authority, marking a progressive approach to the racial dynamics that existed in many movies during the 1980s. As Coleman writes, Childs' character defies stereotypical buddy and sacrificial lamb roles that befell many black characters at the time. He's headstrong, flawed, independent, and heroic. By the time the end credits roll, both he and MacReady have put their prejudices aside and exist as equals, albeit in a hopeless situation.[25]

Of course, these ideas might not have made it into *The Thing* if it weren't for Campbell's original novella. As a writer and editor of the influential *Astounding Science Fiction* pulp magazine, Campbell will forever be remembered as an important literary voice whose contributions to science fiction cannot be denied. However, Campbell also espoused racist views throughout his life, such as showing support for segregation. The author believed that the white race was vastly superior when it came to intelligence, opposed the Civil Rights movement, rejected social evolution, and supported a return to slavery.

Campbell's racist views have added sinister connotations to his fiction, and "Who Goes There?" is no different. As Isiah Lavender argues, the alien shapechanger's assimilation of the white humans symbolizes the author's fear of the white race mixing with minorities. That said, Carpenter's adaptation doesn't adhere to Campbell's racial politics. By adding two black characters who embellish many of the same values and fears as their white counterparts, *The Thing* provides a nuanced examination of racial conflict. And by placing MacReady and Childs on equal footing, the film ultimately rejects the concept of racial superiority.

Racial divides are more overtly displayed in *The Hateful Eight*. Tarantino expands upon the thematic ideas present in *The Thing* and applies them to the racially charged climate of post–Civil War America. The movie locks a group of racist characters in the same room until the brewing tension erupts into full-scale violence. Furthermore, each character's inherent hatred toward the other underpins some of the film's most unsettling moments. In one scene, Samuel L. Jackson's Major Marquis Warren antagonizes Bruce Dern's Confederate war hero, General Sandy Smithers, by confessing that he sexually humiliated and murdered his son. Warren then shoots Smithers for ordering the slaughter of black prisoners during the war. The sequence is arguably one of the cruder moments in

The Hateful Eight, but it's one of many to highlight the hatred these men feel for each other.

The Hateful Eight probes ideas that have informed Tarantino's work for the entirety of his filmmaking career. He's always been interested in exploring race-related issues, and this post–Civil War western is an unfiltered culmination of these ideas. "If I have one serious subject that has carried over with me it is dealing with race in America and in particular between white folks and black folks. It is who I am and what I'm interested in," he told *The Los Angeles Times* in 2015.[26]

Tarantino's films have garnered plenty of criticism because of the controversy they've incited around race, especially in regard to their frequent use of the N-word. Spike Lee once said that Tarantino was "infatuated" with the slur, and questioned whether he hoped to become an "honorary black man."[27] Alternatively, some commentators have praised Tarantino's movies for the way in which they force viewers to engage with these ideas. In his book *Race on the QT: Blackness and the Films of Quentin Tarantino,* Adilifu Nama claims that "his films constantly implicate America's historical angst over race and invite the viewing audience to confront blackness as a source of optic, political, and cultural anxiety."[28]

A substantial portion of Tarantino's output in the 21st century has been interested in exploring real-world atrocities through the lens of alternate history. *Inglourious Basterds* (2009) tackles World War II and culminates with a group of American soldiers slaughtering Adolf Hitler and his closest allies inside a Parisian movie theater. *Django Unchained* (2012) follows a black bounty hunter as he sets out to free his wife from a sadistic plantation owner. Both films have been described as wish-fulfillment fantasies that set out to correct historical atrocities, which has led to further criticism of his work. Critic Danielle Fuentes Morgan stated that this trend allows Tarantino to insert his voice as a savior into the narrative, as opposed to telling stories about the real-life heroes who resisted the Nazis and American slave owners.[29]

Of course, there is a cathartic element to films such as *Inglourious Basterds* and *Django Unchained,* although it can be argued that their slapstick and revisionist elements overshadow the severity of the actual history they draw upon. *The Hateful Eight* is a different animal. The dialogue is pointedly political, the film's tone is oppressive, and the violence is disturbingly nasty. Furthermore, the film was released during a time when racial issues were at the forefront of American political discourse, making the film feel topical. Rather than provide an escapist wish-fulfillment fantasy that offers some therapeutic carnage for the viewer, the icy Western depicts America's racist history in a harrowing, ugly light. Mistrust leads to bloodshed, but none of the violence here feels therapeutic as everyone suffers in the end.

The Thing and *The Hateful Eight* both conclude with black and white characters putting their differences aside and seemingly accepting their tragic fates. In *The Hateful Eight*, Warren and racist sheriff Chris Mannix (Walton Goggins) die by each other's side following a bloody shootout in Minnie's Haberdashery. Much like MacReady and Childs in *The Thing*, some horrific and unfortunate circumstances made them unlikely allies. The closing moments of these films offer no feel-good respite, per se, but there is a sense that the characters have grown to feel ambivalent toward one another's skin colors.

Unfortunately, it took a perilous situation for them to reach that point.

It is our contention that Tarantino is an adapter—a less conventional sort of adapter, perhaps, but an adapter just the same—and *The Hateful Eight* is simply the filmmaker adapting *The Thing* in much the same way he previously adapted *City on Fire* with *Reservoir Dogs*. Taking this a step further, we would assert that *The Hateful Eight* isn't just aping elements of, or finding inspiration in *The Thing*, but is actually a loose remake, as well as Tarantino's most direct "indirect" adaptation to date.

NOTES

1. Wensley Clarkson, *Quentin Tarantino: Shooting from the Hip*, New York: The Overlook Press, 1995, p. 130.

2. Tim Dirks, "Empire's 50 Greatest Independent Films," *Empire*, publication date unknown.

3. Simona Brancati, *Cinema Unchained: The Films of Quentin Tarantino*, Washington, D.C.: New Academia, 2014.

4. Andrew J. Rausch, *My Best Friend's Birthday: The Making of a Quentin Tarantino Film*, Albany: Bear Manor Media, 2019, pp. 10–11.

5. Brancati, *Cinema Unchained*.

6. Gerald Peary, *Quentin Tarantino: Interviews*, Jackson: University Press of Mississippi, 1998, p. 177.

7. Rausch, *My Best Friend's Birthday*, p. 94.

8. Peary, *Quentin Tarantino*, p. 28.

9. Ibid., pp. 16–17.

10. "QT: Five Movies to See Before *The Hateful Eight*," *Premiere* magazine (video), January 5, 2006, https:www.youtube/watch?v=J9nV0a7yHJo,

11. Rausch, *Conversations on Quentin Tarantino*, p. 64.

12. *The Hateful Eight* (film), 2015.

13. Scott Nye, "*The Hateful Eight*: Hard to Hide in a Wide Frame," *Battleship Pretension*, January 4, 2016.

14. Jason Bailey, "Tarantino's *Hateful Eight* Is Nasty, Lengthy, Provocative and Terrific," *Flavorwire*, December 15, 2015.

15. Kyle Anderson, "Why *The Hateful Eight* Is Secretly a Great Horror Film," *The Nerdist*, October 29, 2017

16. "Directors Guild of America Q&A with Quentin Tarantino and Christopher Nolan" (video), December 29, 2015.

17. "QT: Five Movies to See Before *The Hateful Eight*."

18. Ibid.

19. Ibid.

20. Anderson, "Why *The Hateful Eight* Is Secretly a Great Horror Film."

21. Nayman, Adam, *Cinema Scope* (website), September 28, 2017.

22. "Directors Guild of America Q&A with Quentin Tarantino and Christopher Nolan."

23. Ibid.

24. Ed Naha, "Kurt Russell Has SomeTHING on His Mind," *Starlog*, October 1982, p. 50.

25. Robin R. Means Coleman, *Horror Noire: Blacks in American Horror Films from the 1890s to Present*, New York: Routledge, 2011.

26. Jeffrey Fleishman, "*Hateful Eight*'s Quentin Tarantino, Samuel L. Jackson Touch Raw Nerve of Racism," *The Los Angeles Times*, December 17, 2015.

27. Amy Archerd, "Lee Has Choice Words for Tarantino," *Variety*, December 16, 1997.

28. Adilifu Nama, Race on the *QT: Blackness and the Films of Quentin Tarantino*, Austin: University of Texas Press, 2015, p. 134.

29. Danielle Fuentes Morgan, *Laughing to Keep from Dying: African-American Satire in the Twenty- First Century*, Champaign: University of Illinois Press, 2020.

Mashups and Melodrama

More on Men's Emotions, Male Display and Ultra-Violence in Django Unchained *and* The Hateful Eight

SUE MATHESON

As Martyn Conterio remarks in "An Analysis of Quentin Taranti-no's Visual Trademarks and Film Inspirations," Quentin Tarantino is "a bit of a magpie, when it comes to taking inspiration from other movies.... There's nothing original at all about Tarantino's cinema." An expert in the act of cinematic theft, Tarantino began his career as a director making crime films and following in the footsteps of Jean-Luc Godard. Pauline Kael's description of the rule-breaking work of Godard produced a eureka moment for Tarantino: "That's my aesthetic!" he remembers thinking. "That's what I want to achieve!" Tarantino loved Godard's unusual shots— the long takes, the longer closeups—and penchant for cultural transposi-tion. Godard taught him "the fun and the freedom and the joy of breaking rules ... and just fucking around with the entire medium." Tarantino, of course, stole from the master as well as "every single movie ever made." He began by mashing up genres, dabbling in police drama, directing *Reser-voir Dogs* (1992), a heist film with elements of the Spaghetti Western; *Pulp Fiction* (1994), a black comedy crime film; and *Jackie Brown* (1997), a blax-ploitation crime thriller.

Colin Marshall observes, "[F]rom *Bande à part* Tarantino took not just the name of his production company but also the imperfect style of dancing he had John Travolta and Uma Thurman show off in *Pulp Fiction*." Enhanc-ing his reputation as an *enfant terrible,* he moved to other genres. *Kill Bill: Volume 1* (2003) and *Kill Bill: Volume 2* (2004) were stylized as kung fu films by means of Japanese martial arts; *Death Proof* (2007), an exploitation slasher, was released with Roger Rodriguez's *Planet Terror* (2007) under the collective title *Grindhouse* (2007); *Inglourious Basterds* (2009) blended the American war film with elements of the Spaghetti Western.

128

By the time Tarantino turned his hand to the Western itself, his proclivities to borrow and blend had become the stuff of legend, captivating his reviewers, colleagues, and audiences. As Conterio points out, Tarantino lifted the title song from Sergio Corbucci's 1966 cult classic, *Django*, written by Luis Bacalov, and "used almost exactly the same font and coloring for the opening credits sequence" for his first Western, *Django Unchained* (2012). Christoph Waltz has asserted that Tarantino, while making his second Western, *The Hateful Eight* (2015), repatriated the Spaghetti Western, taking "the genre once removed into the Italian and [bringing] it back to America." Tarantino himself only remarks that the *western all'italiana*, interests him because it offers "something new out of an old genre." Of Leone's Westerns, he observes, "They don't seem that violent now, but they seemed very violent then, because they didn't take it that seriously: Italians laugh at violence, that special type of gallows humor."

Released on Christmas Day in 2012, *Django Unchained* was box office triumph, making $15,011,121 on its first day in theaters and remains Tarantino's highest grossing film, boasting a worldwide box office total of $425.4 million, against a production budget of $100 million, in 372 days. The film was also a critical success. David Denby of *The New York Times* proclaimed it "a crap masterpiece … luridly sadistic and morally ambitious at the same time" being "a mock Western," "a mock-revenge melodrama about slavery, set in the deep South and ending in fountains of redemptive spurting blood." Richard Corliss from *Time* deemed *Django Unchained* "[a] pastiche that's nearly as funny as it is long (2hr. 45min.), and quite as politically troubling as it may be liberating … pure, if not great, Tarantino." Roger Ebert judged the film "brilliant entertainment," concluding that its director has "an appreciation for gut-level exploitation film appeal [that is] combined with an artist's desire to transform that gut element with something higher, better, more daring."

Borrowing from Corbucci's degraded West, *Django Unchained* examines "everything America has never dealt with because it's ashamed of it, and other countries don't really deal with … because they don't feel they have the right to." At its base, however, this Western is not as daring as its admirers would have its viewers believe. Tarantino returns to the genre's conservative beginnings to transform what Ebert calls that "gut element" into something better. He uses melodrama to critique racism and make ultraviolence redemptive.

As David Lusted points out, in "Social Class and the Western as Male Melodrama," central conflicts in the Western are those of melodrama, generally belonging to the male hero and the villain, its central relationships are those of male hero and his intimate (or sidekick), and its central group is all-male. *Django Unchained*'s male melodrama first introduces Dr. King Schultz (Christoph Waltz), a German bounty hunter who frees Django (Jamie Foxx) and teaches him the ins-and-outs of being a bounty hunter. Lusted would agree that insofar as *Django Unchained* can be understood as male melodrama, it is homo-social, for gender and social relations determine King's, Django's, and other characters' positions in a class hierarchy. In Tarantino's imagined South, one's social and mate-rial currency largely depends on one's gender and color. Men are privi-leged above women, whites above blacks. Devalued (sold cheap for being a runaway slave), Django begins as the lowest of the low, shuffling through Texas in a chain gang. But unlike the South, in the frontier's social hierar-chy, subject to competing definitions and change, masculine identities are not fixed. Freed, Django's fortunes change. He becomes a bounty hunter operating on the edges of society, and acting with the authority of the law, he regains his freedom.

In *West of Everything*, Jane Tompkins observes that the Western has always been "a symbol of freedom" offering an escape from social entan-glements, unhappy personal relations, and political injustice. Melodrama in the Western has always explored changing expectations and notions of masculine identity, dramatizing psychic and emotional conflicts within and between men. Accordingly, what Lusted would consider convention-ally covert areas of male sensibility are integral to rather than separate from the male action concerned with the recovery of the freedom of indi-viduals in *Django Unchained*. Men's emotional lives are indeed one of Tarantino's primary concerns. Learning that Django's wife speaks Ger-man, Schultz is outraged that she is enslaved. His offended sensibilities immediately prompt him to help Django rescue her. Deeply offended by slavery, Schultz finds feigning a master/slave relationship with Django highly distasteful. As Corliss points out, Django tells the man he freed, "For the time being, I'm going to make this slavery rigamarole work to my advantage. Still having said that, I feel guilty." When the two ride to the South to rescue Broomhilda (Kerry Washington), anger drives them to dispense justice. Incensed, Schultz shoots men dead because of his prin-ciples; Django acts to right personal wrongs and recover his self-respect.

Conventions of distinctive male display that relate to wider pat-terns of identification also convey masculine concerns in Western melo-drama. Horses, for example, are important markers of men's agency and power. Participating in the frontier's social hierarchy, Django immediately becomes horsebound. Affronted by a slave on horseback in the South, Mr. Bennett points out, "It's against the law for n-----s to ride horses in this territory." The Bennett plantation's demands that slaves walk; plantation owners, physically and socially elevated, ride in carriages. Elevated above the carriage, Django on horseback proves to be more powerful than those who depend on drivers to deliver them to their destinations.

Men's clothes also contribute to their wearers' racial and social dialectics. Social binaries in *Django Unchained* are not simple matters of opposites or black versus white. The scurrilous plantation owners, who grace the porches of their Great Houses, are Hollywood stereotypes of 19th-century white supremists. They could not be more "white," wearing snowy linen frock coats accompanied by matching trousers, vests, and sporting anachronistic Panama Plantation hats popularized by Rhett Butler (Clark Gable) in Victor Fleming's *Gone with the Wind* (1939). Blurring the distinction between the white and black masculine displays in *Django Unchained* (and distinctions between whites and blacks), Schultz, dressed in grey, acts a mediator, first between the slavers Ace and Dicky Speck (James Remar and James Russo) and Django and then between the Southern plantation owners and Django. His grey Inverness coat, his conservative black tie and vest, his clean white shirt with its starched collar, and his matching grey trousers and jacket signal wealth, responsibility, and respectability. Like the plantation owners' Panama hats, Schultz's headgear, a grey derby is also an anachronism, signaling the character's mid-range position on Tarantino's monochromatic color scale and his middle-class leanings. Telling, Schultz's costume does not change as the film progresses. Presented as a moderating influence, this character offers emotional, social, and political safety in the company of volatile characters like Calvin Candie (Leonardo DiCaprio).

Django's frequent wardrobe changes mark and comment on the process of his social metamorphosis. Presented first in plantation white, Django wears costumes that change color as his status alters. His identity as a slave discarded, he takes on the role of an indentured servant, and incongruously chooses to dress like Thomas Gainsborough's *Blue Boy*. Belonging to the 18th century, this costume, the Old World codings of its satin jacket and breeches, recalls America's revolutionary beginnings. Django's decision to look like the son of a wealthy British merchant is highly transgressive, reminding viewers of America's antagonistic relationship with its parent country. Django finds Big John Brittle (M.C. Gainey), carrying a bull whip and a Bible, about to punish a young slave (for breaking eggs), and neatly shoots the plantation manager in the heart. Doing so, he not only trades places in the plantation's hierarchy with Big John, he also emasculates him. As Brittle staggers backwards, Django remarks, "I like the way you die, *boy*" (italics mine). After whipping Lil Raj Brittle (Cooper Huckabee), Django empties the man's pistol into him and points out Ellis Brittle (Doc Duhame) who is "hightailing it across" a field.

Operating within his legal boundaries, Schultz effectively ends the brothers' reign of terror, shooting the last Brittle brother off his horse to collect their bounty.

His revenge taken, Django changes his clothes again and becomes a cowboy.

Transmitting the character's increasing agency and power, Django's look, based on some of Tarantino's favorite Westerns, is highly derivative. Joe Leydon points out that one particularly startling item, Django's sunglasses were inspired by the pair worn by Charles Bronson's Wild Bill Hickok character in J. Lee Thompson's surreal critique of racism, *The White Buffalo* (1977). Costume designer Sharen Davis, who worked for more than a year to create wardrobe for Jamie Foxx that satisfied Tarantino, reveals in Leydon's "Wardrobing a Tarantino Western," that the director wanted his protagonist to "look like Little Joe," the hot-headed, highly principled youngest son of *Bonanza*'s Cartwright family. Given Django's concerns and temperament, Foxx channeling this look is highly appropriate. A period drama set near Lake Tahoe, Nevada, during and shortly after the Civil War, *Bonanza* (NBC, 1959–1973) regularly offered television audiences sustained critiques of racism, prejudice, and social injustice.

A model of American morality and positive masculinity, Little Joe was an important element of the series' melodrama, appearing in 402 of *Bonanza*'s 416 episodes, his male display, a sophisticated compilation of colors, signaling the character's similarities with the younger members of his audience. Impulsive, romantic, conscientious, idealistic and at times rebellious, Little Joe looked the part of being his family's free spirit as he learned to be a man, wearing beige, a light gray shirt, a green corduroy jacket, tan pants, and a dark hat. The softer tones and working class texture of his costume contrasted sharply with those of his brothers: Adam (Pernell Roberts) the sardonic, responsible eldest son, dressed in black from head to foot, is a sombre authority figure, clearly the second-in-command to his father; Hoss (Dan Blocker), a conscientious middle child, wore the functional, relaxed garb of Western mellers in the 1920s and 1930s, a conservative white shirt that was always open at the neck, a suede vest, matching brown trousers, and an ivory Trail Boss.

Tarantino's desire to anchor Django's cowboy look with Little Joe's corduroy jacket is highly instructive. Invented as a hard-wearing fabric, corduroy was generally worn as work wear. Now an anti-establishment badge of cool, corduroy signaled working-class identity and political radicalism in the 19th century. "We started the metamorphosis with [Django's] Western costume," Davis observes in her interview with Joe Leydon, "Quentin wanted me to make a costume for Jamie that related to that sexy Little Joe character with that same short jacket. However, this vision had to be his own look and style. It took me 10 different tries to get that jacket just right." Retaining the cut of the jacket to highlight and sexualize Django's hips, she modified the garment's coding from a forest to a Kelly green in order to capture the psychic change involved in Django being a bounty hunter. A true middle green, the Kelly green not only denotes renewal and energy of the individual wearing it, it also symbolizes money and his ambition.

As Leydon points out, Django's transition from Southern slave to a Western-style bounty hunter is not complete until "he throws a saddle over his shoulder and dons a felt cowboy hat." Aptly, Django's Little Joe Cartwright 10x Beaver Stetson, with its lowered crown and turned up brim is no Trail Boss, the classic Western hero's iconic marker. Popular in the late 1950s and early 1960s, the style of Little Joe's Stetson was favored by protagonists of psychological Westerns. Expressing the zeitgeist of America's postwar generation, the lowered crown, associated with existential heroes, warned viewers that its wearer's moral center is his own.

Sporting Little Joe's black gloves, Django also signals he is a professional gunman, living on the edges of society and operating on the margins of the Law. When Django returns to the plantation to exact his final revenge, he appears for the last time in his distinctive cowboy hat, but sporting "new duds," his metamorphosis is complete. "I didn't know burgundy was my color," he remarks, wearing Candie's jacket. Garbed in a dark, turgid, blood red, he guns down Candie's family and the plantation's sub-oppressors before burning the Great House to the ground.

As the house burns, an outrageously long, white, and smoking cigarette holder, jauntily jutting upwards between his clenched teeth asserts the restoration of Django's manhood.

Codified, Django's multi-colored display critiques and complicates the melodrama's race relations. In the end, the South's honor code demanded by law is replaced with the honor code of an individual seeking retribution. Throughout, the struggle for justice is presented in broad terms: as a force, evil is rampant in and even celebrated by plantation culture of the South; Western cowboys are the agents of Law and Order. Good triumphs over evil in the last minutes of the film as in melodrama it should, and those who have been oppressed are seen as being morally superior, but Tarantino's is not a utopian resolution. As a revenge Western, *Django Unchained* delivers a direct, personal, and private critique of antebellum slavery. Django and Broomhilda do not turn and ride towards a hopeful new South. Freed from the past, they ride to the future, away from the scorched earth, into darkness.

A.O. Scott of *The New York Times* points out that *The Hateful Eight* is another "Quentin Tarantino movie" that critiques racism. Arguably,

Tarantino uses *The Hateful Eight*, a postbellum revisionist Western to bookend what appears to be a Civil War critique. Ultimately, Scott finds *The Hateful Eight* unsatisfying, observing Tarantino "repeating himself, spinning his wheels here in a way he has rarely done before." "None of his other films venture so far into tedium or manage to get in their own way so frequently," he says. Other critics also declare the film gravely wanting. Donald Clarke of *The Irish Times* notes that "race, gender, class and nationality divide the dramatis personae," while lamenting "[w]hat a shame the piece is so lacking in character and narrative coherence. What a shame so much of it is so gosh-darn boring." Max Weiss from *Baltimore Magazine* observes, "Some of Tarantino's worst instincts are on display in *The Hateful Eight*, which—damnit!—could've been so great." Scott dismisses the film with the comment, "[I]t's enough to note that 'The Hateful Eight' is, structurally speaking, an Agatha Christie mystery—with Marquis in the Hercule Poirot role." *The Hateful Eight*, however, calls for closer examination. It does not simply mash elements of Golden Age detective fiction into the Western—being a much more radical revisioning of the genre than *Django Unchained*, it deconstructs the Western's melodrama.

Written for an adult audience conversant with the Spaghetti Western, *The Hateful Eight* is a frontier crime drama set in 1854 and shot in Ultra Panavision. A ship of fools, the film's narrative combines elements of the murder mystery and film horror with the oater. Shortly after the Civil War, eight individuals take refuge at Minnie's Haberdashery, a secluded stagecoach stopover located in the Wyoming wilderness. Waiting out a blizzard. the bounty hunters, criminals, and Civil War veterans quickly become a microcosm of America's postwar malaise. One of the travelers, Oswaldo Mobray (Tim Roth) suggests that the haberdashery, split into "'northern' and 'southern' sides," is a house divided, before noting "the pitfalls of frontier justice." These problems become evident as the stranded travelers attempt to address the question of the stopover's missing owner. Poisoned coffee after supper ensures that party dwindles. As the travelers turn on one another, Mobray, Mexican Bob, and John Gage are found to be Minnie's murderers. Then the presence of another killer, hiding in the haberdashery's basement, is revealed. By the time the Minnie's body is located in the well, it is clear that half of the eight are intent on rescuing Daisy Domergue (Jennifer Jason Leigh), a murderer shackled to the bounty hunter John Ruth (Kurt Russell), while the members of the other half are interested in simply surviving the situation in which they find themselves.

Lacking a hero and a heroine, *The Hateful Eight* has only the Western's villains to drive its action. Ruth, who habitually beats Daisy, is not a chivalric figure. Equally vicious, the other bounty hunter and Civil War veterans cannot be considered gentlemen. A foul-mouthed, dirty, psychopathic murderer, Daisy is not an innocent, passive heroine. Her brother's gang, intent on rescuing her, are also foul sociopaths and killers. Only O.B. the stagecoach driver (James Parks) is polite and properly socialized, but he is an unexceptional individual and the first to be poisoned. The members of the hateful eight are simply heinous, and after their crimes have been revealed, all end unhappily, their wholesale slaughter being a matter of *"caedite eos, novit enim Dominus qui sunt eius."*

Sociopaths, the eight have a limited emotional range. Running the gamut of animosity, they express loathing for, dislike of, disgust with, revulsion of, aversion for, and abhorrence of one another. Aptly, every character at the haberdashery lacks guilt. Bob (Demián Bichir), Joe Gage (Michael Madsen), Oswaldo Mobray (Tim Roth), and Jody Domergue (Channing Tatum) are stone cold killers who show no remorse before, during, or after they murder Minnie and Sweet Dave who warmly welcomed them into their home. Major Marquis Warren (Samuel L. Jackson) and General Sandy Smithers (Bruce Dern) do not regret at any time or in any way slaughtering men who surrendered to them during or after the Civil War. A pathological liar, Sheriff Chris Mannix (Walton Goggins), a member of the Mannix Marauders, is also a bushwhacker with no conscience. John Ruth has no qualms about hanging women and expresses no regret that Daisy will be executed. When Ruth begins to vomit blood, Daisy shows no guilt. She instead celebrates her part in his murder, informing him, "When you get to hell, tell them Daisy sent you."

Overall, the limited range of male emotion in *The Hateful Eight* is voiced as anger, fury, and hate, evidenced while the political partisans of the North and South argue and bounty hunters clash with outlaws. Cut from the cloth of the Spaghetti Western, these characters are, as Anthony Mann would say, "professional assassins": they are not "simple men pushed to violence by circumstances [who] have a starting and a finishing line [and] follow a trajectory in the course of which they clash with life." Ironically, each considers the other a social pariah. Accordingly, racial and sexual slurs are commonplace and flung about indiscriminately: the N-word used 57 times, and the B-word, 10 times. Lacking melodrama's morally charged Manichean relationships, *The Hateful Eight*'s masculine concerns are coupled with ultraviolence. Tellingly, Daisy, the only woman outlaw, does not have a gun at her disposal.

Linking violence with the plight of Civil War veterans and the male misery of the post-war diaspora, *The Hateful Eight*'s bounty hunters are not like the sympathetic, victim-identified, moral characters that inhabit *Django Unchained*. Unlike Schultz and Django, Ruth and Warren are mercenaries. At best, their motives are amoral. Purely venal, these men reduce their fellow human beings to cash values. Ruth constantly reminds his colleagues that Daisy is a property that represents $10,000 dead or alive. The viewer is also reminded that the three corpses which ride on top of the stagecoach total their worth to $8,000. Understanding the workings of the bounty hunter's brain, Mobray uses the cash values of his own soon-to-be-dead body and the bodies of his companions to barter with Warren for Daisy's release. Working in the flesh trade, the bounty hunter in *The Hateful Eight* is indeed simply a social pariah. Ruth is the only mercenary whose professionalism is regarded with some respect by others—and awarded to him only by other bounty hunters. As Warren points out, Daisy's captor is known as "The Hangman," because "[w]hen the handbill says dead or alive, the rest of us shoot you in the back from up on top of a perch somewhere, bring you in dead over a saddle. But when John Ruth, The Hangman, catches you, you don't die from no bullet in the back. When The Hangman catches you, you hang."

The film's Civil War veterans are also miserable, displaced, and disrespected professionals. Ironically, the violence that promised them glory has ensured they are despised as war criminals. Counteracting their misery, the men remember themselves as heroes. Sandy Smithers wishes to be referred to as a General. Warren continues to wear his uniform to bolster his self-respect. Remarkably, Warren and Mannix's decision to hang Daisy at the film's end is not intended as an act of justice or even as an act of revenge. Passionate defenders of The Hangman's heroism, they kill her to protect their colleague's reputation, even though they are themselves certain to die and there are no witnesses to relate the significance of their decision. Because Warren and Mannix lack the disposition to behave in what Aristotle would consider as being the right manner, Daisy's end is ultraviolent. Unnecessarily prolonged, her hanging, which demonstrates no Aristotelean mean, is a testament of these men's unhappy and unethical states.

Replete with villainy, life is brutish, competitive, and short on *The Hateful Eight*'s Hobbesian frontier. As the Civil War continues to be waged Red-in-Tooth-and-Claw at the stopover, domination is the order of the day. A *Homo hominis lupus*, Ruth is a predator or a threat to others, exemplifying Hobbes' insights about unpleasantness of human existence. He is a self-interested man to be feared. Physically strong and vigorous, he is what Anthony E. Rotundo would recognize as a Masculine Primitive, illustrating the 19th-century belief that all males shared the same primordial instincts. Savage, Ruth looks and acts like an animal. His long, heavy fur coat signifies his is really an animal's nature. The violence that attends him points to his preoccupation with survival as does his prodigious eating and drinking. Ironically, it is a cup of coffee that proves to be Ruth's undoing. The simple act of satisfying his appetites leads to his excessively violent and messy end, vomiting gallons of blood on the table, onto the floor, and all over his unfortunate prisoner.

As Tarantino says, "You don't go past Leone, you start with Leone." Because the Spaghetti Western's ultraviolence, as an aesthetic, questions our way of thinking via our emotions, excessive gore in *Django Unchained* advances the fortunes of the Western's gender ideal. Django's aggressive action, hard work, persistence, and self-advancement signals him to be a 19th-century Masculine Achiever carrying a gun and riding on horseback. Riffing on the Western melodrama's morally charged relationships, Django's victim-identified look ensures that the ultraviolence in *Django Unchained* is ugly when unwarranted and sweet when the tables are turned. As Django himself points out, when revenge (or retribution) is justified, "[w]hat is there not to like?" *The Hateful Eight*'s excessive bloodiness, on the other hand, counters the assumption that eradicating one's opposition is a desirable activity—all eight expire painfully. Warren and Mannix, in particular, die ignobly, their behavior being immoral and unethical.

Given its production history and carefully choreographed slasher scenes, *The Hateful Eight*'s bloody spectacle calls for the film's narrative to be read as a horror critique. Filled with self-interested killers, Minnie's Haberdashery is what Carol J. Clover terms in *Men, Women and Chainsaws: Gender in Modern Horror Film* a Terrible Place. What makes Tarantino's stagecoach stopover so very frightening is not its decrepitude or even the dead bodies hidden there, but the terrible people who inhabit it with their even more terrible histories. Monsters await unwary travelers at Minnie's. American war criminals, they are accompanied by an unwholesome past that has not been laid to rest. The Civil War, which should have ended at the Appomattox Court House on April 9, 1865, returns like a revenant, and its killers find themselves the horror victims in a house divided. A formal and stylistic feature of Tarantino's male display, the bloody excesses of the ultraviolence which results should have generated matching emotional tensions in its audiences. Remarkably, it did not. Promising fantasies of male power for which those who return to the Western but lacking the morality of male melodrama, ultraviolence in *The Hateful Eight* simply could not sustain its viewers' interest.

Deemed a disappointment at the box office, *The Hateful Eight* runs a distant second to *Django Unchained*, critically and commercially. It is nonetheless important as a cultural document that critiques the use of deadly force and reveals the importance of male melodrama to the Western. Negotiating and shaping concepts of male identity, the eight in this film not only demonstrate the frightening vagaries of our state-sanctioned violence; they also demonstrate our on-going need for morality plays. Considered in relation to the success of *Django Unchained*'s ultraviolence, the failure of *The Hateful Eight*'s reveal how deeply our emotional lives are still rooted in the Founding Father's vision of an ethical America. Tarantino's mashups and melodrama not only question America's past, they also test that past's relationship to our present. Tarantino himself has taken pains to point out that his use of ultraviolence in *The Hateful Eight* is not gratuitous, insisting that it has become "more relevant than we ever could have imagined," being made during the civil unrest that followed the shooting of 18-year-old Michael Brown by a white police officer in Ferguson, Missouri, in August 2014, and the mass shooting that took place at Mother Emanuel Church in Charleston, South Carolina, on June 17, 2015.

In final analysis, and with apologies to Richard Slotkin, America, dealing with issues of race and masculinity, continues to regenerate through violence. Marking a return of what has been repressed, *Django Unchained* and *The Hateful Eight* are important cultural critiques of that process. In them, Tarantino's proclivities to borrow from the past and blend that past into the present themselves are part of this return. As he points out, "[M]e dealing with race in America is one of the things I have to offer to cinema. That is one part of my interest in American society, and so the fact that it bleeds into my work makes perfect sense. In particular, it's what I have to offer the Western genre."

WORKS CITED

Bose, Swapnil Druv. "Quentin Tarantino Named His Greatest Role Models." *Far Out.* September 17, 2021. https://faroutmagazine.co.uk/quentin-tarantino-greatest-role-models/.

Bradford, Amy. "The History of Corduroy." *TOAST Magazine.* November 7, 2018. https://ca.toa.st/blogs/magazine/the-history-of-corduroy.

Clarke, Donald. "*The Hateful Eight* Review: The Wheels Come Off the Wagon." *The Irish Times,* January 7, 2016. https://www.irishtimes.com/culture/film/the-hateful-eight-review-the-wheels-come-off-the-wagon-1.248827.

Clover, Carol J. *Men, Women and Chainsaws: Gender in Modern Horror Film: Updated Edition.* Princeton: Princeton University Press, 2015.

Conterio, Martyn. "An Analysis of Quentin Tarantino's Visual Trademarks and Film Inspirations." *Scene360.* March 15, 2016. https://scene360.com/design/91782/quentin-tarantino-analysis/.

Corliss, Richard. "*Django Unchained*: Tarantino Frees the Slaves." *TIME*, December 12, 2012. https://entertainment.time.com/2012/12/12/djangounchained-tarantino-frees-the-slaves/?iid=ent-main-lead.

D'Alessandro, Anthony, and Anita Busch. "'*Force Awakens*' Will Beat '*Avatar*' Domestic Record Tuesday; New Year's Weekend 219.3M Ticket Sales 2nd Best All-Time." *DEADLINE.* January 4, 2016. https://deadline.com/2016/01/weekend-box-office-star-wars-force-awakens-hateful-eight-new-years-2016-1201674917/.

————, and ————. "'*Star Wars*' Flies to $540M in Second Best Box Office Weekend of All

Time." *DEADLINE*. December 28, 2015, https://deadline.com/2015/12/star-wars-force-awakens-christmas-weekend-box-office-record-joy-daddys-home-concussion-point-break- 1201672899/.

Denby, David. "'*Django Unchained*': Put-On, Revenge, and the Aesthetics of Trash." *The New York Times*. January 22, 2013. https://www.newyorker.com/culture/culture-desk/django-unchained-put-on-revenge-and-the-aesthetics-of-trash.

"Django Unchained." *Box Office Mojo by IMDbPro*. https://www.boxofficemojo.com/release/rl3662644737/.

Ebert, Roger. "Faster, Quentin! Thrill! Thrill!" *RogerEbert.com*. January 7, 2013. https://www.rogerebert.com/roger-ebert/faster-quentin-thrill-thrill.

Frayling, Christopher. *Sergio Leone*. London: Faber & Faber, 2000.

Hiscock, John. "Quentin Tarantino: I'm Proud of My Flop." *The Telegraph*. April 27, 2007. https://www.telegraph.co.uk/culture/film/starsandstories/3664742/Quentin-Tarantino-Im-proud-of-my-flop.html.

Labrecque, Jeff. "The Hateful Eight's Quentin Tarantino Defends How His Films Deal with Race." *Entertainment*. December 21, 2015. https://ew.com/article/2015/12/21/quentin-tarantino-hateful-eight-race/.

Leydon, Joe. "Wardrobing a Tarantino Western." *Cowboys & Indians*. January 2013. https://www.cowboysindians.com/2013/01/wardrobing-a-tarantino-western/.

Lowe, Kinsey. "'*Star Wars*' Now 4th-Biggest Domestic Grosser & Disney's Highest on Way to $700M; 'Hateful Eight' Adds $3.5M in 1st Day of Expansion." *DEADLINE*. December 31, 2015. https://deadline.com/2015/12/the-hateful-eight-star-wars-the-force-awakens-daddys-home-box-office-1201674208/.

Lusted, David. "Social Class and the Western as Male Melodrama." *The Movie Book of the Western*. Eds. Ian Cameron and Douglas Pye. London: Studio Vista, 2006: 63–74.

Marshall, Colin. "An Analysis of Quentin Tarantino's Films Narrated (Mostly) by Quentin Tarantino." *Open Culture*. May 29, 2020. https://www.openculture.com/2020/05/an-analysis-of-quentin-tarantinos-films-narrated-mostly-by-quentin-tarantino.html.

_____. "How Quentin Tarantino Steals from Other Movies: A Video Essay." *Open Culture*. July 31, 2019. https://www.openculture.com/2019/07/how-quentin-tarantino-steals-from-other-movies-a-video-essay.html.

Rotundo, Anthony E. "Learning About Manhood: Gender Ideals and the Middle-Class Family in Nineteenth-Century America." *Manliness and Morality: Middle-Class Masculinity in Britain and America, 1800–1940*. Eds. J.A. Mangan and James Walvin. Manchester: Manchester University Press, 1987: 35–52.

Scott, A.O. "Review: Quentin Tarantino's 'The Hateful Eight' Blends Verbiage and Violence." *The New York Times*. December 24, 2015. https://www.nytimes.com/2015/12/25/movies/review-quentin-tarantinos-the-hateful-eight-blends-verbiage-and-violence.html.

Sharf, Zack. "Quentin Tarantino Pens Heartfelt Essay on Sergio Leone, the 'Greatest of All Italy's Filmmakers.'" *IndieWire*. June 3, 2019. https://www.indiewire.com/2019/06/quentin-tarantino-sergio-leone-essay-Spaghetti-western-1202146940/.

Short, Stephen. "Italian Designer Massimo Alba on Daniel Craig's Last James Bond's Wardrobe." *PRESTIGE*. April 15, 2020. https://www.prestigeonline.com/hk/style/fashion/italian-designer-massimo-alba-on-daniel-craigs-last-james-bond- wardrobe/?fbclid=IwAR3n58y9h42x27UN9rKkL21sLg1HECMPjnMiVkd6V2zBDUkL 3lwXVrGBpc.

Tarantino, Quentin. "Shooting star." *The Spectator*. June 1, 2019. https://www.spectator.co.uk/article/shooting-star.

Weiss, Max. "Review: *The Hateful Eight*." *Baltimore Magazine*. January 4, 2016. https://www.baltimoremagazine.com/section/artsentertainment/review-the-hateful-eight.

"What Is Unique About "*The Hateful Eight's*' Cinematography?" *The Take*. https://the-take.com/watch/what-is-unique-about-the-hateful-eights-cinematography.

The D Is Not Silent

Dangerfield, Django, and Resistance to Slavery

BRYAN M. JACK

> DR. SCHULTZ: "Do most slaves take the institution of marriage seriously?"
> DJANGO: "Huh?"
> DR. SCHULTZ: "Do slaves believe in marriage?"
> DJANGO: "Me and my wife do."

> *Brentville, August 16, 1859*
>
> *Dear Husband,*
>
> *"...Master is in want of monney if so I know not what time he may sell me an then all my bright hops of the futer are blasted ... if I thought I shoul never see you this earth would have no charms for me do all you Can for me witch I have no doubt you will..."*
>
> *Your affectionate wifee wife[1]*

When Harriet Newby, an enslaved woman in Virginia, wrote those desperate words to her husband Dangerfield, he was already committed to a plan to rescue her and their children from being sold to the Deep South. It was a plan doomed to failure, resulting in Dangerfield's death and his mutilated body being desecrated by hogs in an alley in Harpers Ferry, Virginia, 60 miles from Harriet. Within a year, Harriet and some of their children were sold south to a Louisiana planter, and the Newbys became another broken family caught in the tragedy of American slavery.[2]

Till Death or Distance Do You Part

The existence of Harriet's letters to Dangerfield, and Dangerfield's attempt to rescue his wife, make their story somewhat unique, but the Newbys are representative of the assaults that the institution of slavery inflicted upon the Black family, in particular Black marriages. As historian Tera W. Hunter notes, "'To have and to hold, in sickness and in health … till death do you part': these words have been uttered by brides and grooms privileged to enjoy Christian marriage rites since the Middle Ages. African Americans held in bondage were forced to revise the standard wedding vows to make them befit the absence of standing in civil law. As one white minister officiating at a slave ceremony frankly reminded the couple, their marriage was binding only 'until death or distance do you part.' A black preacher named the culprit of this caprice more bluntly; 'Till death or buckra part you'—meaning the white man."[3] As will be discussed later, this built-in limitation to marriage vows meant Dangerfield's status as a free Black man did nothing to protect neither his wife nor their marriage. Marriages involving enslaved people had no legal footing because of the primary right of enslavers to control their property however he saw fit. Harriet was property of her enslavers, at risk of being sold at any time, as were their children, and there was nothing Dangerfield could legally do to stop it. As enslaver and former governor of Georgia Charles J. McDonald stated: "I have a Negro preacher who marries them for the union to last as long as they live or until it is the pleasure of their owner to separate them."[4]

Separation was not the only threat to marriages involving enslaved people. Those who experienced slavery explained what made slavery such a threat to their marriages and relationships: "the separation of parents (especially mothers) from their children, the sundering of ties between husbands and wives, the interference of the third flesh of masters, which violated the marriage bed in its most extreme forms … slave women were often forced to engage in sex against their will with masters, overseers, and other white men. A slave-owner might force a slave husband to exit the marital bed as the slave-owner took his place with the slave's wife. Moments like these diminished the advantages of couples' living together, given the fact that men were told to provide for their wives but could not exercise the prerogatives of free men to protect them."[5] These restrictions meant some enslaved people rejected the idea of marriage while enslaved. In his autobiographical narrative, William Wells Brown discusses his enslaver's offer to purchase Eliza, a woman Brown finds attractive, so they could be married. Brown views this as a "trap," seeing marriage as incompatible with escape. He wrote, "I knew that if I should have a wife, I should not be willing to leave her behind; and if I should attempt to bring her with me, the chances would be difficult for success…. I determined never to marry any woman on earth until I should get my liberty."[6] William and Ellen Craft, a married couple who eventually made a daring and successful joint escape from slavery, spent the early part of their relationship reluctant to marry and start a family because the thought of being separated from one another or their future children horrified them. They did choose to marry but did so with an eye toward escaping together.[7]

For those who did choose to marry or be in relationships, Dangerfield Newby's ill-fated rescue speaks to the lengths people would go to keep their families together, and to resist, sometimes through violence, the forces allied against them. It is this struggle to preserve a slave marriage that is the central premise of Quentin Tarantino's 2012 Academy Award–winning film *Django Unchained*. The film follows the recently freed Django's (Jamie Foxx) rescue of his wife Broomhilda (Kerry Washington) from the horrors of slavery on the Mississippi plantation Candie Land. In the film, we see that Broomhilda has been tortured, branded, and whipped, and is slated to be used as a concubine. Unlike the historical, ill-fated, and all too human Dangerfield Newby, the Hollywood version embodied in Django Freeman not only successfully rescues his wife, he also spectacularly destroys the site of her enslavement, killing their tormentors and burning Candie Land to the ground. This essay uses *Django* as a springboard to explore the story of the Newbys, a couple trying to maintain their marriage within an institution that denied their humanity. Offering neither a full-fledged film critique of *Django Unchained*, nor another tiresome example of a historian point by point chastising a film for its lack of historical accuracy, in the following pages I hope to use Tarantino's film's relationship with history to interrogate African American resistance to enslavement.

When asked about the purpose of *Django Unchained* Tarantino stated, "I think America is one of the only countries that has not been forced, sometimes by the rest of the world, to look their own past sins completely in the face. And it's only by looking them in the face that you can possibly work past them."[8] And his desire for the film: "I don't want it to be easy to digest. I want it to be a big, gigantic boulder, a jagged pill and you have no water."[9] In the film, there are specific scenes that serve this purpose, but the overall tenor of the film and its triumphant conclusion serve do this opposite. Through the lens of marriage, I argue that in his final choices for *Django*, Tarantino made a film that, while it had uncomfortable moments, was ultimately a film that in its depiction of Django's successful rescue of Broomhilda and destruction of Candie Land creates comfort for its audiences rather than discomfort.

Django Unchained *and the History of the Slave South*

In the first few minutes of *Django Unchained*, a title card declares "1858—Two years before the Civil War." Since the consensus date of the beginning of the war is April 12, 1861 (the firing on Ft. Sumter), 1858 is three years before the beginning of the Civil War. Assuming this is not a simple mistake, and again, not pedantically criticizing Tarantino for getting a historical fact wrong, the title card's wrong year implies that the audience is not going to get unadulterated history, but rather something that is history adjacent, a postmodern depiction of the antebellum South. The audience is not seeing a depiction of the historical South, we are seeing a Tarantino depiction of the historical South, a depiction shaped by film history more than academic history.

As many scholars have shown, "The South," as most people understand it, has been constructed in the American imagination, a product of Lost Cause sentimentality depicted in popular culture, especially films.[10] Because the South has been such a frequent Hollywood subject, and feature films reach such large audiences, films profoundly shape public discourse about Southern history. From Hollywood's first blockbuster, *The Birth of a Nation* (1915) to indelible images like the Southern belles and loyal slaves of *Gone with the Wind* (1939), film has been particularly powerful in creating the South in the American imagination. As historian of the plantation South, Catherine Clinton states, "Millions of Americans have had their vision of the South, race relations, and even the entire panorama of our past shaped if not wholly defined by the movie business."[11] Tarantino is, in his own words, "obsessed with *The Birth of a Nation* and its making" because it gave rise to the rebirth of the Ku Klux Klan and resulted in increased violence and racism against African Americans. In Tarantino's view, D.W. Griffith, *Birth*'s director, if put on trial, would be found guilty of a war crime for the damage his film did as propaganda. *Django Unchained*, in Tarantino's telling, is a conscious attempt to respond to *Birth of a Nation* and its paternalistic, benevolent depiction of slavery and white supremacy.[12]

Quentin Tarantino, more than most directors, makes films that are explicitly in conversation with previous films, with homages, allusions, and intertextual relationships with earlier works from both Hollywood and worldwide filmmakers. For a film like *Django*, this is incredibly important to note, because although the story is fictional, the setting is historical, and the antebellum, slaveholding South is quite possibly the most fraught historical setting in American history. When interviewed, Tarantino recognized the responsibility of this, telling historian Henry Louis Gates, Jr., "It was interesting, because on one hand I'm telling a historical story, and when it comes to nuts and bolts of the slave trade, I had to be real and had to tell it the right way. But when it comes to more thematic things and operatic view, I could actually have fun with stylization—because it is taking parts from a spaghetti Western. And I am taking the story of a slave narrative and blowing it up to folkloric proportions and to operatic proportions that are worthy of high opera."[13] For at least a half century or longer, studies of slavery have documented the various ways enslaved people resisted slavery, both overtly and covertly. However, as further evidence of Tarantino's influences, *Django Unchained* is operating within a cinematic history that has frequently presented slaves as victims lacking agency. The enslaved people in Django (including Django before he is freed) are quite remarkably lacking any agency, the exception being Stephen (Samuel L. Jackson), a villain in the film.

In *Django*, despite Tarantino's adamant assertion that he "had to be real" about slavery, his final choices are, as historian Daniel Farrell notes, "often privileged aesthetic choices that made the film simultaneously more profitable and less historical."[14] Django Freeman wears a pair of sunglasses, a stylistic choice that while on the surface is an insignificant historical anachronism, yet their inclusion is also a telling lens into understanding Tarantino. As Andrew Harrington notes, when Sharen Davis, *Django*'s costume designer, "was searching for the perfect pair of sunglasses she knew that Tarantino responded more to film history than real history." She told *Vanity Fair*, "you can show him the actual history, but that won't do it. They were Charles Bronson's from *The White Buffalo*."[15] The importance of this anecdote is not the sunglasses themselves; it is in the telling phrase that in his choices, Tarantino responds more to film history than to actual history. These choices are his right as a filmmaker, and his choices made *Django Unchained* both a commercial and critical success, resulting in a very entertaining film. However, in *Django Unchained*, Tarantino often wants it both ways, falling back on ahistorical styles and Hollywood tropes while simultaneously claiming "his style makes for a more authentic history, saying, 'When slave narratives are done on film, they tend to be historical with a capital H, with an arms-length quality to them. I wanted to break that history-under-glass aspect, I wanted to throw a rock through that glass and shatter it for all times and take you into it.'"[16] I do not disagree with Tarantino about previous films' depiction of slavery being lacking in many ways, including sanitizing and whitewashing the lived experiences of the enslaved, and there is a real need for a corrective in our depictions of slavery.[17] However, because of its style and triumphant ending, Tarantino's jagged pill goes down rather smooth, and perhaps does not accomplish all of his stated goals for making the audience reckon with slavery.

Dangerfield and Harriet Newby

For all of the violence and vengeance in *Django Unchained*, it is important to note that Django's purpose is not to start a slave revolt, or to be an avenger against slavery.

Django's goal is to rescue Broomhilda; he does not rescue any other enslaved people. Django does not even kill Calvin Candie (Leonardo DiCaprio), the lead enslaver in the film, that honor (and the martyrdom that comes with it) goes to Django's white ally, Dr. King Schultz (Christoph Waltz). Django is not Nat Turner, Denmark Vesey, or Gabriel Prosser, all rebels against the institution of slavery who paid with their lives. As Tarantino says, "It's not about him liberating everyone in shack row and them storming Canada together. He's got one mission and one mission only: extract his wife from this hell. And nothing else means a damn compared to that."[18] Django's actions are not an attack on the institution of slavery, but he is instead, according to Tarantino, "going to the evil kingdom" to "rescue the princess in the tower."[19] Slavery just happens to the setting for this fairy tale. And since it is in essence a fairy tale, Tarantino can make it more palatable to the audience by letting Django and Broomhilda win. Django's destruction of Candie Land and the enslavers within provide a cathartic moment for the audience, and his moment of triumph ends the movie. But what happens after? Could Django and Broomhilda ride off into the sunset in antebellum Mississippi and not be caught? Because the purpose of Django's quest is not the destruction of slavery, but simply to rescue and reunite with his wife, perhaps it is better to not ask what happens after. The audience gets to see the fictional Django and Broomhilda win, rather than lose like the real-life Dangerfield and Harriet Newby.

Dangerfield Newby was an impressive physical specimen. Six feet two inches tall, strong from his work as a blacksmith and laborer, Dangerfield was, like Django at the beginning of the film, unfamiliar with weapons and had to be taught how to shoot a gun. But whereas Django was a natural killer, calculating and cool, a Hollywood creation, the Dangerfield Newby who comes to us from history is all too human. His compatriots described the 39-year-old as "a good-natured sensible old man" who was "a quiet man, upright, quick tempered and devoted to his family." The desperation of Harriet's situation, and frustration with her enslaver's refusal to sell her to him made him "low spirited and impatient" and restless for a chance to rescue her.[20]

The Newbys' story began in Virginia, where Dangerfield was born in 1820, the son of an enslaved woman Elsey Pollard and a white farmer Henry Newby, who was not her enslaver. Because of the enormous power differences within the slave system, it is understood that many, if not most sexual relationships between enslaved women and white men were coercive on some level. This does not seem to be the case with Elsey and Henry. By all accounts, Elsey and Henry's relationship was unusual in that they acknowledged each other as family, with Elsey recording their wedding date as

December 1, 1818, even though it was not an official marriage. Elsey and the 11 children she had with Newby were all still the property of the enslaver John Fox, but Fox allowed them to live with Henry Newby as a family.[21]

In 1858, Dangerfield had a difficult decision to make. John Fox was allowing Henry Newby to take Elsey and some of their children, including the 38-year-old Dangerfield, to Ohio, where they would be granted their freedom. But Dangerfield was in a relationship with Harriet, who was enslaved by the Jennings family. Acknowledging one another as husband and wife, Dangerfield and Harriet had several children together. Going to Ohio would mean Dangerfield could have his freedom, but would also mean leaving his wife and children behind in slavery.[22] This was a choice that many enslaved people had to make when they got their freedom, either by running away or by purchase, the decision to gain freedom but leave family behind.[23]

Finally, it was decided that Dangerfield would go to Ohio, work as a blacksmith, and earn enough money to buy Harriet from her enslavers. Dangerfield negotiated with Lewis Jennings, Harriet's enslaver, to buy her and possibly buy some of their children. Accounts vary as to what happened in the negotiation, but many sources state the price was $1,000, a considerable sum in 1858, but an amount that was not impossible to raise. It was reported Jennings took some money then did not manumit Harriet. It was also reported Jennings agreed on a price, then when Dangerfield raised that amount, reversed his decision and held out for a higher price.[24] Regardless, Dangerfield was trying to raise money, and Harriet's letters to him were sounding increasingly desperate.

In April 1859, Harriet wrote a letter that mostly spoke of daily mundane things but closed with: "I want to see you very much but are looking fordard to the promest time of your coming oh Dear Dangerfield com this fall with out fail monny or no money I want to see you so much that is one bright hope I have before me nothing more at present but remain your affectionate wife."[25] Eleven days later, she repeated her plea to see her husband: "you Can not amagine how much I want to see you Com as soon as you can for nothing would give more pleasure than to see you it is the grates Comfort I have is thinking of the promist time when you will be here oh that bless hour when I shall see you once more."[26] By August her desperation of being sold was apparent: "not the trouble I see the last two years has ben like a trouble dream to me it is said Master is in want of monney if so I know not what time he may sell me an then all my bright hops of the futer are blasted for there has ben one bright hope to cheer me in all my troubles that is to be with you for if I thought I shoul never see you this earth would have no charms for me do all you Can for me witch I have no doubt you will."[27]

Dangerfield was also desperate to get to Harriet before she was sold further South, and in that desperation joined the abolitionist John Brown's plot to capture the federal armory at Harpers Ferry, Virginia, and foment a slave rebellion. Most of Brown's followers were either veterans of his conflicts with proslavery forces in Kansas or seasoned abolitionists. Dangerfield Newby joined the group for more personal reasons; it was his last chance to rescue Harriet. By the summer of 1859, Newby had over $700 deposited in Ohio banks, a remarkable amount, but not enough to save his wife. But Dangerfield was going to get to Harriet, money or no money.[28]

Of the planned raid on Harpers Ferry, Frederick Douglass felt John Brown (and his followers) were walking into a "perfect steel trap," and would be surrounded and killed during the raid, unable to escape. This belief led Douglass to refuse to join Brown's expedition.[29] Nothing is known of Dangerfield Newby's thoughts on the efficacy of the plan, but we do have some insight into his state of mind as Brown's followers waited for weeks at their staging area. Annie Brown, John Brown's 15-year-old daughter who was helping care for the raiders, said of Dangerfield, "He had a wife and several children that were slaves, and he was impatient to have operations commenced, for he was anxious to get them…. Poor man, he used to get very low spirited and impatient at what appeared to him the long delay and preparation. We tried to cheer him up, for we really liked him."[30] Brown had drawn up a provisional constitution for the proposed nation he hoped to establish, and Annie Brown recalled Dangerfield Newby was "especially moved by article 42: 'The marriage relation shall be at all times respected and families kept together, as far as possible; and broken families encouraged to unite and intelligence offices established for this purpose.'"[31] After trying to unsuccessfully recruit two of his brothers to join the raid, Newby became increasingly restless, showing Harriet's letters to the other raiders and asking Brown when they could begin the raid, with Brown replying, "Soon, soon, Dangerfield."[32]

On the day of the raid, Dangerfield Newby was the first raider to die. His role, with two other men, was to secure the entrance to the Shenandoah River bridge, one of the few escape routes out of Harpers Ferry. As armed townspeople converged to engage the raiders, Newby shot and killed two of them. One of the men Newby killed was a slaveholder who was taking aim at Newby when Newby fired first. However, more townspeople arrived, and the outnumbered raiders attempted to retreat across an open area to reconnect with Brown's main group. As they crossed the street, Newby fell, shot through the neck. The person who shot him did not have bullets, so had loaded a six-inch metal spike into his rifle. The spike sliced Newby's neck from ear to ear and he quickly died. However, his death was not the end. Enraged townspeople mutilated Dangerfield Newby's body, slicing pieces from his ears for souvenirs.[33]

A newspaper correspondent reported what happened next. "The huge mulatto that shot Mr. Turner was lying in the gutter in front of the Arsenal, with a terrible wound in his neck, and though dead and gory, vengeance was unsatisfied, and many, as they ran sticks into his wound, or beat him with them, wishes that he had a thousand lives, that all of them might be forfeited in expiation and avengement of the foul deed he had committed."[34] Dangerfield Newby's body lay in the gutter for another day and a half. In a scene that would be right at home in a Tarantino film, townspeople occasionally showed up to continue to desecrate it, and drawn by his blood, hogs came to root his corpse, devouring it.[35] By the time what was left of his body was thrown into an unmarked pit, Dangerfield Newby was unrecognizable, and Harriet's dreams of rescue were dashed.[36]

Notes

1. *Governor's Message and Reports of the Public Officers of the State, of the Boards of Directors, and of the Visitors, Superintendents, and Other Agents of Public Instruction or Interests of Virginia* (Richmond, 1859), 116117. Special Collections, Library of Virginia, Richmond, Virginia. "Dangerfield Newby," *Virginia Changemakers*, accessed January 1, 2022, https://edu.lva.virginia.gov/changemakers/items/show/1.

2. Eugene L. Meyer, *Five for Freedom: The African American Soldiers in John Brown's Army* (Chicago: Lawrence Hill Books, 2018), 78, 90–91, 148.

3. Tera W. Hunter, *Bound in Wedlock: Slave and Free Black Marriage in the Nineteenth Century* (Cambridge: The Belknap Press of Harvard University, 2017), 6.

4. Hunter, *Bound*, 12 and 49.

5. Hunter, *Bound*, 41 and 50–51.

6. William Wells Brown, *Narrative of William Wells Brown* in William L. Andrews and Henry Louis Gates, Jr., eds., *Slave Narratives* (New York: The Library of America, 2002), 412.

7. William and Ellen Craft, *Running a Thousand Miles for Freedom; or, the Escape of William and Ellen Craft from Slavery*, in Andrews and Gates Jr., eds. *Slave Narratives*, 696–697.

8. Henry Louis Gates, Jr., "'An Unfathomable Place': A Conversation with Quentin Tarantino about *Django Unchained* (2012)," *Transition* 112 (2013): 61.

9. Gates, Jr., pp. 54.

10. For more on this, please see, Karen L. Cox, *Dreaming of Dixie: How the South Was Created in American Popular Culture* (Chapel Hill: University of North Carolina Press, 2011); Jack Temple Kirby, *Media-Made Dixie: The South in the American Imagination* (Athens: University of Georgia Press, 1986); Karl G. Heider, ed., *Images of the South: Constructing a Regional Culture on Film and Video* (Athens: University of Georgia Press, 1993); Edward D.C., Campbell, Jr., *The Celluloid South: Hollywood and the Southern Myth* (Knoxville: University of Tennessee Press, 1981); Deborah E. Barker and Kathryn McKee, eds., *American Cinema and the Southern Imaginary* (Athens: University of Georgia Press, 2011).

11. Bryan M. Jack, ed., *Southern History on Screen: Race and Rights, 1976–2016* (Lexington: University Press of Kentucky, 2019), 1; Catharine Clinton, *The Plantation Mistress: Woman's World in the Old South* (New York: Pantheon, 1982), 204.

12. Jack, *Southern History*, pp. 51–52.

13. Ibid., pp. 58.

14. Daniel Ferrell, "History Without a Capital H: Violence, Commodification, and the

Perpetuation of the Postmodern Condition in *Django Unchained*," in Jack, ed., *Southern History*, 32–33.

15. Andrew Harrington, "Is Quentin Tarantino Calvin Candie? The Essence of Exploitation in *Django Unchained*," *Black Camera* 7, no. 2 (Spring 2016): 82.

16. Ibid., 81–82.

17. In my opinion, Steve McQueen's *Twelve Years a Slave*, released the year after *Django Unchained*, is a much-needed improvement in these depictions.

18. Gates, Jr., 65.

19. Gates, Jr., 56.

20. Meyer, 22 and 78–79.

21. Meyer, 19.

22. Their exact number of children is unknown, but seven is likely. Meyer, 20.

23. Robert S. Starobin, ed., *Letters of American Slaves* (New York: Barnes and Noble Books, 1988), 107, 153–154.

24. Meyer, 21–22.

25. *Governor's Message and Reports of the Public Officers of the State, of the Boards of Directors, and of the Visitors, Superintendents, and Other Agents of Public Instruction or Interests of Virginia* (Richmond, 1859), 116117. Special Collections, Library of Virginia, Richmond, Virginia. "Dangerfield Newby," *Virginia Changemakers*, accessed January 1, 2022, https://edu.lva.virginia.gov/changemakers/items/show/1.

26. *Governor's Message and Reports of the Public Officers of the State, of the Boards of Directors, and of the Visitors, Superintendents, and Other Agents of Public Instruction or Interests of Virginia* (Richmond, 1859), 116117. Special Collections, Library of Virginia, Richmond, Virginia. "Dangerfield Newby," *Virginia Changemakers*, accessed January 1, 2022, https://edu.lva.virginia.gov/changemakers/items/show/1.

27. *Governor's Message and Reports of the Public Officers of the State, of the Boards of Directors, and of the Visitors, Superintendents, and Other Agents of Public Instruction or Interests of Virginia* (Richmond, 1859), 116117. Special Collections, Library of Virginia, Richmond, Virginia. "Dangerfield Newby," *Virginia Changemakers*, accessed January 1, 2022, https://edu.lva.virginia.gov/changemakers/items/show/1.

28. Tony Horwitz, *Midnight Rising: John Brown and the Raid That Sparked the Civil War* (New York: Henry Holt, 2011), 118–119.

29. Horwitz, 115–116.

30. Meyer, 78.

31. Meyer, 79.

32. Meyer, 79.

33. Meyer, 90.

34. Meyer, 90–91.

35. Horwitz, 153.

36. Walter Johnson, *Soul by Soul: Life Inside the Antebellum Slave Market* (Cambridge: Harvard University Press, 1999), 5.

Fables and History

Tarantino Rewrites Both in Once Upon a Time ... in Hollywood

Scott F. Stoddart

Quentin Tarantino has never been one to simply comply with bound-aries set by genres. From his breakthrough film, *Reservoir Dogs* (1992), Tarantino's work has been scrutinized for its daring, reworking of genre in innovative manners to bring a new sensibility to Hollywood films. Since remixing the gangster film with the heist film with *Reservoir Dogs,* Taran-tino has gone on to redefine the Japanese samurai film with *Kill Bill* (2003, 2004); collaborate with Robert Rodriguez to revive the roadhouse B-movie with *Grindhouse* (2007); reimagine the Spaghetti Western with *Django Unchained* (2012), a loose remake of the 1960s cult Italian export, *Django* (1966), its central character now a free black man and transposing his nar-rative to the American South; and retool the Western again with *The Hate-ful Eight* (2015), denying the redemptive drifter and populating it with a cabin full of anti-heroes.

Reviews of Tarantino's oeuvre often focused on his genius in re-defin-ing genre, but with a distance that appears to underscore his predilection for violence refined through a sense of toxic masculinity. However, the fanfare that greeted his ninth film *Once Upon a Time in Hollywood* (2019)[1] brought a new kind of vocabulary to reviews of his work, with critics char-acterizing the film as "wonderfully comic," "affectionate," "unexpectedly emotional," and "pretty glorious." Such reviews, published in mainstream outlets, mark *Once Upon a Time in Hollywood* as decidedly different, and I will argue that it has much to do with how the critics have defined Taran-tino as a writer-director "practicing a cinema of saturation, demanding audience's total attention," "bombarding us with allusions, visual jokes, flights of profane eloquence, daubs of throwaway beauty and gobs of pre-meditated gore" (Scott 2019). Distinct in its make-up, Tarantino's fairy tale of Hollywood is a love story of epic proportions written against a moment of history that Joan Didion described as "the last extant stable society" before all hell broke loose: the so-called Summer of Love in 1969.

Historian with a Mission

Just as Tarantino displays a playfulness with genre, in *Once Upon a Time*, he demonstrates a playfulness with history. Rather than retelling and depicting the summer of 1969 through a historical/historian's lens, Tarantino rewrites/revises it to accommodate the vision he *desires* us to experience. Tarantino is no stranger to rewriting history in his films, as demonstrated in his previous films *Inglourious Basterds* (2009) and *Django Unchained*. *Inglourious Basterds* revises the known history of the Holocaust film through its inventive creation of a fable where Hitler and his Nazi henchmen are dispensed with via a revengeful cinema owner. Tarantino's handling of history earned the film the label of "postmodern parody" of "historiographic metacinema" that re-envisions the ending of World War II (Setka 141). In an interview with Ella Taylor (154–55), Tarantino speaks about doing little research into the actual history of the timeframe he wants to rewrite. Instead, he admits to being fully conversant in the cinema that he sees as a window into historical context, paying homage to the influences of the Hollywood propaganda films of exiled European filmmakers of the late 1930s and 1940s—films made by the likes of Anatole Litvak (*Confessions of a Nazi Spy*, 1939), Jules Dassin (*Reunion in France*, 1942), Fritz Lang (*Man Hunt*, 1941), and Jean Renoir (*This Land Is Mine*, 1943).

Making historically accurate films is not what interests Tarantino; instead, it is the relevant context that makes them historically sound to him: "I wasn't taking anything from them stylistically, but what struck me about those movies was that these filmmakers probably had personal experiences with the Nazis, or were worried to death about their families in Europe … these movies are entertaining, there's humor in them…. They're allowed to be thrilling adventures" (155). It is this "thrill" that obviously sets the director apart from Steven Spielberg, for example, whose own historical epics take on the sober resonance of epic drama.

As detailed by Stella Setka, while making "pointed references to silenced American histories—such as the genocide of native Americans, the enslavement of African Americans, and the oppression of Jewish Americans" (143), Tarantino's sixth film infuses "the World War II setting with stylistic hallmarks of the Hollywood Western" to turn the Holocaust film into "a concern about the powerful role that cinema plays in the construction of public cultural memory" (144). Setka's analysis rails against the masochistic violence that is a Tarantino staple to argue that the rewriting of history in this vein creates a "metacinematic revenge fantasy" (143) that "calls into question the very essence of what constitutes collective memory, and reveals in the process the extent to which collective memory is defined by how we choose to represent history" (161). In essence, Tarantino's rewriting of history makes for an entertainment that thrills, but that does little to serve as a real testament to virtues of most Holocaust films.

Tarantino's second rewriting of history was markedly more successful than *Inglourious Basterds* according to its critics. 2012's *Django Unchained*[2] re-conceives its source material—the Sergio Corbucci Western of 1966—as "an emancipatory narrative" that uses "hip-hop aesthetics" to provide context for engaging slavery as a physical, cultural, and sonic space of (southern) "black identities" (Bradley 6). In a revealing interview with Henry Louis Gates, Tarantino stresses his desire to set his film in antebellum South, without the trapping of historical accuracy:

> HLG: Well then, what is in the air for *Django*? And why combine the slave narrative with the Western?
> QT: One, I've always wanted to tell a Western story. Two, I've always wanted to recreate cinematically that world of the antebellum South, of America under slavery, and just what a different place it was. An unfathomable place. [I wanted] to create an environment but then not just have a historical story play out—they did this and they did that—but make it a genre story. Make it an exciting adventure [186–87].

Again, focusing on how cinema shapes his version of history, the director looked to D.W. Griffith's adaptation of *The Birth of a Nation* (1915)—adapted from the novel *The Clansman* (1905) by Thomas Dixon, Jr. Once more turning away from the grander epics of Spielberg's *Lincoln* (2012) and, the following year, Steve McQueen's *Twelve Years a Slave* (2013), Tarantino speaks of turning his focus to something more exciting—something more jarring for the more average spectator.

> QT: Well, you know if you're going to make a movie about slavery and are taking a twenty-first century viewer and putting them in that time period, you're going to hear some things that are going to be ugly, and you're going to see things that are ugly.... No, I don't want it to be easy to digest. I want it to be a big gigantic boulder, a jagged pill and you have no water [189].

Casting Jamie Foxx and Christoph Waltz as bounty-hunting emancipators, the film's soundtrack provides the historical revisionism with a foundation that clarifies what other films about slavery seem to lack. According to Regina Bradley, the film works best when it "moves past restricting hip-hop's sonic aesthetics as an anachronistic bridge—life-saver—for contemporary consumers of popular culture to engage slavery as a southern black experience" (5). In one particular sequence, a flashback to when Django and his wife Broomhilda escape (Kerry Washington), the scene borders on looking cliche—a black family pursued by snarling slave catchers with yapping dogs nipping at their heels. But the soundtrack that plays is not the thrilling orchestral track that usually accompanies the action; instead, we hear a mashup of Tupac Shakur's "Unchained" and the baseline of James Brown's "The Payback," symbolizing "Django's transition from slavery to freedom, with Brown and Shakur sonically narrating his emotional response" (Bradley 9). Ultimately, the soundtrack re-channels the rewriting of the historical taking it from the vestiges of the History Channel to make the spectator feel "Django's anger and position as an enslaved man to present the unimaginable: Django's ability to execute and find pleasure in revenge" (Bradley 9).

In both *Inglourious Basterds* and *Django Unchained*, the rewriting of an historical moment creates a new way of imagining cinema's capacity to transport audiences to an event to reconsider the course that history took and the way people at the time could have responded. Such a framework enables us to consider Tarantino's 2019 feature, *Once Upon a Time in Hollywood*, and the writer-director's re-imagining of the events that surrounded that Summer of Love in 1969.

A 20th-Century Fable for a 21st-Century Spectator

Inglourious Basterds, Django Unchained, and *Once Upon a Time* are united in their distinction as fables: modern fairy tales that are not historically accurate, but historically informed. The first words that appear on-screen in opening *Inglourious Basterds* is the phrase, "Once upon a time...," blatantly reminding the spectator that what they will see is not accurate in the least. The phrase "Once Upon a Time..." is significant to most readers as the start of a fairy tale, adventurous stories passed down from the Brothers Grimm to provide moral guidance to young readers in need of "realizing the ground rules of society" (Stoddart 209). Much later, these tales, theorized by Vladimir Propp, resonate more fully as a "quest tale paradigm" designed to show how "protagonists" venture through "situations where obtaining goals results in episodic peril" to highlight the heteronormative processes of the "bourgeois-Capitalist ideology of patriarchal" culture (Stoddart 210). Ultimately, writers like Stephen Sondheim, in his Tony-Award-winning musical *Into the Woods* (1989),[3] rewrite the boundaries set by the fairy tale to explore a more contemporary resonance to the fairy tale.

For film buffs, "Once Upon a Time..." harkens back to a specific Western, Sergio Leone's *Once Upon a Time in the West* (*C'era una volta il West*, 1968), affectionately known as a Spaghetti Western. The tour de force film features Henry Fonda—the hero of many a John Ford feature—playing against type as a murderous thug, with Charles Bronson—soon to be known as the force behind the *Death Wish* franchise—as the considerate "Harmonica" who bands together with the menacing Cheyenne (Jason Robards) to protect a determined widow (Claudia Cardinale). Featuring cinematography from the legendary Tonino Delli Colli and a lustrous score by one of Quentin Tarantino's favorites, Ennio Morricone, the film, like Leonne's earlier Westerns, defies the terms of the traditional genre to "openly take on the politics of the day to bring younger audiences angry about the Vietnam War's escalation back to the cinema" (Stoddart 3).

As in *Django Unchained*, Tarantino is intentional in his evocation of the language of fairy tales to dispel any notion that what will be seen is an historically accurate saga: "And so the thing about [Django and Schultz] in fairy-tale terms: they're going to the evil kingdom. And Broomhilda is the princess in the tower" (190). This alone should be a warning to us that *Once Upon a Time in Hollywood* is a similar type of story. But it does not. Instead, we enter the film knowing of the events that ended The Summer of Love, manufacturing an expectation crafted by Tarantino that sits with us until we reach the film's ending.

Saturday, February 8, 1969

A title card focuses us on the date to situate ourselves in the *mise-en-scene* of Hollywood during the "Summer of Love." We meet Rick Dalton (Leonardo DiCaprio), the aging movie star turned featured villain-of-week supporting player, at a humiliating meeting at Musso and Frank's with producer Marvin Schwarz ("not Swartz") (Al Pacino), who has just watched a "Rick Dalton film festival," made up of *Tanner*—a Western featuring Dalton—and *The 14 Fists of McClusky*—a World War II film that we see an extended clip showing Rick dispensing with a band of Nazis with a flamethrower. Marvin comes with a proposition soaked in reality: He speaks the obvious, reminding Rick (who needs no reminding) that he now finds himself doing "guest shots on episodic television" where the series regular is "whipping Jake Cahill's ass" every week. "Before you know it, down goes your career as a leading man" and Marvin's proposition stings Rick to the core: "Or, do you go to Rome?"—suggesting that Rick turn toward making "I-talian Westerns" for the likes of Sergio Corbucci.

Time is not being kind to Rick already, and it has certainly not proven to be one for his "driver/gopher" Cliff Booth (Brad Pitt) either. Immediately, the film establishes that time itself is the chief antagonism in the narrative. In a few short moments, we learn that Dalton gave up his lucrative stint on the television show *Bounty Hunter* to try his hand at the movies (at a time when television actors did not easily transition from one medium to another) and Booth, his stunt double, cannot find much work (without Dalton's groveling) due to allegations involving the death of his ex-wife. Both men, now in their early '50s, are facing the fact that time is not on their side when it comes to being an actor in Hollywood: "It's official; I'm a has-been" confesses a depressed Rick. Ever the strong silent type, Cliff lends Rick his sunglasses to hide the tears streaming down his face: "Don't cry in front of the Mexicans."

As the pair drive through the Hollywood Hills toward Rick's home, we feel the anguish in both the leading man and his stunt double—time is passing them by, and desperation cannot be too exposed, or their careers will certainly be through. Pulling into Rick's drive, the men spot the other central character in the film, the actress Sharon Tate (Margot Robbie), newly married to the director Roman Polanski (Rafał Zawierucha), and pregnant with their first child. Ensconced in a villa on the hill just above Rick's place on Cielo Drive (the sign shown in close-up), spectators immediately recognize that this is the home where Tate, her friends Abigail Folger, Jay Sebring, and Steve Parent were brutally murdered by members of the Charles Manson "family" some six months later, when Tate was in her seventh month.

Though Rick is cheered by the fact that his good fortune has placed him "one pool party away from starring in a Polanski film," we realize a sense of foreboding; not only does Tarantino make us aware that time is passing Rick and Cliff by, but that time is running out for Sharon—casting an ominous cloud over the dreamlike, sun-drenched Sunset Strip of the late 1960s Hollywood we witness driving through the town, captured through Tarantino's nostalgic lens.

Sunday, February 9, 1969

A new title signals a new day, and the film's structure allows us to follow each character through their routine. As mentioned earlier, *Once Upon a Time* is a bro-mance, and the main focus is the bond between Cliff and Rick, and Cliff dutifully picks up his boss at 7:15 sharp to arrive on set to play Caleb DeCoteau, Rick's latest "villain-of-the-week" on a new weekly television Western series *Lancer*. As Rick leaves the car, instructing Cliff to return home to perform some domestic duties, Cliff calls him back to remind him, "You're Rick-Fucking-Dalton. Don't you forget it"—a sign of encouragement that reveals in a moment the bond these men feel between one another. Cliff knows that Rick's continued success may ultimately mean further work for him, and further glory for them both.

We've heard Rick the night before, swilling "eight whiskey sours" while running lines for this stint, surrounded by his ego in the form of movie posters, magazines, and souvenirs from his film career. But this morning, the director Sam Wanamaker (Nicholas Hammond) finds him sobering up with his head in a bowl of ice. Gleefully enthusiastic, the director has a new vision for Dalton: "I hired you to be actor; not Jake Cahill." While Rick listens dumbstruck, Wanamaker instructs Rebekkah, his costumer (Courtney Huffman) and Sonia, make-up artist (Heba Thorisdottir) to make Rick unrecognizable: "a big, long, droopy Zapata-like mustache" and a hairstyle "more hippie-ish … more Hells Angels." Immediately, Rick flinches: "You want me to look like some goddamn hippie?" But the director, beaming from Rebekkah's inspiration to dress the villain in "a Custer jacket, fringes all down the arm … he could hit the Strip in it tonight" and Rick understands his fate: He's now in hell, consigned here by himself for giving up his series for a fledgling career in film.

Rick's day is plagued by his hangover, and his early scenes with the series lead Lancer (Timothy Olyphant) are pitiful, riddled with missteps and botched lines. In a startling moment, Rick returns to his trailer to wallow in self-pity, tossing furniture and smashing glasses and mirrors, the actor berating himself openly for his drinking, his hubris, his lack of professional foresight. He finds himself with a dime-store Western wandering through the period set, settling to read his book next to Trudi Fraser (Julia Butters), who plays Mirabella, Lancer's eight-year-old sister—and who Caleb will kidnap during the episode—busy reading her own book so as to not "break character" during the union-required lunch break. Wise beyond her years, Trudi finds herself providing Rick with a pep talk while he tells her of his book, *Ride a Wild Bronc* by Marvin H. Albert, and its protagonist Easy Breezy:

> RICK: Well, he's not the best anymore. In fact, far from it. And he's coming to terms with…. What it's like to become … uh … useless.
> TRUDI: It's okay, Caleb. It's okay. It sounds like a really sad book. Poor Easy Breezy. I'm practically crying and I haven't even read it.
> RICK: Wait till you're fifteen, you'll be livin' it.

In telling Trudi the story of Easy's fall from grace, Rick, sobbing and working hard to contain his despair, recognizes his own plight: "not the best anymore" himself, having to take chump roles to keep himself in Hollywood's eye and to keep Cliff on the payroll. The encounter, however, inspires Rick, and when the cameras roll, he is not only on each and every mark, but he excels, turning Caleb into the "mad Hamlet" that Sam desires, and inspiring Trudi to whisper in his ear, "That was the best acting I've ever seen." We recognize the irony, as Trudi is only eight years old, but the performance and the compliment brings a genuine smile of satisfaction to Rick—we imagine for the first time in a very long time.

Cliff's day is, at first, filled with chores around Rick's house, and after donning a tool belt filled with cans of beer, he alights to the roof to fix Rick's television antennae. The moment resonates with the audience as Pitt strips off his shirt and revels in a moment of star wattage, the camera showing the recent dad-bod of the man *People* magazine once named "The Sexiest Man Alive."[4] Cliff might be only Rick's stunt double, but the heat he radiates in the moment reminds us that he once "could have been a contender" in his own right.

The moment gives way to a dual memory from Cliff's own checkered past. The first flashback jogs to his mind once he reflects on Rick's response to his question about any work for himself on the *Lancer* set, Rick reminding him that Randy (Kurt Russell) is the chief of principal photography on the set, and that there is no way that Cliff can be used because of old rumors, "I don't dig him…. He killed his fucking wife"; Rick quickly reminding Randy that "all charges were dropped." The camera boldly cuts to the memory from Cliff's perspective, his gorgeous wife needling him about the size of his boat. As she gets up to confront him, Cliff, dressed in scuba gear and armed with a harpoon, appears to settle in to listen to his harping spouse, the harpoon aimed at her stomach. But just before anything more happens, the scene cuts abruptly back to Cliff on the roof, shaking his head; he then resumes his chores reflecting on the real reason he cannot find work on Rick's set.

The camera cuts once more sharply to the moment when Cliff was confronted by Bruce Lee (Michael Moh) on the set of Lee's series *The Green Hornet*.[5] Lee, bragging about his admiration for Cassius Clay, and his own ability to take down such a fighter because he understands that his own hands are "registered as lethal weapons," confronts Cliff when the stuntman scoffs at the preening star: "I think you ought to be embarrassed to suggest you'd be anything but a stain on the seat of Muhammad Ali's trunks." The remark forces Lee to make an example of the "wife-killing" stuntman, and a contest of sorts takes place. Lee, stripping off his Kato costume, assumes the position, and after squawking like a whooping crane, knocks Cliff down. Cliff, still chuckling over the prissy "dancing" that was Lee's trademark, grabs the star in a lock-hold, and hurls him toward the side of a car, the actor denting the whole passenger side of the vehicle. Just as Lee returns for more, Janet (Zoe Bell), the hypersensitive producer, emerges to take Cliff to task, not only for hurting the star of the series, but for destroying her car. The humorous interlude cuts back to Cliff still on Rick's roof, smirking gleefully at the moment—we now know why Cliff cannot get work of his own anymore.

Cliff's day takes an unexpected turn later in the afternoon, when he drives about Hollywood on some errands. He sees a hippy girl hitching a ride on the corner—the same girl, Pussycat (Margaret Qualley) Cliff has seen at earlier moments in the film, while driving Rick (who refers to the counter-culturists as "fucking hippies"), and the encounter leads Cliff to Spahn Movie Ranch, where he not only used to film stunts for *Bounty Law*, but where the current clan of vagrant teens now live and serve their spiritual guide, Charles Manson. Given the fun and frisky manner that Pussycat uses to tease Cliff, who quickly rejects her offer to "suck" his "cock while you drive," she helps to show that Cliff, while not immune to the occasional affront to the establishment (purchasing an acid-dipped cigarette for 50 cents off one "hippy girl"), he understands there are rules that one must abide by ("What I'm too old to do is go to jail for poontang"), and he drives Pussycat to Spahn for a more specific reason—to check on his old friend George Spahn (Bruce Dern), the proprietor of the ranch, who Cliff gradually begins to believe is being taken advantage of by this crowd.

The visit to the ranch moves this section of the film into its own brand of Spaghetti Western, as Cliff comes face-to-face with members of the Manson clan. Led by the fearless Squeaky Fromme (Dakota Fanning), the cool kids do everything to thwart Cliff's macho sensibility—degrading him by calling him "Hawaiian man" (because of his shirt); halting his entrance to the house with George's "nap time"; gathering outside and calling him names. The camera tracks behind Cliff, as he struts through the ranch toward George, emboldening his movements by focusing on his shadow to make him appear an ominous Gary Cooper, broader against the dusty road to project a long, *High Noon* gun-slinger shadow that dwarfs the Manson members. In this sequence, they appear more as unruly children, attired in hand-me-down nightgowns and skimpy shorts, their flat-chests confined by halter tops, than the menacing maniacs of history. And when Cliff finally finds the now blind George who can barely remember anything but his favorite television programs, Cliff attempts to leave, only to find that one male member has boyishly stabbed the front wheel of Rick's Cadillac. Realizing the entire clan is set for a final showdown, Cliff grabs the knife-wielding Clem (James Landry Hébert) and begins to pummel him, grabbing him by his long hair, and punching him soundly, breaking his nose and humiliating him into repairing the damage. When one of the young women rides to relieve Tex (Austin Butler) from the tour group he leads for money, he arrives back at the ranch to discover the tail end of the cream-colored Caddy leaving in a dusty trail of desert.

The final sequence recording this particular day follows Sharon on a series of errands that seem to be part of the life of an everyday woman. After starting her day by playing Paul Revere and the Raiders' new album *The Spirit of '67* at a high decibel, teasing housemate Jay Sebring (Emile Hirsch) about helping to improve his taste in new music, she heads off to Santa Monica Blvd. in her new black Porsche for a little shopping. One errand she completes first is a stop by a little antiquarian bookshop to pick up a copy of Thomas Hardy's *Tess of the D'Urbervilles* as a present for Roman. This errand resonates with anyone familiar with Polanski's filmography, as Tate really did purchase a first edition of the novel for her husband around that very time—in fact his next film after Sharon's death was *Tess* (1979), dedicated with love to her.

After giving a polite hippie girl a ride to Westwood Village, Sharon spies a little movie theater, the Bruin Cinema, playing her latest film, *The Wrecking Crew* (1968), featuring Dean Martin, Elke Sommer, Nancy Kwan, and herself. The whole segment, from Sharon asking if she really needs to pay for a ticket if "I'm in the film"; to the moment when the usher asks her to pose for a photo by the film's poster; to the interior of the cinema, where Tate sits barefoot reveling in the crowd responding to her screwball antics on screen (the film projects the actual Tate on screen), the spectator even unfamiliar with Tate feels the genuine glee that the actress gets from seeing herself projected on the big screen, and experiencing the joy her work can bring to an audience. Tarantino films the sequence in warm tones, relishing every moment of this private/public moment—it certainly makes you hope that the real Sharon Tate had one such afternoon where she recognized how her talent would one day resonate with the world.

The day ends with the exhausted but exuberant Rick returning home with buddy Cliff at the wheel to watch his latest episode of *The FBI* where he plays another heavy villain-of-the-week. The two buddies sit in front of the color set with a six pack and a newly ordered pizza, toasting to better things coming their collective ways. This extended sequence capturing the cross-cut experience of one day in the life of Rick, Cliff, and Sharon takes up roughly one hour of the finished film. What can be its purpose? The effect, while colorful in its cinematography and constructed to capture the essence of the characters does not really progress plot. Instead, it seems to simply forestall the inevitable, which the suspecting spectator assumes: that the end of the film will recount the effects of August 9, 1969, when Manson's clan murdered Tate and her friends on Cielo Drive.

I believe the key lies, once more, in the film's title: We need to remember that Tarantino is telling us yet another fairy tale, this time taking place in Hollywood, where the handsome princes and beautiful princess, high in the villas in the Hollywood Hills, will one day be confronted with real evil. An evil that, as we know, ended the famed Summer of Love.

Six Months Later: *August 8, 1969*

The final title card takes us to the film's final act, and the date resonates as the day before Tate's murder, so despite the comical documentary that plays recording the re-birth of Rick Dalton's career: The success of *Nebraska Jim* and his subsequent Italian films; his whirlwind marriage to Francesca Capucci (Lorenza Izzo); and even Cliff's own rising star as a stunt man (pointed out to us in all of Rick's stunts), the tone feels elegiac—the feeling that the fairytale is coming to an end.

The faux documentary is a comical recap of what transpired during the six-month gap in the film. Narrated by Randy Miller (who kicked Cliff off *The Green Hornet* set earlier for damaging Bruce Lee and his wife's car), we witness a montage of Rick's new oeuvre—not only *Nebraska Jim* but *Uccidimi Sugito Ringo, disse il Gringo*, co-starring Joseph Cotten (directed by Calvin Jackson Padget); *Red Blood, Red Skin*, featuring Telly Savalas (directed by Joaquín Romero Marchent); and *Operazione Dyn-O-Mite!* (directed by Antonio Margheriti), the former featuring keen stunt work by Cliff.[6] We are told that the sudden renaissance of Rick's career has marked another milestone—once they return to Hollywood, Rick will take up married life fully, and that he and Cliff will part ways. Therefore, the evening of 08 August will resonate for the pair as a celebration of their bro-mance. The sense as we watch Cliff and Rick arrive at Casa Vega cross-cut with the now seven-month pregnant Sharon arriving at the trendy El Coyote with her friends, marks a change in tone: as we watch the simultaneous celebrations, a clock ticks away (represented in the lower left-hand corner of the screen), counting down the moments until the Manson clan arrives at Cielo Drive.

And the build-up to the ultimate attack is fraught with tension as the drunken Rick makes another pitcher of margaritas while Cliff takes Brandy for a walk. Just as Cliff exits Rick's property, the members of the Manson clan arrive, Tex noting that they are supposed to be heading toward Polanski's house to execute the pigs in a "witchy" manner, according to Charlie's instructions. As depicted the frightening clan members, however, appear more like the wannabe teenagers seen when Cliff attacked them at the Spahn Ranch the previous February—the bickering, squabbling hippies do not take on the persona of the cold-blooded killers depicted in any account of the Tate murders, which actually raises the tension as the clock in the corner registers close to midnight.[7]

In fact, Rick confronts the squad when they pull into his drive, afraid the broken muffler will disturb Francesca (who has conveniently gone to bed). Rick retires to the pool, the blender full of margaritas at the ready. As Cliff returns to feed the ravenous Brandy, the effects of his acid-dipped cigarette begin to kick in, and his own efforts to keep quiet make for much hilarity as the scene played earlier with Brandy, where the straight-forward Cliff feeds Brandy in such a regimented manner, repeats itself, but with Cliff's vision impaired via the drug.

Just about the stroke of midnight, the clan breaks into their chosen destination. It is at this moment that we finally learn of Tarantino's scheme to rewrite history. The clan does not break into the Tate home on the hill, but into Rick Dalton's, mainly to settle the score. Cliff readily recognizes the members from his visit to Spahn Ranch, and characteristic Tarantino violence—mixed with many laughs—ensues: Brandy biting Tex's balls; Cliff smashing Katie's face (Madisen Butler) into the mantlepiece; Sadie (Mikey Madison) breaking through a window after her nose is broken with a can of Brandy's "Wolf Chow," only to meet Rick armed with his flame-thrower, looted from the set of *The 14 Fists of McClusky.*

The conclusion of the film, while sweet and wonderfully warm-hearted, is, in fact, a-historical—although Rick and Cliff are fictional characters, we have known this from point one, each figure represents an aspect of the business of Hollywood that become meta-textual with the clips from *Bounty Law*, the *mise-en-scène* of Rick's home, the memories of Cliff's own stunt work. However, the murder of Sharon Tate at the brutal hands of the Manson cult—arguably the destructive end to that Summer of Love—was real, and the left turn that the film takes in its final act, while cathartic (particularly for those who recall the dread of that time frame), is, in fact, a lie. So, what is the point in putting a happy ending on what we all know to be a tragic story?

Looking back at Tarantino's other two films that rewrite history provides a clue. Setka argues that the ending of *Inglourious Basterds*, while outrageously overblown, turns the film into a pure "revenge fantasy film" to "call into question the very essence of what constitutes collective memory, and reveals in the process the extent to which collective memory is defined by how we choose to represent history" (161). In refining an entirely different antebellum South, Tarantino, according to Bradley, focuses on those "hip-hop aesthetics [to] provide context for engaging slavery as a physical, cultural, and sonic space of (southern) black identities (6)." In other words, both critics admit that while bombastic and utterly implausible, the known narratives of both the Holocaust and American slavery are both so horrible—too horrible to imagine fully—that Tarantino is justified in concluding his own narrative take on these atrocities in order to make contemporary audiences applaud the outcomes because we ultimately know that both Hitler and the practice of slavery were defeated, overcome by members of the Jewish and African American communities who triumphed.

This *is not* the effect of rewriting the history that culminates in the activities of August 9, 1969. Tate and her friends did not fight off her attackers; each died horrible painful deaths, Tate most of all who, according to the most famous recorder Vincent Bugliosi, not only watched her friends be butchered, but begged for her own life until she died. In writing his screenplay, Tarantino thought through how Tate's murder has defined her character, and he believes it important to re-think the mythology of Sharon Tate and her death:

> She seemed like an incredibly sweet person. When you talk about the different friends that she had, even acquaintances that she had, they all tell the same story about her, about this unaffected beauty, just this reservoir of goodness and kindness. Now that almost sounds too good to be true, but for whatever reason, as I'm reading all this stuff, I'm really buying it. Every account about her that I found backs up that version of her [Eisenberg].

Believing that her murder was all that people knew of Tate, the writer-director felt that "rather than having that be the defining part of her story in the new film, he wanted to depict her as the good and decent person living her life as an up-and-coming actress in Los Angeles.... I wanted to show people a glimpse of Sharon before the murder, so they think of her as more than just a victim" (Eisenberg). In essence, Tate becomes the fairy princess in Tarantino's fairytale, rescued by the pair of handsome princes who, though a bit long on years, become heroes in the folklore of America, freeing us all from the fear and loathing that marked the end of the Summer of Love. To return to my opening thoughts, Tarantino's ending is similar, in tone, to the ending of Sondheim's *Into the Woods*, where after the threat of evil is upended, the ravaged and beaten remaining members of the fairy tale community—the Baker, Red Riding Hood, Cinderella and Jack—reconstitute a new family, creating a happy ending that entertains the audience while questioning the methods of storytelling and the legacy of those prescriptive tales. Tarantino's fable ends with the wounded Cliff and the new-and-improved Rick reaffirming their love for one another, as Cliff drives off in an ambulance, and Rick joins Jay and Sharon for a rejuvenating cocktail.[8] In a similar manner, in telling his own fairytale about Hollywood, and rewriting the story of just one victim, Tarantino redefines the reason we go to the movies—not just to be entertained, but to think about how the stories that shape our collective memories define the kind of humans we are—and the kind of humans we want to be. Remember, the final words on-screen do not read "The End" (the standard closing for a Hollywood comedy)—but "Once Upon a Time … in Hollywood."

I want to thank my creative team for always watching films with me and listening to my ideas: Stephanie Prugh, Rachel Wifall, Stephen Mathis and Travis Wicklund. Special thanks to my editor supreme Michael Samuel. —Scott F. Stoddart

Notes

1. *Once Upon a Time in Hollywood* was nominated for 10 Academy Awards, including Best Picture, Best Director, and Best Writing, Original Screenplay. It won two: Brad Pitt, for Best Performance by an Actor in a Supporting Role, and Barbara Ling and Nancy Haigh, for Best Achievement in Production Design.

2. *Django Unchained* was nominated for five Academy Awards, including Best Picture. It won two, another for Christoph Waltz for Best Performance by an Actor in a Supporting Actor and a second for Tarantino for Best Writing, Original Screenplay.

3. *Into the Woods* was written with music and lyrics by Stephen Sondheim and a book by James Lapine; it was nominated for 10 Tony Awards and won three (Best Score; Best Book; Best Actress in a Musical). It lost the Tony for Best Musical to Andrew Llyod Webber's *The Phantom of the Opera*.

4. In fact, Pitt is the only man to be named *People*'s "Sexiest Man Alive" twice, the first time in 1995 and the second in 2000.

5. *The Green Hornet* ran on ABC for one season (1966) and starred Van Williams, as Brad Reid (aka The Green Hornet) and Bruce Lee, as Kato, Reid's limo driver and sidekick in fighting crime.

6. The hardback edition Tarantino's novel of the film contains an appendix featuring each of the film posters for Rick's Italian films.

7. According to all accounts, the Manson clan broke into the Tate home just before midnight; the killings actually taking place on 9 August 1969.

8. Of course, this is not the final image of the film. In order to keep the audience engaged during the lengthy credit sequence, Tarantino films a mock cigarette ad for Big Apple cigarettes featuring Rick Dalton. The humorous parody not only pokes fun at the sincerity of such ads, but once the director calls, "Cut." Rick breaks character and begins complaining about how lousy the cigarettes taste, and how unhappy he is with the life-size cut-out being sent to stores.

Works Cited

Bradley, Regina N. "Re-Imagining Slavery in the Hip-Hop Imagination." *South: A Scholarly Journal* 49, no. 1 (Fall 2016): 3–24.

Bugliosi, Vincent. *Helter Skelter: The True Story of the Manson Murders.* New York: Norton, 2001.

Burr, Ty. "Tarantino Is at the Top of His Form with *Once Upon a Time in Hollywood*." *Boston Globe*, July 24, 2019.

Didion, Joan. "Hollywood Having Fun." *The New York Review*, March 22, 1973.

Django Unchained. Dir. Quentin Tarantino. Columbia Pictures, 2012.

Eisenberg, Eric. "*Once Upon a Time in Hollywood* Ending Explained: What Happened and Why." *CinemaBlend*, January 1, 2020.

Gates, Henry Louis. "Tarantino 'Unchained': *Django* Trilogy." *Quentin Tarantino Interviews*, ed. Gerald Peary. Jackson: University of Mississippi, 2013.

Inglourious Basterds. Dir. Quentin Tarantino. Columbia Pictures, 2009.

Once Upon a Time ... in Hollywood. Dir. Quentin Tarantino. Columbia Pictures, 2019.

Scott, A.O. "We Lost It at the Movies." *New York Times,* July 24, 2019.

Setka, Stella. "Bastardized History: How *Inglourious Basterds* Breaks through American Screen Memory." *Jewish Film and New Media,* Fall 2015, 141–169.

Stoddart, Scott F. "Happily ... Ever ... NEVER: The Antithetical Romance of *Into the Woods.*" *Reading Stephen Sondheim,* ed. Sandor Goodhart. New York: Garland, 2000.

———, ed. *The New Western: Critical Essays on the Genre Since 9/11.* Jefferson: McFarland, 2016.

Taylor, Ella. "Quentin Tarantino: *The Inglourious Basterds* Interview." *Quentin Tarantino Interviews,* ed. Gerald Peary. Jackson: University of Mississippi, 2013.

Turan, Kenneth. "A Quentin Tarantino Skeptic Takes Great Pleasure in *Once Upon a Time in Hollywood.*" *Los Angeles Times,* July 24, 2019.

Vineberg, Steve. "Alternate History." *The Threepenny Review,* Spring 2020, 23–24.

Zacharek, Stephanie. "*Once Upon a Time in Hollywood* Is One of Quentin Tarantino's Most Affectionate Films. It's Also One of His Best." *Time,* May 22, 2019.

About the Contributors

Katharine **Coldiron** is the author of *Ceremonials* (2020) and *Junk Film* (2023) as well as a standalone monograph on the 1959 film *Plan 9 from Outer Space*. Her book criticism has appeared in the *Washington Post*, the *Guardian*, on NPR, and many other places. Find her at kcoldiron.com.

Vlad **Dima** is a professor and chair of the Department of African American Studies at Syracuse University. He has published numerous articles, mainly on French and Francophone cinemas, but also on Francophone literature, comics, American cinema, and television. He is also the author of three books.

Kieran **Fisher** is a journalist and lifelong action movie aficionado from Glasgow, Scotland. He works as a writer and editor for Static Media, and he has contributed to various print and online outlets, including Fandor, Arrow Video, Starburst, and *Diabolique* magazine.

Bryan M. **Jack** is a professor of history at Southern Illinois University Edwardsville, teaching African American history. He has published two books, *Southern History on Screen: Race and Rights, 1976–2016* (2019) and *The St. Louis African American Community and the Exodusters* (2007), and articles in numerous academic journals.

Sue **Matheson** is an associate professor at the University College of the North, teaching in the areas of American film and popular culture, Canadian literature, and children's literature. She is the book review editor for *The Journal of Popular Film and Television*.

Kevin **Quigley** is a novelist, monographer, and nonfiction writer in Boston, Massachusetts. His young adult novels *I'm on Fire* (2015) and *Roller Disco Saturday Night* (2017) have received critical acclaim, and his short work has been featured in books alongside writers like Peter Straub and Stephen King.

Andrew J. **Rausch** is the author of more than 60 books, including *Conversations on Quentin Tarantino* (2016), *My Best Friend's Birthday: The Making of a Quentin Tarantino Film* (2019), and *Generation Tarantino: The Last Wave of Young Turks in Hollywood* (2025). He is a regular contributor to several film publications.

Charles J. **Rzepka** is a professor of English at Boston University teaching British Romanticism and detective and crime fiction. He has published essays on Raymond Chandler, Todd Downing, and Earl Derr Biggers. His books include *A Companion to Crime Fiction* (2010) and *Critical Essays on Elmore Leonard* (2020).

Troy D. **Smith** is an associate professor of history at Tennessee Tech University, where he teaches on a variety of subjects including American Indian Studies, the origins of race, the American West, and comic books. He is also a novelist, primarily of Westerns and mysteries.

Scott F. **Stoddart** is a professor of English and president of the Faculty Senate at Saint Peter's University. He teaches courses in British and American literature, cinema, theater, and television studies. He is the editor or *Exploring Downton Abbey* (2018), *The New Western* (2016), and *Analyzing Mad Men* (2011).

Dara **Waldron** teaches in the Critical and Contextual program at Limerick School of Art and Design at the Technological University of the Shannon (Midlands/Midwest). He is the author of two books and has published extensively in international journals. He is a regular contributor to Irish independent media and politics journal *Cassandra Voices*.

Index

167

www.ingramcontent.com/pod-product-compliance
Ingram Content Group UK Ltd.
Pitfield, Milton Keynes, MK11 3LW, UK
UKHW031832040626
6257IPUK00002B/24